HALLIWELL'S HORIZON

Leslie Halliwell and his Film Guides

by

Michael Binder

First published 2011

Copyright © Michael Binder, 2011

PAPERBACK ISBN: 978-1-4477-4821-2

For Graham

Michael Binder was born in St. Albans in 1970, and works as a software developer for a market research company in London. In 2006 he wrote the website www.lesliehalliwell.com to celebrate the author who, more than any other, enriched his knowledge and appreciation of the cinema.

Author photograph by Graham Turner.

Contents

Acknowledgements .... *vii*

Introduction *1*

1. *Like a Duck to Water* *5*
   The Golden Age, 1929-39

2. *No Concessions to Low-brows* *29*
   Bolton School and the Army, 1939-49

3. *The Scarcest Commodity* *53*
   Cambridge University, 1949-52

4. *A Dream Come True* *78*
   Picturegoer *and the Rex, 1952-56*

5. *Just like Ealing Broadway* *103*
   Marriage and Granada, 1956-67

6. *For People who like the Movies* *124*
   The Filmgoer's Companion

7. *Things became Fraught* *145*
   Buying films and shows for ITV, 1967-81

8. *Two Untrained Index Fingers* *174*
   Halliwell's Film Guide

9. *A Store of Riches* *197*
   Channel 4 and the return to Shangri-La, 1981-87

10. *A Matter of Life and Death* *220*
    The final years, 1987-89

11. *A Tough Act to Follow* *245*
    Legacy

References *253*
Bibliography *283*
Index *287*

Acknowledgements

Many thanks to the following splendid institutions:

Bolton History Centre; British Film Institute Library, London; British Library, London; Cambridge Archives; Cambridge Central Library; National Archives, Kew; National Newspaper Archive, Colindale; Slough Library.

With very special thanks to my brother Stephen for proof reading.

In addition, these people were all immensely valuable in the creation of this book, and I am most grateful for their contributions –

Halliwell's family and friends: James Beattie, Joanna Harrison, Denise McKemey, Michael Wright.

Bolton School Development office: Stuart Chell, Jenny Salerno, David Shaw.

Old Boltonians: Ron Edge, Ronald Lowe, Irving Wardle, Lindsay Williamson, James Wood, Malcolm Worrall.

St. Catharine's Alumni Office: Kevin Bentley, Lizzie Perdeaux, Elizabeth Ennion-Smith.

The Cath's alumni themselves: Michael Collie, Eric Cross, Peter Darby, Laurence Fleming, Allen Freer, Sir Peter Hall, Robert Jervis, Michael Millgate, Jim Norris.

Independent television: June Dromgoole, Sir Denis Forman, Sir Paul Fox, Alan Frank, Bamber Gascoigne, Sir Michael Parkinson.

Authors and critics: Philip French, Leonard Maltin, Philip Purser, David Quinlan, Jeffrey Richards, Shaun Usher.

Other contributors: Edgar Metcalfe, Ian Payn, William Russell, Peter Sheil, John Michael Swinbank, Marco Trevisiol, Michael Winner.

Introduction

On any given night in the 1930s, Churchgate positively teemed with life. This short cobblestoned stretch of Bolton's municipality, a market place through the ages, was the centre of town life and a hive of activity. Bound at the western end by the stone cross – near which the 7th Earl of Derby was executed during the Civil War – and at the other by the commanding presence of the Parish Church, its square tower dominating the scene, Churchgate packed in three pubs, two cinemas and a theatre.

Round fronted double-decker trams ('bone-shakers', 'rattle-traps') would clank their way up Bradshawgate and swing left onto Deansgate, swaying and juddering as a white-gloved policeman on point duty waved them on, their path to Churchgate seemingly blocked by the stone cross – it would be several years before public transport encroached upon the market place. Doormen resplendent in epauletted frock-coats competed for the patronage of the paying public with cries of "Seats in all parts, twice nightly!" or "Seats in the one-and-nines; standing room only in the circle!" Buskers with piano accordions or harmonicas serenaded the waiting crowds as they queued for their evening's entertainment, the men dressed in threadbare suits with flat caps or homburgs, the ladies in long coats and cloche hats. Pony-pulled carts stood by outside Sabini's ice cream parlour and hungry customers waited in line at Ye Olde Pastie Shoppe for one of their legendary meat and potato turnovers. The Grand Theatre of Varieties, just opposite the church, was the preserve of music hall stars, comedians, novelty acts and even a circus, the elephants for which would be led in via the rear stage door – it was said that more than one unlucky punter had his pastie filched by a swaying trunk…

On Monday, 31st January 1938, a young boy and his mother hurry towards the bright lights and noise of this very scene, as a blustery wind whips across the town bringing thundery showers. The boy is a few weeks short of his ninth birthday and for half his young life has been captivated by the magical world of the cinema. He is surprisingly advanced for his age, with an extremely sharp mind, and he has already grown contemptuous of the frivolous entertainments enjoyed by his contemporaries. Some of the more sophisticated comedies may go over his head, and the finer points of film-making currently elude him, but it will not be long before he begins to document his frequent trips to the movies in an exercise book. He will record the significant details of each evening's entertainment: title, studio, principal cast list and a brief précis, as well as giving a terse assessment of the film's qualities – or otherwise.

These opinions, combined with his star ratings, will one day make him famous, and infamous, as nearly thirty years after this night he will publish *The Filmgoer's Companion*, the first one-volume encyclopaedia covering all aspects of the cinema. He will follow it a dozen years later with his *Film Guide*, another monumental undertaking, its subsequent editions eventually encompassing some sixteen thousand individual titles. Furthermore, he will use his role as a cinema manager and then as a film buyer for a major television company, to tap into enthusiastic interest in movies of a certain vintage, his work helping to preserve many negatives of films which would otherwise have decayed to dust.

His mother is a heavy-set woman in her early fifties, whose complaints about her swollen ankles fall on deaf ears as the boy leads her round the corner into Churchgate, eager to catch the 'first house'. They know they will have to queue in the rain and cold for it, however, as they pass newspaper seller "Chronicle" Tommy making a dash to a slowing car. The boy stops for a quick sup from the drinking fountain outside the Swan Hotel before they proceed past the Man & Scythe pub, where that unlucky Earl spent the last few hours of his life, and arrive at their destination: the arcade-fronted Theatre Royal, known locally as the The*a*tre. It has been ten years since a live performance was seen there, however, as the venue transferred its allegiance to the silver screen upon reopening after a fire.

Queues stretch in both directions, for tonight sees the opening of one of the biggest Hollywood productions of the decade. After standing in line, the boy and his mother pass under the Theatre's iron-pillared glass canopy to reach its marble entrance hall. They will have to forego their usual seats (front row of the rear stalls – easier on Mum's ankles) and take whatever tickets are offered, which turns out to be separate singles. A cheap wooden category board attempts to advertise the night's entertainment but some of the letters have fallen off – not that these two need reminding what they have come to see.

They enter through one of eight sets of swing doors and find themselves inside the auditorium, with its plush red upholstery and grand proscenium arch decorated with a frieze depicting a Greek chariot race. The house lights remain on for a few seconds, and after a quick negotiation with a couple of seated patrons the pair eventually occupy adjacent seats in the rapidly filling stalls. Unusually, tonight there is no supporting programme: it is just the main feature, and as the house lights dim an usherette emerges from the wings with a brass scent sprayer, to pump sweet-smelling perfume into the atmosphere, droplets of which fall irritatingly on the heads of nearby audience members – air conditioning 1930s-style.

Light from the projection booth flickers into life and the British Censor's certificate appears in wavy form over the red velour curtains as they draw back. The image straightens itself out on the large four-by-three screen as dramatic music fills the room. The Columbia torchbearer comes into view, followed closely by a vision of snow-capped mountains. Cigarette smoke wafts around in the beam which passes over the heads of the transfixed audience, and as the reflected light hits the young boy's face his eyes grow wider with anticipation, for he is held in thrall by those gleaming monochrome images in the dark. The silver screen, with its glamour and adventure, has offered him an escape from the humdrum existence of a soot-covered mill town. He is living through what he will later refer to as the "Golden Age of the Cinema", the period when the big Hollywood studios churned out movies on a production line basis, with stars, directors and writers all under contract. They were film factories, producing, distributing and exhibiting multi-million dollar dreams for the likes of this Boltonian boy and his mother.

The music drifts into a sweeping melody as the film's title appears in an Oriental font, annoyingly bathed in a green glow courtesy of the projectionist's penchant for using stylised coloured filters over the opening and closing titles of each film. He would sometimes add equally unwelcome kaleidoscopic images into the mix, no matter if important action was taking place beneath the credits. Breakdowns were frequent, and one will happen this very evening during a particularly dramatic moment. At times it seemed as though the management *wanted* the movies to fail, so that they could return to the old days of live performance.

Nevertheless, the boy is about to watch a film that will become an instant favourite and will resonate throughout his life. It is an adventure story set in a distant land which no-one in the audience is ever likely to visit. It was shot in black and white by possibly the most famous director then working – Frank Capra – and it stars one of the finest screen actors of the age, Ronald Colman. It contains action, suspense, mystery, excitement and, above all, a sense of wonder…

The boy's name is Robert James Leslie Halliwell, and the film is called *Lost Horizon*…

1

Like a Duck to Water

- The Golden Age, 1929-39 -

Bolton in the 1930s might not have been many people's idea of Shangri-La. Lying in a natural basin a few miles to the northwest of Manchester, Bolton-le-moors – as it was still officially called at the time – was at the height of its powers as a cotton spinning town. The mill factories, over two hundred of them, covered the local area: huge rectangular blocks of burgundy brickwork, with rows of closely spaced arched windows seemingly too dark for light ever to pass through them. Chimneys pierced the sky and, six days out of seven, belched plumes of smoke which hung over the town like ominous clouds, soot falling like acid rain to blacken the hard cobblestoned streets and the densely packed houses – which contributed their own share of pollution to the grimy atmosphere, courtesy of fifty-thousand coal fires.

Housewives fought a constant war against dirt, scrubbing front steps and skirting boards with materials that were far from labour saving, in their attempts to hide the effects of the industry which dominated the town. Men, women, and even children ran their sets of wheels in the factories – but only when there was cotton to spin, as the nature of the business led to frequent periods of unemployment. Women gathered in doorways or on street corners to discuss the latest social news, and after supper their husbands would head off to the local for a pint of mild, or to the Spinners' Union to socialise with the same folk they had likely spent all day with.

A strongly developed sense of community existed, where everyone knew everyone else's business and whole conversations could be had by simply scanning the "births, marriages and deaths" column in the *Bolton Evening News*. People accepted how things were and maintained a light-hearted, philosophical outlook, proud of the fact that they survived in an environment where complaining was regarded as weak, and any adversity could be laughed off with a bit of that old Lancashire wit.

And they sure went to the movies. Cinemagoing was the most popular form of entertainment in Britain in the 1930s. It is estimated that on average 19 million tickets were sold every week at around 3,000 cinemas nationwide. Both figures would rise steadily over the next few years to a peak of around 30 million tickets per week in 1946, sold at nearly 5,000 cinemas – an impressive forty-seven of which were either in or around Bolton. Such overwhelming demand for the 20th Century's newest art form was created by one thing: the desire to escape. Those mills must have cast a long shadow indeed to bring about such a regionally disproportionate need to be transported, but the barest examination of the cinemagoing habits of the time turns up frequent mentions of the wish to be "taken out of oneself" or to "live in another world for a little while."

For an easily affordable price one could exchange the cold and drab surroundings of one's own home for a couple of hours sitting in the plush warmth of a picture house, watching glamorous stars leading lives of adventure and excitement, and with a thousand other like-minded folk to laugh and to cry and to dream alongside. It is no wonder that the cinemas themselves became known as 'dream palaces', for the best of them were indeed sumptuous in design, with ornate furnishings, lush carpets and luxurious seating. Cinemagoing was also a cheap way of keeping warm during winter.

With regards to the exhibition of films, there was a hierarchy of cinemas from the 'majors' down to the 'fleapits' or 'bug hutches'. A big release would normally play for one week only at a major on its first run, returning in subsequent weeks to the theatres lower down the scale for second, third and fourth runs if demand was high enough. Up until 1937, Bolton's first-run cinemas were the Theatre Royal, the Capitol, the Hippodrome, the Rialto and the Queen's… and it was to the Queen's on a blustery afternoon in late July of 1933, that Leslie Halliwell's mother Lily took him for what would be remembered as his first official visit to the cinema. His first *actual* visit occurred two years before, after Lily had cancelled an afternoon shopping trip due to inclement weather. She decided to take her son to the pictures and chose the Queen's because it was one of the closest cinemas to their home on Parkfield Road, and because the Great Lever tram stopped nearby. However, on that first occasion – perhaps overwhelmed by the darkness and the crowds – the two year old boy went into a panic and had to be carried out screaming. Unfortunately, the title of the movie which provoked this outburst is lost to history.

In later life, Halliwell would attain front page headlines for running the only cinema to show a banned movie in England. He would contribute to one of Granada Television's most popular shows and become a household name for compiling nine editions of *The Filmgoer's Companion* and seven of *Halliwell's Film Guide*. In addition, he would be responsible for bringing to British television screens some of the most popular films and shows of the 1970s and 80s, as well as contributing articles to *Sight & Sound*, *The Spectator* and *The Times Literary Supplement*. His promotion of the cinema through his encyclopaedias would win him awards from the London Film Critics' Circle, the British Film Institute and the British Academy.

But it could all have been very different. His father James "Jim" Halliwell was born in 1883, one of nine children of whom only six survived infancy. Jim's brother Henry then died tragically at twenty-one due to seemingly no more than a bad cold. One of his ancestors must have taken the name Halliwell from the local parish of the same name, which itself derived from the Old English "halig wella" or "holy well". What passed for normal life in Victorian age Bolton seems scarcely comprehensible nowadays. As a child, Jim's day would begin at 5:30am, when a tall-hatted gentleman known as a 'knocker-up' tapped on the window to wake the family, a service he provided for tuppence a week. Jim's first task would be a trip to the mill to take his father's and elder brothers' breakfast, wrapped in a red handkerchief, before returning home for his own. The streets were full of beggars and striking mill workers, who slept rough because there was no union money to support them during disputes. Sewage was collected from the 'privy middens' and taken away on steaming carts by the council-employed 'muck misers'. The undertaker was a common sight, and all too often the coffins were small.

Jim went to work in the mill at the age of eleven, on half time for two years until he passed his labour exam, which entitled him to leave school and to start work properly. He would eventually work there until the age of *seventy-eight*, with the last few years being on a part time basis – he couldn't give it up because he felt he could not socialise with his mates if he had not done a day's work beforehand. In his twenties, Jim was a popular character about town and did his 'courting' along Bradshawgate and Manchester Road, where it is assumed that on one such occasion he met Lily Haslam, herself a mill worker from the age of eleven, although she would retire after they got married. They had two daughters, Edith and Lilian, and almost thirteen years later a boy came along whom they named Robert James Leslie. 'Robert' was Lily's father's name but it is not clear where 'Leslie' came from, which the boy eventually adopted as his first name. He was born on February 23rd, 1929, and referred to himself as his mother's "afterthought" – Lily was forty-four at the time.

The family lived in a simple terraced house up a hill at the southern end of town, across the road from a mill pond from where it was said that Jim had once rescued a drowning man. The young Halliwell, having quickly discarded conventional children's toys such as a rocking horse and a tricycle, would lie on the rug in their front room watching his sisters put the finishing touches to their make-up, and listen to their conversations about the likes of Clark Gable and Claudette Colbert and Ronald Colman. The cinema was important to them for social reasons: they needed to be *au fait* with the latest star stories. As he read his sisters' glossy film magazines and gazed at the cinema advertisements which dominated the front page of the *Bolton Evening News*, Halliwell's interest grew and he began to pester his mother to take him again. Lily was understandably reluctant and reminded him of the previous occasion, but he reasoned that since by then he could no longer *remember* the previous occasion, he should not, therefore, be held responsible for it.

The Queen's was at the time Bolton's most highly regarded picture house, advertised as "the coolest cinema in town" – which was unlikely to have been a reference to its social standing, but may instead have been due to the projection booth's door opening out directly onto the street. The projectionist himself could often be seen on the pavement having a quick smoke during the film, or on occasion nipping over the road for a bag of chips.

When Lily finally plucked up the courage to take him again, Halliwell, then four, was destined to see as his first film a rightly forgotten, non-singing production of *Madame Butterfly*, starring Sylvia Sidney and Cary Grant, and advertised rather whimsically in the *Bolton Evening News* as "the loveliest love story ever told." Despite tripping over a piece of torn carpet on his entrance to the auditorium, the young boy this time managed to retain his composure and was captivated from the moment he saw the huge four-by-three screen, and the giant faces projected onto it.

"The screen was astonishing," he later wrote, "It astonished by its size, by its simplicity, and by its gentle brilliance. It was a window through which I could gaze into an incredibly glamorous, magical, monochrome world. And it really did look silver, just as the film magazines said." Halliwell was fascinated as much by the trailers as he was by the main feature, and the whole experience, including the tram rides and a quick post-film trip to Catterall's the bakers, would remain in his memory for over half a century.

In one sense it might seem a shame that such an important event in this boy's life should have been defined by such a lacklustre film, especially as on the very same day Clark Gable and Jean Harlow were smouldering in *Red Dust* over at the Majestic, and Halliwell's soon-to-be favourites Laurel & Hardy were at the Capitol. But in another sense it was quite appropriate: over the next fifty-five years he would see literally thousands of movies… and the vast majority would leave him unimpressed. He would, however, retain a vivid memory of almost all of them.

> *For me, the greatest days of the cinema were the days when the cigar-chomping moguls sat in the front office, instinctively knowing better than their employees what was best for both of them, and when every studio under contract had an army of master craftsmen capable of producing almost any kind of magic on command.*

In 1933, when the young Halliwell took that first successful trip to the pictures, the Golden Age was in full swing. During the silent era it had been the movie stars – the likes of Fairbanks and Chaplin – who had begun to exert a degree of influence in Hollywood, but the arrival of sound in 1927 changed all that. Suddenly everyone, whether established star or newcomer fresh off 'the Chief', had to pass a sound test. Many failed, and the influx of theatre-trained actors prepared to accept lower pay enabled the studios to regain the power they had lost, by establishing the star system whereby actors were tied down by the notorious 'seven year' contract.

The cost of converting to sound had almost bankrupted the studios, but after financial intervention, and various mergers and acquisitions, five major movie factories came into being which would dominate the American film industry: MGM, Warner Brothers, 20th Century Fox, Paramount and RKO. In addition, there were smaller studios such as Universal and Columbia, and independents like Samuel Goldwyn. For the first couple of years, with noisy cameras housed in soundproof booths, the early 'talkies' were hampered by static actors and dialogue said to be "ponderously and portentously spoken." But, as sound techniques improved and the camera was freed from its chains by innovative directors like Rouben Mamoulian, the era of talking pictures was off and running. Some felt, however, that one Golden Age had in fact just ended.

Outraged at the content of some of Hollywood's output, the Catholic Legion of Decency was formed and persuaded Will Hays, the president of the Motion Picture Producers and Distributors Association of America, to draw up a Production Code. Every script had to be submitted to gain a seal of approval or the resulting film would not be released. The Code forbade among other things, "excessive and lustful kissing," "brutality and possible gruesomeness" and "profane or vulgar expressions." With explicit sex, violence and bad language off the menu, film-makers had to find more ingenious ways of getting their messages across.

The Hollywood studios not only controlled the actors and the technicians but in America they owned cinema chains, making them at once manufacturers, distributors *and* exhibitors. In the UK, cinemas were forced by a system of 'block-booking' into renting a whole clutch of films they did not necessarily want, in order to get at the few choice titles they did. As Hollywood grew in confidence the quality of its output improved, especially in terms of dialogue. Halliwell observed, "To this fluency with words was added an increasing mastery of the visual medium by directors like John Ford and James Whale. Filmland was entering its golden age, [a] period when audiences were constant and enthusiastic, and both reality and the world situation could safely be excluded from the gaze of the producers."

With production overseen by front office 'moguls' like Louis B. Mayer and Darryl F. Zanuck, the studios themselves began to take on distinct characteristics. MGM, the largest and grandest of them all, was famous for its lavish historic or literary adaptations, such as *David Copperfield*, *Mutiny on the Bounty* and *Grand Hotel*. Halliwell wrote, "You really felt sometimes that MGM were in the business not for profit but for what they could do to educate the masses; then you remembered the length of the queue you had stood in, and realised your error." The studio proudly boasted that it had "more stars than there are in heaven," including Greta Garbo, the most enigmatic and enduring screen legend of them all. Garbo mesmerised audiences the world over with her radiant beauty and devastating screen presence. Her torrid affairs and avoidance of publicity only enhanced the air of mystery that surrounded her, and which MGM used to full advantage.

Halliwell always felt he was in the presence of a goddess when Garbo was on the screen. She tended to portray tormented or tragic women in films like *Queen Christina*, in which she plays a monarch who forsakes her country for love, only to end up with neither. Although he confessed to not exactly *enjoying* her pictures, the young Halliwell was nevertheless impressed by their production values, and of the star herself he said, "It was the indestructible, almost hermaphroditic loveliness of the unsmiling Swede that crowds clamoured to see. No star before or since has been placed on quite so high a pedestal by a public so eager to live up to her."

Paramount was renowned for its sparkling society comedies and "agreeable light entertainment" provided by directors such as Ernst Lubitsch, and with debonair charm supplied by the likes of Maurice Chevalier and Herbert Marshall. They were further responsible for bringing the Marx Brothers to the screen, whose unique brand of lunacy it would be a few years before Halliwell fully appreciated. Paramount was also home to the epics of Cecil B. DeMille, perhaps the best of which was *The Sign of the Cross*, which featured Charles Laughton's Nero muttering "delicious debauchery..." as well as Claudette Colbert bathing in asses' milk and – according to publicity – "Christians killed in a novel and diverting manner." These scenes greatly disturbed the young Halliwell, but he remained alert to any implausibilities of plot as he asked his mother why, if the Christians wanted to keep their organisation a secret, they went around drawing easily interpretable symbols in the sand. He was nevertheless inspired to emulate their actions but found that Bolton "did not seem to have the right kind of dust."

Warner Brothers was "all cheap sets and shadows," and its gangster films featuring its roster of heavies – James Cagney, Humphrey Bogart and Edward G. Robinson – brought the studio much criticism for glamorising crime in the likes of *The Public Enemy* and *Little Caesar*. So, instead, they began to tell the same stories from the FBI's point of view in films such as *G Men*, claiming somewhat disingenuously that they were merely highlighting the futility of a life of crime. Warners were significant in the emergence of the musical, with the kaleidoscopic routines devised by Busby Berkeley being particularly groundbreaking. *42nd Street* remains perhaps the best example and still stands up today as a great movie. It was released a year before the Production Code came into effect and its frankness would raise a few eyebrows even now, especially as its jaunty title number depicted begging, prostitution and domestic violence.

RKO was distinguished by the tapping feet of two legends of the age: Fred Astaire and Ginger Rogers, who danced their way into the hearts of millions in a series of productions throughout the thirties. Fred's seemingly effortless grace and elegance lit up the screen, and Ginger's vivacious charm provided him with the perfect partner. Their pictures usually began with an initial rapport upon 'meeting cute', followed by a series of misunderstandings forcing them apart. Various comedic or musical episodes would follow, leading to reconciliation and the inevitable closing dance routine. They were often set in foreign locations wholly recreated on studio sets, which never made any pretence to reality, and the mixture would include some choice wisecracks and *double-entendres* delivered by a supporting cast of "friendly show-offs," adding comic value. Indeed, Halliwell began a repertoire of impersonations inspired by the character actors who provided such solid support in the films he saw. He would mimic the "wounded but threatening tones of Eric Blore" and the "dithering of Edward Everett Horton," who became a particular favourite of his.

When *Top Hat* came to town, it was deemed a big enough event for Halliwell's whole family to attend, queuing at the Queen's and sitting through most of it twice. The film contains the archetypal Astaire number, 'Top Hat, White Tie and Tails', which, according to Halliwell was "the image that made Fred a star and stuck with him all through his career, that of the cheerful, elegant man about town, lighting up the city with his optimism, delighting with the precision of his movement, setting an example for the world."

Universal would make its name with a string of monster movies featuring a host of ghoulish characters such as Frankenstein, Dracula and the Mummy. Halliwell was unable to see these on first release, being too young, but when he did finally make their acquaintance it became one of his favourite genres. These, then, were the Hollywood film factories which supplied the product so eagerly consumed by that young Boltonian boy – and millions like him – throughout those golden days of the 1930s. Days which may have been characterised by hardship and privation, but which he would nevertheless spend the rest of his life recalling and celebrating.

I have no idea why, like a duck to water, I took so easily and instantly to the cinema.

Following that first successful trip, Halliwell and his mother went regularly for weekday picture outings until he started school, when instead they would troop off after supper hopefully to catch the first house, but more likely having to queue for the last. The Queen's would be their venue of choice for some considerable time as it was so comfortable and convenient for the tram. They mostly sat in the five-penny stalls on account of the stairs to the circle putting too much of a strain on poor Lily's ankles, especially after what might have been two hours waiting outside. Halliwell recalled, "It was with my mother that I saw my first few hundred films. Our frequent outings strengthened the natural bonds and made us pals, diminishing to almost nothing the years between us." Indeed, Lily's interest in the cinema was almost the equal of her son's, and they would often go for fish and chips after a showing to discuss and critique the evening's fare.

Jim and Lily generally sought separate interests for most of Halliwell's childhood, their initial romantic spark having long since expired. Jim had no great fondness for the cinema and preferred to spend his evenings at the Spinners' Union or the local. After supper he would tiptoe upstairs to shave and put on his suit; he would light his pipe and slip out the back door, taking care to return home late so as to avoid any arguments. Lily had become by then a large, "often ailing" woman, but she had come from a family which liked to be entertained and educated. "She looked for excuses to take her 'out of herself'," Halliwell wrote, "and she found them through me, and through our joint fascination with the movies."

At the time, cinemas had only one screen and showed the same film for a week at most. Queuing to get in was as much a part of the experience as the film itself: there was no advance booking, you simply stood and waited. On visits to the Capitol, Halliwell would often leave Lily in the queue and venture off to sample the atmosphere of Churchgate. He would chat and tell jokes to other waiting filmgoers or nip to the pastie shop, recalling, "I wandered delightedly down the hundred yards of brightly-lit Churchgate, the most exciting theatre street I had seen." If he stayed away too long he would have to fight his way through the crowds exiting the first house, in order to be reunited with his mother.

There was a certain sense of achievement in gaining admittance to the auditorium, not least because of finally being able to warm up after standing out in the cold for so long. But also because these palaces of public entertainment were often exotically decorated, with gilded proscenium arches and friezes depicting scenes from Venice, Spain or the Middle East. The cinemas operated a policy of 'continuous performance', which meant that patrons could turn up during a film – if space was available – and watch it round, a custom which gave rise to the phrase "this is where we came in." The big cinemas employed an organist to entertain the audience, typically rising from the orchestra pit and with the organ itself often decorated with coloured lights. Halliwell soon formed a deep hatred of them after a traumatic incident when the organist rose *during* a musical's climactic number, and attempted to accompany the film, creating what he described as a "discordant nightmare."

In addition to the queuing and the organ performances, another feature of moviegoing in the thirties now sadly lost is the 'full supporting programme'. This could stretch a night's entertainment to three hours by including any combination of cartoons, short films – maybe a serial episode like *Flash Gordon* or a detective drama – documentaries and newsreels, and finally the main feature. Indeed, the Halliwells' decision on which cinema to visit often rested upon which offered the more attractive supporting programme. The young boy usually found at least some interest in whatever was served up, but it was the short films of two comedians in particular that would stand head and shoulders above them all, and remain his lifelong favourites: Laurel & Hardy.

Stan Laurel was actually born in Ulverston, not far from Bolton, and had travelled to America with Fred Karno's troupe of actors, which included Charlie Chaplin. There, he met Oliver Hardy and one of the most fondly remembered partnerships in entertainment history was formed. Their characters were basically overgrown children in suits and bowler hats. Ollie was the large round one with the insufferable pride – which more often than not came before a fall – and Stan was the thin one, famous for his curiosity which would land them in one fine mess after another. Their essential appeal was based on familiarity: once you knew Stan and Ollie, you knew what was coming next, and that anticipation made the inevitable all the more hilarious when it duly arrived. A major characteristic of their comedy was the tit-for-tat routines of escalating destruction, which in the case of *Two Tars* and *Big Business* made up almost the entire twenty-minute running times. The violence would usually begin with an accidental injury which would be assumed deliberate by its victim. "Each injured party," Halliwell wrote, "instead of exacting immediate revenge on his attacker, would quietly simmer while thinking up his next onslaught, an onslaught which his victim would make no attempt to avoid, watching instead with interest as the scissors or the eggs or the gluepot were procured and wielded."

Possibly the most famous of all the Laurel & Hardy shorts was *The Music Box*, in which the pair try to push a piano up an enormous flight of stone steps, and inevitably wreak havoc as they go. It was not even necessary to know the title of their latest release, as on one occasion the advertising board at the Capitol read simply, "In addition we have pleasure in presenting our dear old friends Mr. Laurel and Mr. Hardy." And dear old friends they indeed were, to millions.

I was always grateful for the traditions inherited from my father's time, and it was generally not to my own generation but to my elders that I looked for guidance.

Jim was content to hand over his pay packets to his wife as he left the running of the house to her. Despite frequent periods of unemployment, his wages were enough to cover Lily and their son's almost nightly visits to the cinema, as well as 'wakes week' holidays on the Isle of Man and bank holiday excursions to Blackpool. More surprisingly, in 1934 Lily had managed to save enough for them to move house – not far, just a little further up the hill of Bradford Road to a semi-detached. Relatives and friends 'down below' felt the Halliwells were getting too big for their boots by moving to the area of Great Lever, but although the conditions were a marked improvement on Parkfield Road, their exposed position now meant that they were susceptible to the soot showers of the entire county.

The new house had a small front garden in which the young Halliwell was photographed, sitting cross-legged on a rock, with a neat driveway and a bay window behind him. He wears a shirt, short trousers and sandals, and has parted hair with one side combed forward. His rounded face shows no sign of the jutting chin which would later characterise his appearance. Despite Lily's efforts, the payments for the new house were steep and it remained sparsely furnished and poorly maintained as a result. But, her striving to better the family and to rise above their circumstances was clearly in evidence. Over the next few years this drive would have more far-reaching effects on her son's life.

Due to illness or simple misfortune, Halliwell's sisters had never received any secondary education, both eventually drifting into retail. Lily was determined that this was not going to happen to her son, and so over the next few years she encouraged him to seek out knowledge and to improve himself at every opportunity. She enrolled him at the Central Library, and whilst she was well aware of the questionable accuracy of Hollywood's attempts at history-telling, if such entertainment provided a stimulus for her son to learn, then that was all the better. Thus, the young Halliwell's interest in the Romans was encouraged by Eddie Cantor in *Roman Scandals*; in the British Empire by *The Four Feathers*, and in art by *Rembrandt*. He eagerly sought out the literary sources of films he had seen, such as *Alice in Wonderland*, *David Copperfield* and *Treasure Island*. It was already clear that the boy had a sharp mind: he had learned to read almost by himself at a very young age, and when he started at St. Simon's and St. Jude's elementary school he made an immediate impression on the teachers. However, he struggled to make friends as he seemed to have very little in common with the other children, later conceding that he was "an inward-looking child." He loathed sports and games, and whilst his contemporaries were flocking to the Saturday matinees to see cowboy films and detective serials – and usually behaving badly to boot – Halliwell, even then, preferred a little sophistication in his entertainment. Simple slapstick or farce bored him: "I looked for some cleverness in the presentation, some wit in the dialogue, some hint of the magician's wand."

He found it in films such as *The Thin Man*, in which William Powell and Myrna Loy play a husband and wife team who solve a murder mystery on New Year's Eve, with the help of several martinis and plenty of wisecracks. In keeping with the idea of the cinema as escape, Halliwell wanted to see life depicted as it was in his sisters' magazines, "replete with champagne cocktails and Alpine holidays and dinner jackets and grand pianos." He especially valued films which contained a 'lightness of touch', but if the productions of the 1930s possessed one characteristic which he appreciated more than any other, it was *optimism*.

Not surprisingly, with all their cinemagoing and with her desire to improve him, Halliwell was much closer to his mother than he was to his father. However, he did often accompany Jim on his weekly visits to the Grand Theatre, to watch music hall stars such as Max Miller and Sandy Powell. He found the theatrical atmosphere exciting and especially enjoyed the good-natured barracking from the bar. He also joined his father on walks up on the high moors, where he found the fresh air and open spaces a tonic compared to the grime of the town. Halliwell would retain a fondness for barren places for the rest of his life.

> *Even the more expensive* [British] *movies tended to be stilted, class ridden or downright foolish.*

In contrast to Hollywood's almost unbroken period of success throughout the 1930s, the British film industry at the time was struggling. The public in general did not care for its output as the pictures often lacked action, substituting instead excessive dialogue spoken by stiff actors. The American films, on the other hand, were slick, professional and often spectacular, with players adopting a more natural, wisecracking manner which greatly appealed to audiences in Bolton and elsewhere. An Act of Parliament was brought in to force the American studios to plough back a percentage of their profits into British production, and the exhibitors were similarly required to show a certain quota of homemade films. But it was a grave mistake, as it led to the creation of the infamous 'quota quickies' of which Halliwell observed, "These were incredibly cheap productions flung together by American distributors ... the quality was unspecified, in practice it was always abysmal."

But there were exceptions. Due to a downturn in the standard of presentation at the Queen's, Lily and her son transferred their allegiance to the Hippodrome, a converted music hall at the western end of Deansgate. It was there that they experienced the productions of mainly British stars of what Halliwell termed "low comedy": the likes of Will Hay, the Crazy Gang and the Aldwych *farceurs*, which proved at least that not all British product was of a poor standard. In addition, at the Hippodrome they enjoyed many of the films featuring one of the biggest entertainment stars Britain has ever produced: Gracie Fields.

It is almost impossible now to comprehend how big a star Gracie was in the thirties, and how cherished she was by the British public. The Rochdale-born former cotton spinner may not have been blessed with film star looks but she had a singing voice of almost unmatched range and quality. She was equally at home performing comic ditties in a croaky Lancashire accent as she was mocking maudlin Victorian songs of hardship, or moving hearts with a perfectly pitched ballad. She was the local girl who had made good, and yet, despite fabulous wealth and stardom, still managed to retain that down-to-earth quality that made people feel they knew her. To Halliwell, and the millions who adored her, she was simply 'Our Gracie'.

To achieve such enormous popularity almost *required* conditions of hardship, so that her independent spirit could offer people a beacon of hope. They could be inspired by the sight of Gracie holding her head high, marching proudly along, cocking a snook at pomposity and exalting the audience to "look on the bright side" or to "look up and laugh." She made them feel that any adversity could be overcome by the application of a bit of industry and optimism, and that self pity was to be shunned. *Sing as we Go* remains perhaps her most representative film, made especially relevant to Halliwell's life as it was partly shot in Bolton. "Lancastrians preferred to laugh at hardship," he wrote, "and if Gracie Fields was their inspiration then this film above all was their shield." Gracie stayed at the Swan Hotel on Churchgate during the shoot and Jim Halliwell actually watched some of the filming on one of his out-of-work afternoons. She played a cotton spinner, one of many laid off when a mill is forced to close, whereupon she travels to Blackpool in search of work. After various escapades, a last minute plot contrivance sees the mill reopened, enabling Gracie to lead her colleagues triumphantly back to work. As Halliwell observed, "If the film had been set in Timbuctoo, Boltonians would still have flocked to hear the performer we most loved … Gracie was one of us; and as J. B. Priestley's boisterous script unfolded, you could almost smell the tripe and onions."

As an illustration of how popular she was, particularly in the North, *Sing as we Go* had its first run in Bolton at two majors, the Rialto and the Queen's, eventually playing at *eight* different cinemas in the town. By contrast, Garbo's *Queen Christina* – with all the might of Hollywood's grandest studio behind it – opened only at the Capitol and went on to limited success in the lower houses. Halliwell would see *Sing as we Go* many times during his life and referred to it as "a joy in itself and as a revered relic of my own childhood." Years later, for a television programme, he tracked down the mill gates through which Gracie marched at the end of the film, and whenever he hummed the film's title song it brought a lump to his throat.

On the male side, and almost as popular, there was George Formby, whose 'character' could not have been more removed from Gracie's, although his catchphrase "turned out nice again" appeared to convey the same message of hope that she did. George was the gormless stumbler who overcame adversity usually by accident and quite implausibly ended up with the girl, often charming her with a saucy song on his ukulele. *Let George Do It*, perhaps his most representative outing, contained a fantasy sequence in which George flies a balloon to Germany, interrupts a rally and punches out Hitler! Halliwell wrote, "Anything starring the lad from Wigan could be revived again and again in the town centre, for all the staff had to do was open the doors and stand well back." On one of their cinema trips, as Halliwell and his mother settled into their seats for an evening's entertainment, a gawky-looking man shuffled onto the stage quite unannounced… it was George Formby himself. He had been passing by and noticed the film was on, and so dropped in to wish his patrons a good evening. Unfortunately, he had not brought his ukulele and so managed only a few nervous words before vanishing from view. Halliwell was thrilled to find himself in the company of such a major star.

If the contributions of Gracie Fields and George Formby were fairly primitive entertainments based wholly on star personalities, those of a young British director named Alfred Hitchcock were another matter. This directorial genius would be snapped up by Hollywood before the decade was out, but before he left he made two gilt-edged classics in his home country: *The 39 Steps* and *The Lady Vanishes*. Most of his signature aspects are to be found in these two, and it could be argued that he spent the rest of his career imitating them. Both films contain a character who nobody believes and a piece of information valuable to spies, which is the excuse for the action – a cinematic device known as a McGuffin.

In *The 39 Steps*, Robert Donat is pursued across the Scottish moors; he finds himself handcuffed to Madeleine Carroll and ends up having a confrontation at the London Palladium. Halliwell and Lily were warmed up by its mixture of suspense, excitement and comedy on a cold night when the Hippodrome's heating broke down. He described it as "the electrically vivid first flowering of a brilliant young British film-maker who hopes we will enjoy his bag of tricks and not reproach him for the backcloths and non sequiturs."

In *The Lady Vanishes*, Margaret Lockwood meets an old woman on a train who then mysteriously disappears. Halliwell saw it on a return visit to the Queen's and went again a few nights later. It quickly became one of his favourites, as it contained so many of the qualities he enjoyed: sophisticated entertainment, intrigue and mystery, and supporting actors providing comedy asides. He later wrote, "It is still among the most entertaining ways one can find of spending eighty minutes in a cinema."

These two films offer marvellous if completely implausible adventures, which proceed at such a pace that the audience has no time to question the plot. Hitchcock firmly established his reputation with these two, and when Hollywood beckoned he went on to become the world's most famous film director. He remained so for three decades… and he even played a small role in Halliwell's future career.

Another giant of the cinema at work in the thirties was Alexander Korda, a Hungarian-born journalist who became a producer and put British film on the map with *The Private Life of Henry VIII*. Masterpieces such as *Rembrandt* and *The Four Feathers* would lead Halliwell to call him "the saviour of the British film industry," and one of Korda's films in particular always reminded him of his family's annual holidays to the Isle of Man. The whole family went on these trips but in later years Halliwell's sisters preferred to stay in different digs, and would only remain with the others until the dance halls opened. In a curious arrangement, cottage apartments were rented from a landlady, with the occupants buying their own food which was then labelled up and cooked by a maid, resulting in many occasions where guests ended up eating someone else's meal. Halliwell observed, "The cheapness of this arrangement when compared with full board can scarcely have compensated for the immense confusion it caused." He was pictured with his parents outside one such cottage, wearing shorts with a button jacket and a cap, and standing smartly to attention.

On these holidays he would be up early on the first morning to scout the fare at the local cinemas, such as the Crescent Pavilion in Douglas, where he encountered *Things to Come*. This remarkable film, made in 1936 from a screenplay by H. G. Wells, follows a fictional English town through several ages. An accurately predicted war in 1940 is followed by famine, disease and the town's eventual rebirth as a futuristic utopia, where technology rules peoples' lives. The film was characterised by the brilliant design of its director, William Cameron Menzies, who would go on to grace *Gone with the Wind*. Halliwell had seen nothing like it: "For a small boy on holiday in 1936 ... it was a new and awesome concept of a world which had hitherto seemed rather grimy and hard."

Despite the contributions of Korda and Hitchcock, and Fields and Formby, it would be the best part of ten years before British cinema truly blossomed. But in one area of the entertainment business Britain led the way, with a development which would one day have serious ramifications for the entire cinema industry. On 2nd November, 1936, the BBC started the world's first regular television service, an epoch-making event that later shaped Halliwell's own career. Approximately three hundred receivers within a few miles of London's Alexandra Palace could pick up the signal; by the end of the decade there would be more than twenty thousand. A film magazine of the time announced gravely – and could not possibly have known quite how presciently – "We warn the industry: television is a serious danger."

The décor was undeniably sumptuous. My first impression, after I got my breath back, was of rounded corners everywhere, without a right-angle in sight.

As the thirties progressed and movies came to form such a vital part of the fabric of everyday life, new and better houses in which to present them were springing up almost every week. One day in 1936, Halliwell observed some workmen clearing a site in Ashburner Street, near the old market. He read with excitement that it was to be a new Odeon cinema, the latest addition to the chain founded by entrepreneur Oscar Deutsch. However, because work progressed so slowly, in the time it took to build the Odeon another picture house was begun and completed. This was the Lido (pronounced 'Leedo'), a little way along Bradshawgate from the Queen's. It was duly assessed upon its opening by Halliwell, but although he was impressed by the Venetian frieze around its proscenium arch, he found the ice cream queues too long and the stalls too shallow for him to see. Furthermore, the Lido devoted too much of its performance time to the organ, as a cheap alternative to running a supporting programme.

However, he did see one undeniable classic there: *Dr Jekyll and Mr Hyde*, directed in 1931 by that master of film technique, Rouben Mamoulian. This was the version of the famous story for which Fredric March received an Academy Award as the tormented split personality of the title. Halliwell wrote, "It was my first experience, in our well-behaved town, of an audience cat-calling and rough-housing during a performance. Mum said comfortingly that they only did it to prove they were not scared by Jekyll's transformations into Hyde; I was, but tried not to show it."

The film was made in the pre-Production Code era and positively strains with barely suppressed sexuality. The garter scene, in which Miriam Hopkins dangles her naked leg over the edge of the bed, was one example, but the film additionally features some extraordinarily suggestive dialogue and shocking brutality for its time. It further abounds with innovative tricks of technique, such as subjective camera, extreme close-ups, match cuts and dissolves – and possibly the slowest screen wipe in history. Mamoulian displayed a sense of visual grammar that any present day director could (and certainly should) learn from. Halliwell thought it "a masterpiece of cinematic flow and invention."

When the Odeon was finally finished, it turned out to be a 2,600-seat work of art. The cinema looked positively futuristic set against its drab surroundings, with its art deco curves and lines and its cream faience frontage. Inside, the emphasis was on comfort and ambience, with every seat of "precisely the same type and standard," as the free programme placed on every seat on opening night asserted. Halliwell and his mother were in attendance, of course, on Saturday 21st August, 1937 – in fact so were his whole family, although his sisters typically sat separately with their boyfriends. He was excited about being part of a real *occasion*, and was impressed by "the immensity of the red velour curtains; the cunningly concealed lighting [and] the great golden honeycomb grills on each side of the screen."

The entertainment began with a Compton organ rising from the orchestra pit, playing 'Entry of the Gladiators'. This was followed by another live performance from a military band and an opening speech from the mayor. The enormous luminescent screen was eventually set to work with a Mickey Mouse cartoon and a colour musical providing support to the main attraction: Conrad Veidt in the spy thriller *Dark Journey*, in which secrets are woven into the fabric of a costume seller's dresses. Despite the café serving the "toughest buttered crumpets" around, the Bolton Odeon would prove to be one of Halliwell's favourite cinemas, and he referred to it as "that palatial hall." He would enjoy many great films there over the next few years, including two westerns, *Stagecoach* and *Destry Rides Again*, for which he retained a special affection even though it was a genre that never greatly appealed to him.

Half-employed people in a Lancashire mill town had more need than most of a Shangri-La to turn to.

In early 1938, the *Bolton Evening News* trumpeted the impending arrival of a production which would prove to be truly a landmark in Halliwell's life: "Next week: the supreme film achievement of all time, *Lost Horizon* … by any standard of comparison, the greatest picture ever made."

Lost Horizon was directed by Frank Capra and adapted from the novel by James Hilton. It starred the elegant British actor Ronald Colman as Robert Conway, a diplomat who escapes a political conflict in Nepal only for his plane to be hijacked and diverted to the Tibetan Himalayas. After crash landing, he is taken to Shangri-La, a place of wonder on "the other side of the mountain," where the weather is always warm and people are kind and live to a very advanced age. Conway is smitten by the place, and when events force him to leave he tries desperately to find his way back.

The film was very much an 'event movie' of the time: it was said to have cost over two million dollars – easily Columbia's most expensive production – and principal photography alone took ten months. Halliwell had been eagerly looking forward to its release as there had been much talk of it in the film magazines, especially concerning the lavishness of its sets. On the Friday before it opened, the local paper devoted a full page to what appears at first glance to be an article about the making of the film. Closer examination reveals the piece to consist entirely of adverts for local businesses tied in to the release – an inspired piece of publicity which probably paid for itself with subscriptions:

> The magic of Shangri-La is that it has a perfectly equitable climate in the midst of Tibet's ice and snow. In such a place you might not need Mason's fireplaces, but in Bolton…

> Should the film *Lost Horizon* give you any ideas for original silverware, jewellery or table decorations, discuss them with Prestons the jewellers.

> Indian ponies were used in the film to represent the primitive transport of the Tibetan Eden … but for good transport in Bolton there is nothing better than a Ford car from Gordon's.

The film was big enough to gain a first run at both the Hippodrome and the Theatre Royal, and after the first day the paper announced, "Instantaneous Success! Record crowds endorse the critics' verdict of Frank Capra's terrific production … you are advised to come early." Halliwell and Lily braved the crowds and were not disappointed. He later called it "a haunting piece of Hollywood moonshine ... a thoroughly entertaining film and a thrilling adventure of the mind." It would remain a firm favourite for the rest of his life and it also came to represent his entire career. He was ever after celebrating the films he saw in his youth, as if trying to find a way back to his own Shangri-La – those golden years in Bolton.

Lost Horizon still has great power. In addition to a vivid sense of adventure the film features a haunting score by Dmitri Tiomkin, some impressively staged scenes and the inevitable supporting characters, including Halliwell's favourite ditherer, Edward Everett Horton. He was, however, disappointed to find that *his* character was not actually in the original novel, which predictably enough he immediately borrowed from the library. This was one of many changes from the book which even its author felt were improvements. The main reason why the film succeeds so effectively, however, is the presence of Ronald Colman, that fine and distinguished actor with the pencil moustache and the velvety voice. Halliwell wrote that he was "never observed to raise his voice, lose his temper or speak unkindly to a lady. His image was compounded of three-fifths British reserve, one-fifth debonair optimism and one-fifth idealistic dreamer." Colman captivated audiences with his elegant style: the wonderment of Shangri-La and the pain of losing it are etched into his face.

In one sense *Lost Horizon* could be thought of as the ultimate Golden Age movie, as it represented the very reason why people went to the cinema in the first place: the wish to escape reality and to live in a fantasy world. Whenever I watch it, it stays in my mind for days afterwards.

> *Black and white, for certain purposes, is richer than colour, as poetry is to prose; for colour can only show the world as it is, whereas black and white in the hands of skilled photographers and set designers can encapsulate a dream.*

Towards the end of the decade, and at his mother's suggestion, Halliwell took his first solo trip to the pictures. He spotted a tear in her eye as he left the house that evening, and did not enjoy the experience very much. However, Lily appears to have been insistent, perhaps seeing it as some sort of rite of passage for both of them. Without her presence, he occasionally overdosed on sweets or lost track of time and was late home, but he gradually became accustomed; he began to enjoy observing the people around him as they laughed and cried and gasped together. As he grew in confidence, the young boy began to explore the picture houses all over town – and there were plenty to choose from. Halliwell reckoned there to be twenty-eight cinemas within easy reach of his Bradford Road home, and nearly all are described in detail in his memoir, *Seats in all Parts* – "the Atlas was incompetently run and maintained … the Regal was untidy and uncomfortable … the Royal had a mock-Tudor façade but the interior was very seedy…"

It was never questioned, a boy not yet ten years old venturing out to cinemas on his own, and wandering about town often after dark – "He'll come to no harm," Lily confidently asserted. She did, however, ban him from visiting the Tivoli, as it was frequented by cotton spinners who came directly from a nearby mill. The air was consequently thick with linseed oil which stuck to her son's clothes.

Halliwell grew to love exploring his environment and heading off to visit his many aunts, uncles and cousins scattered across the town. He would stroll across the high metal footbridge which still to this day crosses the railway tracks, and as puffs of smoke from trains billowed around him he would dream of what life was like in the far-off places he had only ever seen at the movies. One incident points up the innocence of that vanished time in particular: when he attempted to see *King Kong* at the Odeon. On finding that adult supervision was required, Halliwell tried to persuade total strangers in the queue to act as his guardian. That is, until an officious commissionaire spotted his attempts and shooed him away. He consoled himself by gazing at the pictures in the stills cabinets, but they were only artists' impressions as RKO had refused to release any actual shots of the great monster. The images were in colour, of course, as was all publicity material. Indeed, it was often said that the brightest things to be seen about town were the movie posters, standing in direct contrast to their bleak surroundings, as well as to the vast majority of the films they advertised.

Despite the arrival of Technicolor, there seems to have been no great demand for colour pictures. One would have thought people in such an environment, so starved of colour elsewhere, would have relished the idea but box office takings appear not to have been especially affected. Halliwell's own preference was for black and white, as he felt it more in keeping with the expressionist nature of the films themselves, although he did grudgingly admit that there were some admirable colour films around. The studios themselves seemed to make no firm attempts to adopt the process permanently, mostly because of the extra expense involved but the technique was also difficult to master, and bad colour was worse than none at all. However, as Halliwell observed, "By the time *Gone with the Wind* was presented, the hues had almost all the richness and definition one could desire."

That particular masterpiece was made in 1939, widely regarded as the Golden Year of the Golden Age, a year in which the Academy was fully justified in nominating ten films for the Best Picture Oscar. Out of them, only *Gone with the Wind* itself, the eventual winner, was wholly in colour. Although it would be another three years before David O. Selznick's Civil War soap opera finally arrived in Bolton, Halliwell called it "a magnificent monument to the Hollywood which, like the old South, has been swept away." Despite the enormous success of even this film, however, colour remained over the next decade the exception rather than the rule.

Lily had one more rite of passage in store for her young son, in her determination to keep him out of the mills and away from shop work. She persuaded his school's administrators to let him sit for a scholarship to Bolton Grammar School, the most prestigious centre of learning in the town. He took the examination a year early, and was subsequently interviewed by an imposing headmaster in full gown-and-mortar-board regalia. Halliwell felt the pressure, knowing what it meant to his mother and observing for himself the snobbishness of the other parents whose children were in competition, most of whom came from much more upmarket areas than Great Lever. But Lily had the last laugh when the *Bolton Evening News* announced his success: her son was one of only five children in the county who had won scholarships.

At the end of the 1930s, the young boy was on his way hopefully to a promising future, thanks to a combination of his own abilities and Lily's resolve. His lifelong love affair with the cinema was firmly established, although the era he would recall so fondly was drawing to a close. The Golden Age itself still had many years to run, however: techniques would improve greatly over the next decade and some of the most talented actors and directors ever to work in the medium would emerge. In many ways the best was yet to come and –

astonishingly enough – the cinema's popularity was still increasing.

Halliwell's future was far from certain but at least he now had a chance of a brighter one than many of his family's previous generations…

But this was September 1939, and more important events were about to intervene…

2

No Concessions to Low-brows

- Bolton School and the Army, 1939-49 -

In the late 1930s, a London-based social research project was established to study the everyday lives of ordinary folk in Britain. It was called Mass-Observation, and one of its founders was a documentary film-maker named Humphrey Jennings. Paid investigators were dispatched across the country to observe the movements and conversations of people in a variety of public situations, and voluntary contributions were received from individuals regarding their own behaviour. The study into the habits of cinemagoers eventually formed one of the largest collections on a single theme produced by the project. Its research work was carried out in Bolton, just after the war began.

Questionnaires were distributed to three cinemas in the town, and despite the relatively small sample sizes the responses revealed that Bolton audiences generally enjoyed Hollywood's costume films and musicals a great deal more than their British equivalents. They preferred comedies to dramas and enjoyed topical films provided they were not "excessively realistic or particularly unpleasant." It was observed that the Odeon responses displayed a higher "literary fluency" than the others, and that its respondents tended to be from more upmarket areas, which led to the conclusion that there was a greater proportion of middle and upper working class patrons of that cinema in particular. The Embassy was another picture house examined and its manager was interviewed:

If business is bad, the cinema is bad. You take any dispute concerning working people, in any mill or foundry in Bolton. During that dispute your evening takings drop, but your afternoon goes up. It proves that however hard up they are they still want the cinema, so they take the cheaper seats in the afternoon.

Since the Lido and Odeon have opened, there are three to four thousand more seats in the town, yet I've had no drop. Last night I was boozing with two friends, both in the cinema business, who had had the same experience.

Week in week out I get six thousand people or more who come here regularly twice a week. They won't only go once, but two and even three times to a good musical. Musical pictures in Lancashire go the best for any. Five years ago I gave the cinema three years. My view now is that it will always be here.

Leslie Halliwell never forgot that fateful Sunday morning, when his mother gave him his breakfast "with the most serious look, and said we had to listen to the wireless at 11 o'clock because Mr Chamberlain would be speaking." The whole family listened in silence – as millions did – to the announcement that Britain and France were going to war. After the broadcast, Halliwell wandered out into Great Lever Park and gazed up at the sky, to see whether he could spot any German planes overhead.

"All our lives were instantly affected," he later recalled in a television programme, "Blackouts, war work, food rationing – every kind of shortage. I didn't get to go to my new school for a week until it was properly sandbagged, and worse still… all the cinemas closed." An outcry resulted from the closures, with even George Bernard Shaw writing to *The Times* to complain. The government was eventually persuaded that the need for people to escape was greater during wartime and – more importantly – that the cinema could be used as a powerful propaganda weapon. The picture houses were duly reopened after a couple of weeks.

When he finally made it to his new school, the young Halliwell stepped off the tram on Chorley New Road, one of the major arteries which lead uphill out of the town. He was wearing his blue blazer with shorts and a cap, and carried a satchel over one shoulder and a gas mask over the other. He must have felt a chill at the sight of the long, low, brown building which loomed in front of him, set back from the road by its tidy green lawns. He would have walked under the archway of its intimidating turreted gatehouse, which separated the boys' section from the girls', and arrived in the main courtyard. Beyond this are more lawns and smaller school buildings leading to the playing fields which descend in levels towards the town. From this vantage point, Halliwell counted sixty-three mill chimneys – a view which served as a chilling reminder of the life to which he would return if he failed to live up to his potential.

Almost from the very first day he struggled. Intimidated by the grandeur of the place, he felt as though he did not belong – a feeling exacerbated by the resentment he received from some of the children whose parents were *paying* for their education: Halliwell had got in for free. The schoolwork itself, algebra and geometry, befuddled him at first and he could get no help at home as such subjects were a foreign language to his family. He hated games and resented being thrown into the pool during swimming. His old schoolmaster at St. Simon's was disappointed to hear of his first term's performance and rather unkindly told him so. Halliwell had been top of the class there, and the master had assured Bolton School they were getting something special. With the pressure mounting, coupled with the added privations brought by the onset of war, the young boy retreated within himself, and more and more turned to the cinema for solace.

Ronald Lowe was in the same class as Halliwell, and since he was another scholarship winner I asked him about this situation:

> Perhaps he personally felt some resentment but I don't recall that at all. I mean, there *was* a difference, and the difference was really in intellectual ability, because the scholarship boys were the sort of *crème de la crème* of the district, who were grabbed by Bolton school. He was extremely bright – he was a born intellectual, really, and a tremendous film enthusiast.

With the trams and buses working out conveniently, Halliwell found that he could catch the first house on his way home from school and only have to pay matinee prices. The programmes were usually quite short and by half past six he could be home for dinner. He recalled, "At seven o'clock I would then do my homework, with a cup of tea in the one hand and a pen in the other." As more and more men went off to war, he observed that cinema staff were becoming increasingly female or "semi-disabled." He further noticed that queues formed earlier and contained many servicemen, who got in for half price. The bigger releases were then filling two or three houses a day instead of the usual house and a half – cinemagoing was more popular than ever.

American films were still dominating the industry, not only in terms of box office success but they were also reaching hitherto unscaled heights of artistic quality. The output of the early 1940s reads like a roll call of Hollywood's finest ever directors, all making their finest films:

Hitchcock made *Rebecca* and *Foreign Correspondent*; John Ford made *How Green Was My Valley* and *The Grapes of Wrath*; Howard Hawks made *His Girl Friday*; William Wyler made *The Letter*; John Huston made *The Maltese Falcon*; George Cukor made *The Philadelphia Story*; William Dieterle made *All That Money Can Buy*; Michael Curtiz made *Yankee Doodle Dandy* and *Casablanca*; Preston Sturges made *Sullivan's Travels* and *The Miracle of Morgan's Creek*... and Orson Welles made *Citizen Kane* and *The Magnificent Ambersons*.

What other equivalent period in cinema history has produced such supreme examples of the combination of entertainment and craft? All of the above are intelligent films, whether comedies or dramas, and yet with one or two exceptions they managed to appeal to large audiences – thus proving the maxim which Halliwell would always hold to, that great art *could* also be popular. He wrote of this particular period, "I already sensed that I was living through a golden age of cinema, a time when filmgoing had become an occupation not merely to pass an evening but to stimulate the mind."

One of the strangest, most unsettling but impeccably produced films of the era is now all but forgotten. *Kings Row*, directed by Sam Wood, tells the story of a group of children who grow to adulthood in a seemingly pleasant turn of the century town which hides dark secrets behind its doors – a theme that would be mimicked many times over the years. It had no major stars, although one of its principals, Ronald Reagan, would go on to become President of the United States. The distinguished British character actor Claude Rains played a physician who uses draconian methods to treat his daughter's mental illness, and Charles Coburn played another who takes sadistic pleasure in performing unnecessary amputations. The film was essentially a soap opera, before such things were invented, laying on plenty of melodrama and family intrigue, as well as possessing a brutal edge.

Halliwell first read about the film in *Picturegoer* magazine, a publication which he had found to be "sound, reliable and friendly." Paper was scarce during wartime so he had to make sure of being at the local newsagent on a Thursday morning for eight o'clock, to queue for his copy. Indeed, at this time the *Bolton Evening News* shrank from its previous twelve or so pages to just four very cramped ones, with the cinema advertisements that had previously dominated the front page, reduced to a single column. *Picturegoer* ran a special feature on *Kings Row*, describing it as "an adult film with no concessions to nitwits." Halliwell was intrigued as he felt he was now approaching the age where he could appreciate the screen's more cerebral entertainments. He saw the film on his own at the Capitol on its first run but then took both his mother and sister for a second showing. He found it to be "a supreme example of the challenging, thought-provoking and memorable melodrama which the Hollywood studio system could provide in its heyday." He commended in particular Erich Wolfgang Korngold's haunting score, which "floods this entire movie with its subdued light. Its effect is minatory, ominous; it makes one think of cheerless times of history."

Another film Halliwell read about avidly in *Picturegoer* was *Citizen Kane*. He wrote, "I devoured all the critical analyses of its story structure, its photography, its acting, its narrative art; and when our local number two hall, the Lido, announced it as a forthcoming attraction I literally jumped for joy." Unfortunately, his joy was short-lived: when he arrived on the Tuesday evening he found that the film had already been taken off owing to a poor reception on the Monday. It would be ten years before he finally caught up with Welles's masterpiece.

Picturegoer rapidly became Halliwell's moviegoing bible and his gradually rising stack of copies on top of the meat safe was protected by a 'keep off' notice. He especially enjoyed its double page spread of reviews by Lionel Collier, who usually covered seven or eight new releases a week and gave each one a star rating of up to four asterisks. After a couple of paragraphs of précis Collier would begin his critique, culminating in a clipped sentence of summary: "Ingenuous stuff, sentimental and quite well put over ... Romance and slapstick are competently blended but the picture never really touches the high spots ... The humour is of the stereotyped domestic order but is put over slickly and is well directed."

Collier's style greatly appealed to Halliwell, who found himself more often than not in agreement with his opinions. His own reading habits had by then widened to include more serious works on film appreciation, such as Paul Rotha's *Movie Parade* and Alistair Cooke's *Garbo and the Night Watchmen*. He began to cast a more critical eye over the fare being served up at the local picture houses, and recorded the details of each programme he encountered in an exercise book purchased from the school shop. With one page reserved for a whole evening's entertainment, space was at a premium and so he adopted Collier's style of terse assessments, as well as borrowing his star ratings. He went through several books in this fashion and kept the process going for many years. In addition, he would spend his Saturday nights drawing up "amusement guides" which detailed all the available entertainment in the town each week. As Jim and Lily had temporarily begun once again to go out together, he would sit for hours composing his guides with the wireless for company.

And there was more variety than ever to report on. With stage actors deserting the cities for fear of being bombed, provincial towns like Bolton suddenly found themselves overwhelmed by live performance. The demand was such that the Hippodrome went over to musicals and shows, and the Theatre Royal – whose presentation of films had been so shoddy – jumped at the chance to revert to live entertainment. The City Hall began hosting classical concerts and the Lido, with its reportedly cramped backstage area, went semi-live, presenting pantomimes and music hall evenings as well as films. Halliwell sampled as much of this activity as he could and developed a strong affection for the theatre which he would retain for the rest of his life. He had previously gained some limited stage experience himself, performing in plays at his previous school. He then joined the St Mark's Church Youth Club where he began to produce and appear in revue shows, impersonating Al Jolson in one and playing Widow Twankey in another. Indeed, it would be this activity more than any other which eventually brought him acceptance among his classmates.

He did form a small group of friends in those early years at school, however, and by then his physiognomy had led to him being given the nickname "Chinnie." One of his group was Ron Edge – "Eggie" – himself a scholarship winner, and he spoke to me nearly seventy years later from his home in South Carolina:

> We had something in common, going to the same school as the prestigious people, the children of mill owners who could pay. We were in the same class … you tended to befriend people in a similar situation to you. We all had to play games but he and I did so more or less under protest. We were often put in the outfield.
> I enjoyed the movies, perhaps not quite as much as him. I went regularly about once a week with my parents. As I got older I went on my own or with Halliwell. I would guess he went at least twice a week – it didn't really cost very much. He was particularly definite about what he liked but our taste was very similar: if he recommended a movie, I knew I would like it.

Malcolm Worrall, another contemporary, further confirmed that Halliwell went to the cinema at least twice a week after school, as well as attending the occasional weekend performance. These were rarer as he was expected to contribute to the housework at weekends. Halliwell enjoyed going in a group, although he later recalled that they did not converse all that much, except about the films they saw.

He and his new friends – "social misfits" as he called them – were especially fond of horror films and felt sophisticated enough to bring an intellectual approach to them. Universal had presented both *Dracula* and *Frankenstein* to huge success in the 1930s but were slow to follow them up. By the early forties, however, the studio had made a name for itself with a series of these relatively cheap forms of entertainment. Halliwell wrote, "The best of them were fairytales for grown-ups; the worst were comic-strip adventures for mental incompetents." Officially, one had to be sixteen to see a film with an 'H' – for horror – certificate but Halliwell found that if he took off his school cap he could usually pass for it. In addition, at the Lido, he was actually assisted on several occasions by a friendly commissionaire who helped him in through a side entrance.

One day a schoolteacher took Halliwell's entire class to see a propaganda film called *This is England*, thinking they might find it instructional. However, the film turned out to be a disappointment and the teacher allowed the children to stay and watch whatever came on after it, as he was going home. Halliwell and his friends knew full well that next on the bill was *The Mummy's Hand*, the first film in which a slow moving, malevolent, bandaged protagonist stalks its victims. The boys were pleased with themselves for keeping quiet but an hour or so later were feeling rather green, and despite it still being light they found the walk home distinctly uneasy. He later commended the film as a "pretty efficient little movie of its type," although admitted that it had soon lost any power to frighten – not least because of the dozens of variations on the same theme there had been over the years. He further observed, "In this kind of film the heroine cheerfully retires to her tent alone despite three violent deaths that evening." In fact, it is difficult now to imagine that any of these films once frightened people, but there are accounts from the time of cinemagoers being genuinely terrified, even fainting during performances.

Other works in the genre which Halliwell especially appreciated were Val Lewton's series of low budget occult thrillers for RKO. He recalled, "My friends and I were impressed by Lewton's daring to deal with devil worship in *The Seventh Victim*." Their B-movie titles, such as *Curse of the Cat People* and *I Walked with a Zombie*, often belied the thoughtful, character driven stories they contained, with subtleties that reward repeat viewings. Halliwell pursued them to "remoter spots" once he became aware of their quality and also recalled venturing to the Manchester Odeon with a friend to see *The Uninvited*, in which Ray Milland inherits a haunted Cornish cottage. They challenged each other to write ghost stories when they got home – indeed, it was around this time that the vicar at St. Mark's, Canon Stanley Leatherbarrow, introduced Halliwell to the supernatural tales of M. R. James. After Leatherbarrow moved to Malvern in Worcestershire, Halliwell would visit him during the summer holidays and years later was inspired to write three volumes of ghost stories himself.

Artistically speaking, Universal's horror genre had peaked in 1935 with *The Bride of Frankenstein*, one of the most surprising and original horror movies ever made. The film was intended more as a black comedy by its eccentric British director James Whale, responsible for the original *Frankenstein* as well as *The Invisible Man* and *The Old Dark House*. Halliwell saw it on re-release, paired with

Dracula's Daughter at the Rialto, and he was accompanied by schoolmate James Beattie, who went on to become a popular actor in Australia. They formed a lifelong friendship and Halliwell later dedicated a book to him, with the words, "To Jimmie Beattie, in whose company on a stormy night in 1944 I saw my first horror film, *The Bride of Frankenstein*. It still seems the best."

I managed to catch up with Mr Beattie at his home in Brighton, and he reminisced about his old friend:

> Well, he was very shy, until he started to act… it was dreadful really, they used to tease him because he had this rather large chin. I got to know him about 1944 – there was a play called *Gallows Glorious* which I did, and he was in, about John Brown. But I think I knew him the year before that, at the Literary and Debating Society, which he was very fond of. He joined all these societies. I didn't – I just wanted to act.
>
> We were great friends. We used to go to Blackpool together. I think we shouldn't have done it but we used to go and drink six penny-worth of champagne at Yates's Wine Bar. Then go on to the pleasure beach and the fun house, rolling the few pennies that we had. We used to cycle a lot, on the moors around the town – Scotsman Stump we used to go to, and pick things: dandelion and burdock… then we'd have tomato sandwiches and Tizer lemonade…

I asked Mr Beattie if he recalled the night they saw *The Bride of Frankenstein* together and he replied, "I remember it was very wet – well, it was always wet in Bolton. It was quite frightening but I remember laughing a lot." An appropriate reaction, as director James Whale had brought a unique mixture of horror and camp humour to the film, which Halliwell called "a simply marvellous piece of Grand Guignol which from the very beginning laces its horrors with wit and laughter." The story followed directly on from the events of its predecessor and featured the gargoyle-like Ernest Thesiger as Dr Praetorius, persuading Victor Frankenstein to resume his work. Praetorius himself has been dabbling in reanimation and feels that together they could make a mate for the monster, at the time thought burned 'alive' in a windmill but is in fact roaming free in an entirely fake countryside, expertly recreated indoors on some imaginative sets. The mad scientists' fiendish collaboration results in the creation of a 'bride' in the shape of Elsa Lanchester, previously seen playing Mary Shelley in the nineteenth-century-set prologue. Her electric shock hairstyle and Hawaiian theme tune only add to the bizarre concoction that this movie undoubtedly is. Halliwell found the creation sequence in particular especially riveting and became aware, perhaps for the first time, how much work went into the production of a motion picture, with master craftsmen in each field all contributing to its artistic success. He described the sequence as –

> *Cinematically quite breathtaking ... a perfect masterpiece of direction, photography and editing, and could be used even now as a showpiece for film students who want to learn something about film as a narrative art. These extraordinary six minutes would not have disgraced Eisenstein and have no parallel in Hollywood.*

There were no casualties among Halliwell's family and friends during the war, and he only experienced its effects second hand. One night he stood in Great Lever Park – as he had on the day war was declared – watching a pink glow in the sky to the southeast. That was Manchester ablaze, but few bombs fell close to Bolton. Rationing affected everybody, however, and since it was Halliwell's duty to go to the shops to get the food, he would always pick the assistant he knew to be a film fan. He could chat to him enthusiastically about the latest Cary Grant film, say, in the hope of gaining slightly larger portions.

Hollywood's only significant attempt at depicting the war in Britain was the sentimental Oscar-winner *Mrs Miniver*, with Greer Garson maintaining a stiff upper lip while her eldest son is away fighting. All Halliwell's family went to see the film, which presented an England far removed from that which the average Boltonian of the day would recognise. Indeed, he was not wholly convinced that it presented an accurate portrayal of the South, which he visited for the first time to see his sister Lilian, then married and living in Surrey. He and Lily took the night train to London, with a brief pause in Stockport whilst bombs fell again on Manchester, providing them with an unexpected and chilling firework display. Halliwell became enchanted by the gentle suburban feel of Weybridge and its sweet-smelling pines – and, of course, the local picture houses. He wrote,

"The Surrey climate was as balmy as I had expected, and most of the local cinemas had a cool modernity to which I was unaccustomed… at last, I thought, I have found Shangri-La." Many years later, he would make Surrey his home.

On the whole, he felt that the war had more emotional effect on him in screen terms than in reality, not least because of the resurgence in British films. After hostilities had begun, the Ministry of Information incorporated under its wing a ready-made film unit which had previously produced documentary shorts for the General Post Office. Its directors included Humphrey Jennings, one of the founders of Mass-Observation. The team was renamed the Crown Film Unit and set to work making five-minute instructional films, informing people what to do in the event of invasion or reassuring parents about the need for evacuation. By 1942, eighty-six of these films had been made, all distributed freely to cinemas to be included in their usual programmes. Initially, Halliwell found them to be quite dull and observed "sporadic booing" at some showings: he felt they lacked both entertainment value and any sort of craft. As the film-makers grew in confidence, however, the quality improved and more ambitious, feature length projects were undertaken. The special talents of Humphrey Jennings came to the fore in the likes of *Fires Were Started*, which depicted a night's work for a London fire brigade during the Blitz. *Western Approaches*, directed by Pat Jackson, concerned the perils of merchant seamen bringing cargo from America, under fire from German U-boats.

Another Jennings piece, which was designed for the American market, was *London Can Take It*, in which Londoners are shown finishing their working day, before taking shelter in time for the sirens to sound and the night's attack to begin. The following morning they go about their daily lives amid bomb craters and ruined buildings. The film closes with its American narrator announcing, "They'll be over tonight; they'll destroy a few buildings and kill a few people. Probably some of the people you're watching now." Halliwell found that line in particular "marvellously chilling." He recalled seeing the film at a second-run theatre in his hometown and wishing initially that the supporting feature had been "an Edgar Kennedy or a Mickey Mouse. I soon realised that this was quite different, something very acutely observed. That image at the end of a violin over the shadow of a cannon stayed with me."

Possibly Jennings's finest work, though, was *Listen to Britain*, credited to both him and Stewart McAllister, a film whose 20-minute running time consisted entirely of images and natural sounds from a single day during wartime. It shows leaves rustling in a tree being drowned by the roar of a Spitfire, and the conversations of girls at a dance. A lady plays piano to a group of wardens, and music hall stars Flanagan and Allen entertain factory workers with a song. It was a collage of everyday life in Britain – like a mini Mass-Observation report. The film has an emotional effect one would scarcely countenance from such a simple idea. Halliwell said it showed "the British people making the very best of a desperately bad situation," and that the last few moments formed one of his "favourite film sequences of all time. The swell of the music for 'Rule Britannia' – that's still a great emotional experience for anybody, whether or not they lived through the war. It's all pure cinematic magic." He grew so fond of these films that years later he presented two television series celebrating the wartime documentary movement. He felt that Jennings "brought to the cinema a form of poetry" and was not the first to note that particular quality. Alexander Korda, that pioneer of British films who by then was working in Hollywood, called Jennings "the only poet of British cinema."

The documentary movement had more far-reaching effects than mere morale boosting, however. It additionally helped to train up a whole generation of film-makers and taught them to look to real life for inspiration. Thus, feature films began to take on a more realistic edge, with outdoor location photography and a more authentic style of acting. Britain was depicted not as a class ridden society but as a single people grouping together for a shared cause. Halliwell wrote, "It was the documentary which first showed the new spirit. The Ministry of Information employed writers, directors and administrators who subsequently proved to be amongst the ablest men in their field."

In Which We Serve, Noel Coward and David Lean's masterpiece, depicted the sinking of a fictional ship, with survivors clinging to a life raft and recalling their past lives. *The Way to the Stars* examined events on the ground at an airfield in England and featured scarcely a single aerial shot. Others included *The Way Ahead* and *This Happy Breed*, all showing the British people pulling together in the face of a common enemy. And *Went the Day Well?* was a remarkable tale about the German infiltration of a sleepy English village, which builds to a surprisingly violent climax.

In 1942, *Picturegoer* ran a competition to find their readers' top ten favourite films. Halliwell observed that there was "not much wrong with the general cultural level" of the fans who chose among others, *Goodbye Mr Chips*, *Mrs Miniver*, *Gone with the Wind*, *Rebecca*, *How Green Was My Valley*, *Wuthering Heights*, *Citizen Kane* and *The Good Earth*. Halliwell was in step; his opinions were in tune with the majority – for possibly the only period in his life. There would be other times when he would take advantage of more marginalised interest in his favourite subject, but here in the 1940s he was firmly representative of the masses. The general cinemagoing public was being positively spoiled by the high quality of both Hollywood and Britain's output, and he and millions of others were loving every moment.

Gradually my multifarious school activities enabled me to command some kind of tolerance and even respect from those who had initially despised me as an intruder into their closed society.

As he progressed through school, Halliwell was able to join various societies not open to younger pupils, and these group activities helped him to become more confident in his surroundings. In fact, the course of his rejuvenation can be plotted through the articles of the school magazine, *The Boltonian*, published at the end of each term. This was a round-up of every event which took place at the school, with reports for each society and the details of sporting results. It featured reviews of films, books and plays, and was written mostly by pupils but with the occasional contribution from teachers. During wartime, the magazine included a Reported Missing column as well as listing those captured by the enemy: "We hear that Bill Howard and Ronnie Smith are in Japanese hands … Sydney Rowall sends his greetings from Africa…" One Old Boltonian wrote of his experience of being taken prisoner after the fall of Singapore: "For nearly two years we lived a life in the jungle with no facilities for plays or concerts."

After being listed in the *salvete* (Latin for welcome) section of the December 1939 edition, upon joining the school, there are no mentions of Halliwell for three years. Then, in March 1943 he is included in the round-up for the Philatelic Society: "In the last term's competition L. H. Jones was first in the senior section; R. J. L. Halliwell and W. H. Stott were second equal." In addition, he was reported as having given a talk on 'National Emblems and Symbols on Stamps'. From then on his name appears in more and more articles, such as the report for the Poetry Society where he gained further experience speaking in front of a group. His delivery of *Prospero* was described as "polished if superficial," whereas that of *The Poetasters of Ispahan* was commended as "polished and mature."

Throughout his time at school he was listed as R. J. L. Halliwell, making him easy to spot among the other names, being the only boy with three initials. Of the Old Boltonians I spoke to, not one remembered him as Robert, and even Leslie was rare. Ronald Lowe told me, "No-one ever called him Leslie in my hearing. It was always 'Chinnie' or 'RJL'. Of course, I come from the era when people were not referred to by their first names at school."

Halliwell was included in a list of some eighty boys who took part in an agricultural trip to Mowbreck Hall in Kirkham, which ran for five weeks but "most boys stayed for two." Their duties involved "stoking, lifting potatoes, weeding kale, and loading and housing oats and wheat" – surprising activity for someone who had previously shown no affection for outdoor pursuits, except for long walks on the moors. The report for the August 1945 trip, when Halliwell would have been sixteen, includes the comment "the baths and cinemas in Kirkham must have benefited from our presence." This trip coincided with the end of six years of bloody conflict, the event being duly commemorated: "On V. J. Day most boys were given a holiday, and practically everyone returned home to enjoy the celebrations and local thanksgivings."

By this time, Halliwell was being listed among the editors of the magazine, and in the following issue he had become secretary of his House and Treasurer of the Film Society, a group which was run for many years by the art master George Higginson, himself an amateur film-maker. He had to depart for Army service and so the physics teacher, Miss Waterhouse, took over as president of the society. The report for December 1945 includes the comment, "Looking ahead to next term, it is hoped that, when we are not restricted by the blackout, longer and better films will be shown." The Film Society held its meetings in the oak-panelled school library, using a 16mm projector which Mr Higginson had taught Halliwell how to operate. At 4.15pm the heavy curtains would be drawn and a showing would commence.

They had initially featured many of those Crown Film Unit documentaries as they were free to acquire, but once Halliwell became secretary he was able to advise on more adventurous bookings. He remembered fondly a performance of D. W. Griffith's epoch-making silent *The Birth of a Nation*. The report for that term remarked that the "attendance broke the Society's record, over two hundred people being crowded into the Library." A sprinkling of school masters and even the local press had helped to swell the numbers, and the projector had to be moved back to accommodate everyone, thus resulting in a reduced image. Halliwell supplied cocoa during reel changes and the evening was an unqualified triumph.

His reputation as a film buff was firmly established by this time and one day at lunch the headmaster approached him with a question, "Well, young Halliwell, will *Henry the Fifth* ever be shown in Bolton?"

"I think in view of the money J. Arthur Rank has poured into the production, he would be bound to ensure that it was played at his local flagship Odeon."

"And do you think it will draw the crowds?"

"It might surprise everyone, Shakespeare or no Shakespeare."

Halliwell notified him when the film finally arrived in town and instead of going after school on the Monday it opened, he felt it was enough of an occasion to go home and change first. Disappointingly, though, the Odeon was mostly empty when he arrived, with no queue and a "cathedral-like air." The word 'Shakespeare' had indeed put most people off, but had instead brought to the fore that better class of customer which frequented the Odeon: Halliwell observed for the first time a distinct lack of cigarette smoke in the air. He supplied a review of Laurence Olivier's epic to *The Boltonian*, in which he wrote of the dilemma facing any adapter of the Bard's work: "Give rein to the visual, and where is Shakespeare? Concentrate on the words, and you fling away the real asset of the screen…" He went on to describe it as "a serious film which makes no concessions to low-brow taste." Contrary to the clipped style he had adopted for his notebooks, his reviews for the magazine were lengthy, often stretching over two pages, although extremely well written for a teenager.

The Ministry of Information had tasked Olivier to bring to the screen something stirring for a wartime audience. The result was a masterpiece of cinema, opening with a Tudor setting in which the play is being performed at the Globe Theatre. The film becomes more and more cinematic as it progresses until the Battle of Agincourt is staged in full glory, with camera techniques liberally borrowed from Eisenstein's magnificent *Alexander Nevsky*. Halliwell wrote, "The battle sequence is breathtaking in its Technicolor array, the charge being particularly glorious. William Walton's lilting music does much to keep one excited, though there is rather too much of the choir."

Another project commissioned by the Ministry of Information – though not as a morale booster – was Michael Powell and Emeric Pressburger's *A Matter of Life and Death*. The producer/director team were obliged to make a film which would improve Anglo-American relations in the post-war period. The result was one of the most startling and imaginative fantasies ever filmed. David Niven plays a pilot who falls in love with an American radio operator as his plane is in the act of crashing. Finding himself unexpectedly still alive after bailing out without a parachute, he begins to suffer hallucinations about being summoned to the hereafter. In the real world he undergoes brain surgery to cure his condition, whilst in the imaginary world he stands trial in a great heavenly court, his life depending on the outcome of both events.

Halliwell first saw *A Matter of Life and Death* at the Lido, although he was semi-conscious at the time on account of having spent the previous night in a prison cell. He had been hiking with a friend through Brontë country and after spraining his ankle in a fall he limped into Todmorden at two in the morning, whereupon a kindly desk sergeant offered him the only 'room' available. He returned to the Lido the following night in a more alert state to reappraise the film and found it to be "spectacular moonshine with a welcome dash of vinegar." The film would become one of his favourites and – like most of Halliwell's selections – it is a picture which works on both an entertainment level as well as a cerebral one. He especially commended "the insistence that the audience's mind shall be put to work," and called it "a true work of the intellectual imagination."

Michael Anderson, director of *The Dam Busters*, thought *A Matter of Life and Death* to be "a unique masterpiece, technically and artistically light years ahead of its time, and a great influence on me."

Martin Scorsese, a lifelong fan of Powell and Pressburger's output, called it "a romantic, daring and beautiful allegorical fantasy."

> *By the war's end no purely patriotic reason need be sought for watching a British film ... British films had reached maturity, and I felt I had done so along with them.*

Towards the end of his school years, Halliwell's confidence was sky high and he began to write letters to film magazines, as well as the *Bolton Evening News*. One requested that more foreign language films be shown in the town and he briefly got his wish: the local Empire cinema was taken over by a Pole who proceeded to bring in a selection of continental films. Halliwell managed to catch Marcel Carné's masterful period epic *Les Enfants du Paradis*, but the endeavour was not a profitable one and the cinema soon reverted to type. Another request he made was for a repertory cinema to be set up in the town to show old classics – that dream *would* come true, but not in Bolton.

He also wrote to *Picturegoer* and one article was actually printed in August 1946, his first for a national publication. The headline, 'Do we need plots in musicals?' was provided by the magazine and gave a slightly misleading impression of the article. Instead of calling for the removal of plots entirely, he was merely suggesting that they not be allowed to get in the way of the entertainment. "Music and comedy," he wrote, "blended into an agreeable confection, are the only ingredients either expected or wanted from musicals." The piece was fairly representative of his later output: a generalisation backed up by myriad examples to show off how cinematically learned he was.

That summer he spent a "delirious week" at Stanford Hall on a Co-operative College Film Study Course. His father had been invited to send a delegate to attend and so picked his son. Finding the place to be a "small-scale Xanadu," Halliwell played croquet and spent the week watching films and listening to lectures by the likes of Dilys Powell and Paul Rotha. He was observed on his return to have given a talk to the Co-operative Guild on film criticism.

He joined the Bolton Little Theatre, a dramatic group whose plays were performed in a converted chapel in the centre of town, and there he was watched by a school party playing Le Beau in *As You like It*. Indeed, at this time the theatre was seriously challenging the cinema for his affections, and he often ventured to Manchester with James Beattie to watch the likes of Ralph Richardson and Vivien Leigh on the stage. If that was not enough activity for a boy in his teens, Halliwell took part-time jobs at the post office and on the buses in order to help his family during their post-war struggle. Although by then he was fully accepted by his peers, he described himself as "still oddly shy except with people I knew well, to whom I was unforgivably bossy."

He gained more experience speaking in front of a group at the Literary and Debating Society, which discussed such topics as 'Is Bolton the Geneva of the north?' In addition, they performed scenes from plays and Rene Fauchois' *Prenez garde à la peinture* brought "noteworthy support from J. I. Wardle and R. J. L. Halliwell." J. I. Wardle, known as Irving Wardle – another who used a middle name as his first – later became drama critic for *The Times*, and he was kind enough to invite me to his house to talk about his old school friend:

> He was very good at organising people, especially at the Literary and Debating Society. I can remember him arranging the chairs and deciding who should sit where. He was also a great reader: Somerset Maugham was his favourite author, and he had a huge memory for facts about the cinema. I remember at times finding this a little irritating. We used to go for tea at one of our teacher's houses, and whenever the subject got around to the cinema he would come alive with information. It was a constant stream of facts which never seemed to *mean* anything – it was just trivia, apart from the occasional adjective.

A major event in the academic calendar was the school play, which took place usually in March and with performances starting promptly at 6.30pm. Halliwell remembered the great hall's conversion to a theatre, "The platform was augmented into a genuine stage complete with proscenium, orchestra pit, rich drapes, side scenery, steps, a lighting switchboard, the lot." He worked his way up through a succession of small roles such as Fourth Servant in *She Stoops to Conquer*, until in 1946 he landed a major role in *Richard II*. The notice praised him for being "most successful as Bolingbroke, strong, commanding, ruthless yet sincere, with a good voice and sharp, effective command of gesture." He would have his finest school moment in the following year's production of *Hamlet*, in which Irving Wardle played the doom-laden prince. Of his acting in particular, Wardle recalled, "He had a sharp, hammer-tap voice. He was not a narcissistic actor; he was more superficial." James Wood, who played 'A Gentleman', remembered, "Leslie played Claudius, King of Denmark, and I can still see him now resplendent in his robes."

Several pictures were taken of this production including a group shot of the entire cast, captured on the lawns just inside the main entrance to the school, with one of the gatehouse turrets visible in the background. Halliwell sits in the front row of three, wearing his stately ermine robe and crown, and with a fake beard and moustache hiding that prominent chin. Wardle sits alongside him in a black gown, looking rather uncomfortable. Halliwell wrote that the pair argued over which of them was to roll down the steps upon his death scene: Halliwell apparently won, although Wardle did not recall the incident. That he fell down the steps is not in dispute, however, as the reviewer for *The Boltonian* observed:

> R. J. L. Halliwell gave a polished performance in the difficult part of Claudius; he was most convincing in his later scenes when we know him for what he is, unscrupulous, shrewd, plausible, yet inwardly quaking. His soliloquy was impressively delivered and his final fall a most effective touch.
>
> The contrast was here well drawn between Wardle and Halliwell, the latter with his quick, not the less effective, use of slight gesture. This production will remain long in the memory…

Another photograph was taken during a performance showing the enormous drapes which dominated the rear of the stage. Halliwell sits on a throne alongside his queen (played by a boy) gazing sternly at one of his courtiers, who kneels before him at the foot of the grand set of steps he is later to fall down – how he must have loved this part!

It is entirely likely that Lily attended one of the performances, as her son later observed of his school life, "My mother loved it. I am sure that she got more out of it than I did, coming to the school plays and various functions." Her son's talents had not gone unnoticed: he was urged by one of his teachers to seek a university scholarship, and after three attempts he was accepted to St. Catharine's College,

Cambridge, to read English Literature. Before commencing his university education, however, he would have to serve two years' National Service in the Army.

For the July 1947 issue of *The Boltonian*, Halliwell writes almost the entire magazine and appears to be running the school at the time. The review of *Hamlet* was one of the few pieces not actually supplied by him – as well as the sports section, obviously. Having risen to the heights of school monitor and house secretary, he was further commended for his "excellent services" as an assistant librarian. He had given a talk on the novels of his favourite author, W. Somerset Maugham, whose "casual and disjointed first person narration and his flawless prose style" he greatly admired. Halliwell concluded that Maugham should be regarded as "the best of the twentieth-century storytellers."

He contributed an essay, 'Novel into Film', which told the sorry story of cinematic adaptations of literary work, observing, "Many of our great novelists, classic as well as contemporary, have suffered much at the hands of Hollywood." Again he got the chance to mention his favourite author, who had been particularly badly treated "in every sense but the financial one," and he concluded, "There is little point in being proud of our separate art forms if one is to reign supreme at the expense of another." The Film Society report was predictably his own, and he further reviewed *Cymbeline Refinished* by George Bernard Shaw as well as writing yet another essay, this time on 'The Development of the Dramatic Society, 1919-1947'. He later claimed to have belonged to the chess club, but his talent must have been lacking as that was one of the few societies in which his name never once appeared. There was no end to his literary expertise, though, and in another edition he even supplied a poem, apparently inspired by the view from the school playing fields –

PASTORAL

Thy levels, Bolton, war-like Mars' retreat,
At once the sportsman's and the scholar's seat,
Invite my lays. Amid the snowy plains,
A sky-dropp'd Swan, no mortal, Monarch reigns,
For lo! the levels shine with sudden frost,
Their beauty wither'd, and their verdure lost,

> All Nature mourns, the Skies ne'er cease their show'rs,
> Gone are the Pigs, asleep the shiv'ring flow'rs,
> And all the youthful flocks to shelter tend,
> As from the Heavens snow-fill'd clouds descend,
> The white Orbs harden on the scene of strife,
> Once host to lusty Youth, which now seeks indoor life.
>
> R.J.L.H (H. VI.A).

Halliwell reported for duty with the Lancashire Fusiliers at Bury Barracks in June 1947, thinking himself "weedy, long-chinned and bespectacled: not a good bet for the army." By feigning a foot condition he managed to get himself excused from most of the intense physical activity which accompanied basic training, and with his intelligence standing out clearly he was assigned to the Army Education Corps, which came with an instant promotion to sergeant. He was dispatched to Buchanan Castle, near Glasgow, where he received some limited teacher training but by December he was already indulging in the creative arts. In a letter sent to his old school he related having appeared in two variety shows, giving his rendition of *The Lion and Albert* in one, and further stated he was hoping to stage a play he had written, *Twice Two are Five*. He had in addition started a Film Club, predictably enough, comprising three evening showings a week with "discussions and debates."

Halliwell spent the next two years at various postings across the country, attempting to educate small classes of recruits in the "rudiments of citizenship" and – of course – seeking out all the local ABCs, Regals and Odeons of every town he found himself in for more than five minutes, be it Figsbury, Chester, Oswestry, Salisbury or Portsmouth. He was still diligently filling in those notebooks with his evaluations back at barracks, whenever he returned from an afternoon's or evening's entertainment. As he observed, "Rough-hewn army ways could make one more than usually grateful for the comfort and luxury which a well-run cinema provided in those days."

An embargo on new Hollywood imports imposed after the war was still in place and subsequently many of the cinemas were forced to show re-runs, often in the form of double-bills. It was then that Halliwell managed to catch up with more of the films he had not been allowed to see as a child, such as the Warner gangster movies *The*

Public Enemy and *Little Caesar*, and "the greatest monster movie of them all," *King Kong*. However, he sometimes found the films cut for the purposes of timing and was outraged enough to complain to the management on more than one occasion. Years later he would find himself on the receiving end of similar criticism.

Around this time Halliwell very nearly secured an interview with Stan Laurel. He and his famous comedy partner were undertaking a tour of music halls, including Bolton, and Halliwell wrote to request an interview which Stan obligingly granted. Unfortunately, an army posting was unexpectedly brought forward and his leave was cancelled just prior to the big day. He was inconsolable, but Stan sent him a photo to commiserate, on which he had written "Hello Leslie" and which was signed by both him and Ollie. Halliwell treasured the photo and more than one person recalled seeing it pinned to the wall of his office many years later.

By March of 1948, he was ensconced in Winterbourne Dauntsey, near Salisbury, although by then he was missing his old life as he wrote, "How I long for what I suppose I must call the good old days, when one might sandwich between breakfast and supper, literature and history and perhaps even a film. I am in the process of writing my second full-length play [and] I am becoming adept at leatherwork and, I confess, at billiards."

Halliwell found his students to be generally reluctant to participate in the learning process but he usually managed to win them over via a compromise. He would talk for ten minutes; then ask questions on what he had spoken about, and finally as a reward he would round off with a general discussion. Once his knowledge of the cinema became apparent, his class would often try to test him. He would challenge them to pick a film title and if he failed to name at least one of its stars he would pay out threepence. He claimed never to have paid out once.

The Army obligingly granted whatever requests Halliwell made for outings he felt his charges might find instructional. At Figsbury, he persuaded his Commanding Officer to let him take his pupils on day trips to London. With the post-war feeling toward servicemen still warm, they were able to visit Ealing Studios where John Mills was filming *Scott of the Antarctic*. They finished the day at the theatre watching a Ben Travers farce called *Outrageous Fortune*, and Halliwell even managed to meet the star before the show. In Devizes, he was allowed to undertake a two week course in twentieth century literature, in preparation for Cambridge.

To his great delight, he was then seconded to the Southern Command Drama Company, and for "nine outrageously sunny weeks" he and a group of instructors toured camps in the south west, giving acting lessons and teaching how to stage theatre productions. They performed one-act plays which were always well attended – not least because entrance was free of charge – and he described the whole experience as the peak of his "career in khaki." It gave him an opportunity to explore the countryside and he grew to love the sight of old churches, winding lanes and "unexpected views." But, like all good things, it had to end, and did so thanks to the appointment of a new education officer, who decided that they were all wasting the Army's time and money, something Halliwell could not wholeheartedly dispute.

With his period of National Service drawing to a close, he was dispatched to Aldershot, from where he could spend weekends with his sister in Fareham, "a straggly town saved by the more westerly of its two cinemas." Halliwell introduced himself to the delights of the West End picture houses and caught Olivier's production of *Hamlet* at the Odeon Leicester Square. A relentlessly gloomy piece, the film might have impressed the Academy but it was a world away from the splendour of *Henry V*. Nevertheless, it would have brought back fond memories of his own experience in the play, two years before.

Of the whole widespread Halliwell clan only I seemed to have before me the possibility of a shining future, and that meant deserting the streets where life had had most meaning.

Halliwell returned to Bolton in 1949 to find post-war austerity had taken its toll on the town's palaces of public entertainment, which during the war had seen such feverish activity. Several of the old cinemas were closed and the remaining ones were in disrepair – "the Lido shrieked neglect, and ran only cheap exploitation programmes." A general tone of gloom hung over his hometown, with mills closing, rationing still in place and a fuel shortage occurring. The positive attitude of the war years – when everyone pulled together to fight for a common cause – was absent, and with the conflict over by several years no-one could understand why they were still so poorly off.

Halliwell and his mother attempted to relive their past by visiting as many of the old picture houses as were still open, but they both knew full well that the glory days were behind them. No longer did frock-coated commissionaires compete for patronage amid star struck crowds: the age of the dream palace was over. In addition, Lily seemed to be permanently unwell and her marriage to Jim was more strained than ever before.

Hollywood's output seemed to mirror this general air of despondency, the productions becoming more realistic and cynical. The movement later referred to as *film noir* was going strong, with its dark shadows, anti-heroes and downbeat endings. Very few of them matched the class of Billy Wilder's *Double Indemnity*, and fewer still offered any of that pre-war optimism which had been so prevalent. Gone, it seemed, was the innocent magic of *Lost Horizon* and *Top Hat*, and Halliwell came to regard the year 1949 as "the nadir of film art."

Three years before, actress Olivia de Havilland had won a legal battle against Warner Brothers over the infamous contract system, and a little later the American Supreme Court divorced the studios from the cinemas and outlawed the practice of block-booking. The post-war baby boom brought about a decline in cinema attendance, and over the next few years a certain distraction in the living room would keep yet more of the audience at home. Meanwhile, the studio system, which had served the industry so well for two decades, eroded from within.

The outlook for Hollywood was bleak, but Halliwell had every reason to feel positive about the future…

He was about to dive into the cultural whirlpool of Cambridge, where he could let his literary and dramatic impulses run free…

3

The Scarcest Commodity

- Cambridge University, 1949-52 -

St. Catharine's is set back from the main thoroughfare on which both King's and Trinity Colleges stand, exuding a rather more austere appearance than its ostentatious neighbours – no spires, turrets or crennelations adorn the roofs of *its* buildings. It occupies three sides of an open courtyard with a lush green lawn, and with a wrought iron gate rather ominously closing off the fourth side. St. Catharine's dark red brickwork further stands in contrast to the light brown stone of the more majestic Cambridge learning centres, and its stocky buildings and closely-set windows are reminiscent of those mill factories which dominated Leslie Halliwell's hometown.

St. Catharine's was in the late forties, as it is now, a medium-sized college admitting around three hundred students a year, compared with Trinity's nearly seven hundred. Halliwell's path from matriculation to graduation was negotiated, as with all honours candidates, by being resident at the University for nine terms and passing two parts of a Tripos ('try-poss') examination in his second and third years. The terms – Michaelmas, Lent and Easter – lasted around eight weeks each and alternated with three periods of what amounted to "virtual expulsion" according to one contemporary guidebook, "during which the undergraduate is expected to complete at home the reading squeezed out by the congestion of term [and] to recover enough freshness of mind for the ensuing term, when the process begins all over again."

University rules dictated that cap and gown must be worn at college and in the streets after dark. Discipline, what there was of it, was enforced by the Proctors, the 'University Police', who patrolled the streets at night and had the right to "enter licensed premises and places of public entertainment … in the prevention and detection of undergraduate misdemeanours." The front door of the college was locked at 10pm but the errant student could be let in at any time up to midnight with the imposition of a nominal fine – unless he climbed over the railings, as many did.

In contrast to his experience at school, where he took several years to find his feet, Halliwell spent only one Cambridge term acclimatising. He recalled, "I missed the discipline of both school and army, not yet feeling ready to select my own star and follow it." Graham Dukes, in *Portrait of Cambridge 1952*, made the point that because the modern undergraduate had completed two years' National Service, he required a period of adjustment which the student of 1938 would have been free of. He added, "The danger, on present experience, is not that he will slack and abuse his freedom, but rather that he will work too anxiously. Being older and more mature than his pre-war counterpart … he tends to think almost too much of ends and of results."

Halliwell didn't. After his brief period of settling in he immersed himself in the social life of Cambridge to such a degree that his supervisor actually took him aside, and told him that if he would only cut down on his "extra-mural activities" he might rate a 1st. Halliwell was honest enough – and brazen enough – to respond that if he did that he would likely be so depressed he would fail anyway. He later referred to Cambridge as "that joyous intellectual backwater" which offered him "a life of bewildering richness," with Union debates, societies, theatres and cinemas. He could spend long afternoons discussing Proust or Hemingway in cafés; cycling the lanes or relaxing on the Backs, the green areas on the western side of the River Cam. He could drink beer in the evening with his contemporaries, and hold late night discussions over a chicken biryani at the Koh-i-noor restaurant in St. John's Street.

But mostly he went to the cinema. As early as December 1949 another Old Boltonian reported that Halliwell could "frequently be seen in his spare time making a furtive egress from some local cinema or other, at least once a day." The choice might not have been anywhere near as abundant as in Bolton, but almost every film of any note was screened somewhere in the city during his time there, whether old or new. Allen Freer was up at the same time as Halliwell and recalled:

> He was always a very congenial person. Even back then it was obvious that he was mad on cinema ... and if the conversation ever turned to the subject, he would have huge amounts to say. He would always be very pleasant when you sat with him in the dining hall. You couldn't help but be impressed by his personality.

Another contemporary remembered seeing the walls of Halliwell's dormitory room covered in movie posters and stills. Michael Wright found himself on the same course as Halliwell, and noted in his diary, "He is full of vitality, which is good, but is unfortunately always letting it off at someone else's expense, and since that is usually mine, not so good. His voice is very loud. His mind is agile, but material, unoriginal and repetitive." Despite that less than glowing first report, Wright and Halliwell bonded at Cambridge and remained friends for forty years.

Wright recalled the two of them exploring their surroundings: taking the bus to Ely Cathedral and cycling or walking to the nearby villages of Coton, Cherry Hinton and Grantchester. "We took tea at the Dorothy," he wrote, "coffee at the Whim, and drank beer at the nearby Mill." Halliwell's confidence and enthusiasm were in marked contrast to Wright's more reserved nature and the pair seemed to complement one another perfectly. Wright was himself a film fan – "though I could not match Leslie's obsession with the form" – and they went at least once a week to the pictures. On one occasion he recorded in his diary, "L dragged me away from *Road to Xanadu* and we saw Bob Hope in *Fancy Pants*." He further recalled them having to climb the railings (on 12th March, 1951, no less) "after an excessively long undergraduate production of *Hamlet*."

Eric Cross was another reading English at the time, and remembered Halliwell to me in a letter, "He was clearly very intelligent, very knowledgeable, and very ready to express his views. There was nothing quiet or withdrawn about him; on the contrary, his voice was quite loud and clanging." Mr Cross recalled that Halliwell was sometimes out of step with the company in which he found himself, and to illustrate this he related an incident where a group of undergraduates were discussing modern poetry. Halliwell began quoting G. K. Chesterton and Wilfrid Gibson, with unashamed enthusiasm – quite out of place with modern poets – and the response was stony silence. Cross was embarrassed for him but regretted being so, "I should have admired his honesty. To be sure, there were some poseurs around. Leslie was not one of them."

Ah, to be young again, and seeing The Lady Eve *for the first time on a Sunday night at the Arts Cinema, Cambridge, during the autumn of 1949. It was the last performance, and tickets were like gold dust.*

Although the exhibitor chain ABC dominated the Cambridge circuit, with five major cinemas in and around the city, Halliwell found himself drawn to the more specialist houses such as the Arts Cinema, just off the market square. It was here that he received his long awaited education in films not in the English language, such as Jean Cocteau's dreamlike *Orphée*, which he referred to as "the closest the cinema has ever got to poetry." In addition at the Arts, Halliwell managed to catch up with *The Philadelphia Story*, whose sparkling wit had passed over his head on first release, but from here on the film would remain a firm favourite. He went with a friend on the first night and returned for a second helping a day later with some more acquaintances in tow. By the end of the week, the picture was booked solid and its witticisms were being quoted by the undergraduate *cognoscenti* at society events the length and breadth of the town. This 1940 George Cukor-directed comedy about the Philadelphian upper class had resurrected the career of its star, Katharine Hepburn, previously labelled "box office poison." It featured two of the most fondly remembered leading men of the Golden Age, Cary Grant and James Stewart, and of the cast itself Halliwell wrote, "If the talents listed above had found no other showcase, for their felicitous teaming in this magical film they would be rightly cherished."

ABC's largest picture house was the Regal, still a functioning cinema today and perfectly positioned on the main road which cuts right through the city. Halliwell called it "shapelessly designed … a charmless hall whose vast empty spaces could be guaranteed to depress the spirit even if the temperature had risen above 58 degrees"

– which it failed to do on the occasion he was introduced to *The Third Man*. He had to pull his overcoat around him to enjoy Carol Reed's classic Vienna set, zither-haunted thriller. Familiarity with Orson Welles's famous cuckoo clock speech subsequently became another piece of film culture vital to acceptance within undergraduate society.

Also essential to the avoidance of social embarrassment was a good working knowledge of the Marx Brothers, whose anti-establishment zaniness appealed greatly to students. At the time, the ageing Marxes were way past their best, having just released the dismal *Love Happy*, which would prove to be their last film. However, revivals of their earlier triumphs of crazy comedy made them a cult among undergraduates, and packed houses ensured that hardly a week went by without one of their films being shown somewhere in town. One observer called the Marx Brothers the "patron saints" of the city, adding, "their hilarities may be recalled over anything from coffee to Curaçao; they are an essential part of the escapist dream-world of Cambridge."

Perhaps the most famous – and probably the most accessible to a modern audience – of all the Marxian extravaganzas is *Duck Soup*. Released in 1933, it was the brothers' final effort for Paramount before Irving Thalberg snapped them up for Metro. Halliwell was introduced to it at the Cambridge Film Society, which at the time boasted over a thousand members – "embracing both town and gown" – and held its principal meetings on Sunday mornings at the Central cinema, another house controlled by ABC. 35mm film was required for these showings, which was more expensive than the 16mm the society preferred for its usual weekday meetings held in the college examination hall, far from the comforts of a major cinema.

Halliwell's Sunday mornings became something of a ritual. After a "leisurely breakfast" he would stroll down to Hobson Street, which runs alongside Christ's College, and arrive at the Central. He would "enter the wide and sweet-smelling circle at 10.25," where he would be "deafened by the rustle of six hundred copies of *The Sunday Times*, and blinded by the whiteness of newsprint held in undergraduate fists." That particular screening of *Duck Soup*, in which the Marxes encounter dictatorship politics in the fictional country of Freedonia, would remain in Halliwell's memory for the rest of his life. He kept the programme, which gave "little impression of the permanent and renewable joy the movie would bring."

However, his enjoyment was tempered slightly by the knowledge that the brothers were at the time all washed up, as he recalled, "To see them now so buoyant at the apogee of their careers was somewhat too sharp a contrast. But at second viewing – and the Film Society hurriedly arranged one – *Duck Soup* could be confirmed as a comic masterpiece of its own time." The film was so popular that Paramount was persuaded to strike a brand new print, which according to Halliwell "must have cost all of forty quid. It staggered round the art houses and film societies of Britain until it ran minutes short from splices."

The satirical aspects of the movie are especially notable as real dictators were at work in Europe at the time the film was made, but as Halliwell observed, the references appear to have been unintentional. *Duck Soup* contains none of the musical or romantic interludes that characterised the Marx Brothers' later MGM productions, which some viewers felt were to their detriment whereas others appreciated the mixture. But it does contain several classic routines and wisecracking exchanges, such as this one between the cigar-chomping Groucho and his long suffering comic foil, Margaret Dumont:

"Where is your husband?"
"He's dead."
"I'll bet he's just using that as an excuse."
"I was with him to the end..."
"No wonder he passed away."
"I held him in my arms and kissed him."
"So it was murder!"

Halliwell concluded, "The pure undiluted essence of these primitive zanies, for whom nothing is sacred, is to be found in the earlier movies with their abhorrence of love interest, their loathing of establishment ethics, and their generally unswerving endorsements of corruption, incompetence and greed."

The Film Society provided additional opportunities for him to sample foreign language films, such as Eisenstein's *Ivan the Terrible* and Dreyer's *The Passion of Joan of Arc*. Peter Darby was the Film Society representative at the time and remembered Halliwell joining; they became friends and often went to the cinema together. He recalled Halliwell being especially enthusiastic about the cinema as an art form, and described an incident when the society was refused permission to show the German film *Der Apfel ist ab* (*The Apple*

Fell), an updating of the Adam and Eve story. The film was considered blasphemous and banned by some theatres. Darby and Halliwell instead formed the German Society, for the sole purpose of exhibiting this film, which for some reason exempted them from the ban. They advertised by word of mouth and brought in a full house.

Halliwell's feverish interest in the medium inspired everyone around him, as Eric Cross recalled:

> His film knowledge was extraordinarily wide. The names not only of actors but also of directors, studios, photographers, were constantly on his lips. I am certain I saw *The Lady Eve*, *The Philadelphia Story* and *Destry Rides Again* on his recommendation (at his insistence), and that his enthusiasm rubbed off on me. I'm sure he was aware of recent trends in, say, French and German 'art' cinema, but they by no means supplanted his childhood affections. He had a real love affair with Hollywood glamour, and Hollywood comedies.

Another picture Halliwell saw for the first time at the Film Society, and which would make it into his list of favourites, was Ernst Lubitsch's *Trouble in Paradise*. Although he later rarely managed to catch up with this 1932 romantic comedy concerning jewel thieves, he maintained, "It has been in my mind and my heart since that Sunday morning in 1949 when Cambridge's Film Society, a thousand strong, rose to it as one man and gave it a deafening ovation." The film starred Herbert Marshall, a debonair light comedian with a soft, elegant voice, and sassy Miriam Hopkins as his partner in crime. Together they attempt to relieve an heiress of her valuables by insinuating themselves into her life: she as a maid and he as a potential suitor – thus causing friction between the swindlers and creating plenty of scope for comedy. *Trouble in Paradise* has a sophistication which belies its age, and its cleverest lines are often suggestive, as Marshall, expecting company, says to a hotel porter, "It must be the most marvellous supper. We may not eat it, but it must be marvellous…"

The film is perhaps the best example of the 'Lubitsch touch', as promoted by Paramount, and which can be described as many things: sophistication, style, elegance, and the compression of ideas and situations into brief scenes. Halliwell further observed that the director "tried to tell his society comedies by picture as well as dialogue; in his hands a doorknob turning or a clock ticking could mean as much as a page of script." Lubitsch's huge influence on film-making in general, and the genre of light comedies with subtle sexual suggestions in particular, was only a contemporary one, as the style itself went out of fashion – and out of the movies, where subtlety was no longer welcome. However, virtually any romantic comedy from the Golden Age owes a debt to the German-born director, so much so that Billy Wilder had a notice pinned to his office wall which read, "How would Lubitsch do it?"

Also popular among the Cambridge in-crowd were the comedies of a writer/director who showed no lightness of touch whatsoever: Preston Sturges. Halliwell called him "a wacky and unpredictable near-genius whose drive, imagination and facility with words and actors took him in the mid-forties to the highest pinnacle of Hollywood success." Sturges established himself with 1941's *The Lady Eve*, in which Henry Fonda is outwitted by a father and daughter team of con artists. Sturges was famous for screwball comedy and freely admitted that most of his films were really about 'Topic A', his codename for sex. Indeed, Halliwell would later call *The Miracle of Morgan's Creek* a "one-man assault on the Hays Office."

It would be easy to dismiss films like *The Philadelphia Story*, *Duck Soup*, *Trouble in Paradise* and *The Lady Eve* as being the products of a vanished time; to say simply that they don't make them like that any more and to leave it at that. But since they all managed to be popular, and with a relatively young audience, long after their time – in Lubitsch's case *seventeen years* after – is it outrageous to suggest that their appeal might be timeless, if perhaps a modern audience were prepared to give them a chance? And if they did, they might recognise many of the elements present in more recent movies that seem to be oblivious to their own influences.

> *Wit and style are what I miss, heroes who are at home in any society, and that marvellous repertory of versatile supporting actors which vanished without trace and has never been replaced.*

After that first Michaelmas term, Halliwell returned to Bolton where he visited his old school to give them an update on his progress. He informed them that he had accepted a small part in the

Cambridge Mummers' production of James Elroy Flecker's Middle Eastern epic *Hassan*. The play was staged the following February and his part seems to have been tied inexorably to one of his co-stars, as the reviewer for *Varsity* noted, "McGregor and Halliwell were good as the Chiefs of Police and of the Military, whose slapstick is one of Flecker's tricks to make the atmosphere bearable." However, *Varsity Supplement* was less complementary, saying, "John McGregor and Leslie Halliwell should have injected something more of the Eastern art of insult into their playing."

Varsity itself was a weekly student newspaper founded in 1947 and staffed by around twenty-five undergraduates at its office in the market square – "a scruffy editorial suite above the Scotch Hoose restaurant," as Halliwell described it. Each edition ran to around twelve pages, printed at the *Cambridge Daily News* press and published on Saturday mornings. The paper boasted a circulation of 6,700 – which is suspiciously the exact number of students reported to be in attendance at the University (according to the book *Portrait of Cambridge 1952*). Within a few months of joining St. Catharine's, Halliwell was flexing his journalistic muscles and contributing reviews of books, plays and films to *Varsity*, as well as other articles related to the University. He would often write under pseudonyms, usually variations on his own name, a practice which was widespread at the newspaper. One issue contained an article called 'Twenty-eight miles of books in the University Library, but no *Winnie the Pooh*', by a 'Leslie Halliwell' – as well as featuring a piece entitled 'Such Shocking Vice!' with the by-line 'James Leslie', which concerned an 18th Century pamphlet discovered in the library complaining of licentious student behaviour. Another article in the same edition, called 'Boater to Bow-Ties: Fashions of the Half-Century', dealt with student clothing trends and was credited to a 'Robert James'.

1950 saw Halliwell's first appearance at the Cambridge Old Boltonians' Dinner, an annual event held at the University Arms Hotel, with his old teacher and Film Society associate Miss Waterhouse in attendance. He appeared on stage in his hometown, in the Bolton Little Theatre production of *Alice in Wonderland*; achieved a 2:1 in his preliminary examination for Part I of the Tripos, and rose to the position of Features Editor for *Varsity*. In addition, he accompanied a group of boys from Bolton School on a trip to Italy "as a kind of surrogate teacher." After spending one night on a coach and the next two on a train they all arrived in Rome, and the first thing they saw was a poster for the film *Harvey*, in which James Stewart played a character convinced he is best friends with a seven foot tall white rabbit. Halliwell promptly took his charges to see it at the first opportunity, and fortunately for him it was in English.

Two articles he contributed to *Cambridge Today*, a supplement to *Varsity*, are worth examining as they reveal his insight into the changing face of the movie business. The first, entitled 'Exit the Monsters', dealt with the winding down of Universal's horror movie series, which had so delighted him a few years before.

"Horror films have for some years been precariously balanced on the edge of an abyss of absurdity," he began, "and not many more blows are needed to pitch them into it." He proceeded to blame the war for producing so much real horror that latter day audiences found little about the likes of Dracula and Frankenstein that could frighten them. The quality of the films had noticeably depreciated, though, with Boris Karloff and Peter Lorre sending themselves up in *The Boogie Man Will Get You*. Halliwell remarked, "This abominable tardiddle might have ended the horror genre for good and all."

The article itself was essentially a review of *Frankenstein Meets the Wolf Man*, which was on re-release at the Cambridge Playhouse and was the studio's first attempt at packaging its monsters to stimulate interest. Whilst in itself it was a creditable effort – and Halliwell's hopes had been raised by this and Robert Siodmak's *Son of Dracula* – he admitted that "the improvement was momentary." Further packaging resulted in two unintentionally funny compendia, *House of Frankenstein* and *House of Dracula*, which killed off the series altogether. "Where do they go from here? Can they regain their former distinction?" Halliwell enquired. The simple answer was "not at this studio," for there would one day be a revival but it would happen across the Atlantic, in a small studio on the banks of the Thames, called Hammer.

Whilst 'Exit the Monsters' mourned the passing of one genre, another article appeared to do the same for musicals, but perceptively offered some hope. 'Music without Charms' traced the history of the genre from its birth at almost the very moment sound was invented. "No sooner had the cinema learned to talk than it began to sing and dance too," he observed. Whilst the early musicals of Busby Berkeley and Astaire & Rogers had been built upon the talents of star personalities, and film-makers who "had a firm grip on the effects of black and white photography," the latest efforts were overloaded with plot and lacked charisma. Halliwell had previously made a similar point in *Picturegoer* magazine but here complained, "Musicals have become so stodgy and tedious that they are not only unentertaining but intolerable to sit through." However, he added a note of optimism, "More recently hope has been raised by Gene Kelly's *On the Town*."

And that hope, for once, would be fulfilled, for in a small department in the largest Hollywood studio, a mini-revival of the Golden Age was underway at this very time. The Arthur Freed Unit at MGM, considered separate and untouchable from the rest of the studio, managed over the next few years to produce some of the finest musicals ever made, including *An American in Paris* and *Singin' in the Rain*. It was all the more surprising that this outpouring of old-style creativity should have occurred at the very time when Louis B. Mayer, "the beating heart of MGM," was ousted from the studio. Of *On the Town* specifically, Halliwell wrote, "It sparkles in my memory as the one movie which really lit up the chill anonymity of the Cambridge Regal."

In January 1951, Halliwell was appointed Literary Editor of *Varsity*. He was regularly churning out articles at the time and enjoying the experience so much that he seriously contemplated a career in journalism. On Fridays, after dinner in the Hall, he would cycle down to the *Cambridge Daily News* press and watch them set the type and run off the next day's edition. He recalled, "Soon after midnight the newspapers came flowing down to be collected in bundles, just as I had seen it happen in a hundred American movies." One of his articles contained the remarkably prescient headline, 'A Filmgoer's Guide', which managed to predict the titles of his future encyclopaedias, fourteen years before the first was published. The article itself was a round-up of the local cinemas for the benefit of incoming undergraduates, featuring typically idiosyncratic synopses:

"The Regal has all the trappings of the modern super-cinema ... but what tawdry stuff it sometimes offers! ... Programme-planning at the Playhouse and Tivoli appears to be somewhat slapdash, and the cinemas are both unpleasing to the eye and inconveniently far away for most of us ... the Arts is, of course, the Mecca of undergraduate filmgoers, and it is an institution we are grateful for ... The serious filmgoer will of course belong to the Film Society..."

On that note he suggested that the Film Society should show *all* of its films at the Central Cinema, rather than just one a week, and for his temerity he was roundly rebuffed by the Chairman of the Society. In a letter to the newspaper he wrote, "In reply to Leslie Halliwell's suggestion ... I should like to point out several factors, of which he, and others may not be aware." He explained that the Central was only available on Sunday mornings and that, because 35mm films were more expensive to rent, showing them exclusively would necessitate a rise in subscription fees, which would have the self-defeating effect of causing reduced renewals.

One other forward looking aspect of 'A Filmgoer's Guide' is to be found in its conclusion, which speaks of the need for improvements to the presentation of films in Cambridge, such as the addition of "a repertory cinema on the lines of the London Classics, which presents revivals of English-speaking productions that qualify not necessarily as great films but as undoubtedly good entertainment." Halliwell had previously called for something similar in a letter to the *Bolton Evening News*, but he would have to wait a little over a year before he got his wish.

Another article he contributed to *Varsity* – which he later claimed to be his own invention – became a regular feature in the paper. 'Next Week's Films', a round-up of the following seven days' fare at the local picture houses, publicly introduced for the first time his talent for brief assessments – the 'Halliwell touch' – not as light as the Lubitsch one, but for which his future film encyclopaedias would become famous. As with his exercise books – which he was probably still filling out at this time – space was at a premium, and with each of the eight available cinemas requiring a mention, Halliwell had to get his points across in the most economical fashion.

The Robert Donat comedy *The Ghost Goes West* was described as "a whimsical fantasy ... technically it is surprisingly naïve but it is likeable for its witty script and an attractive performance." *Laughter in Paradise* prompted "Although there is neither pace nor style, there are a great many laughs." *Captain Horatio Hornblower* received "A good sea story for those who like sea stories. Rambling and overlong, but certainly crammed with incident," and *Night unto Night* rated 'A gloomy psychopathic drama produced with great care but little skill; often interesting, though, and intelligently written and acted."

Halliwell's succinct dismissals were not universally popular, and one complaint was prompted by the very edition from which the above examples were taken. The 'Letters to the Editor' page of the following week's *Varsity* featured this reaction, with the headline 'Invective':

> Sir, - Seeing a new name at the foot of 'Next Week's Films,' I read it hoping for a change from the superior carping of your previous "critic." What unrewarded optimism! Once again we appear to be in for a weekly column drooling over anything continental or by the Marx Brothers, and sneering with a cocktail party type of wit at anything else. Let us glance at some of the week's remarks by our dictator of taste: "neither pace nor style," "does not convince," "can be safely missed," "hotch-potch," "very silly," "rambling and overlong," "patchy," "cheap," "not good," "wearisome," "depressingly vile," "gloomy." A nice effusion and by no means unusual!
>
> Since our national newspapers run columns of more reliable and less adolescent criticism, it would be an improvement were you to turn Leslie Halliwell out to grass and leave us a blank column on which we could write our own comments. - Yours etc., MIKE SHEARMAN, Trinity Hall.

Halliwell was moved to respond, "I fail to see a point in Mr Shearman's letter; if I sincerely believe a film to be bad, it is hardly 'superior carping' to say so. The column is intended as an acceptable guide for the majority of intelligent filmgoers, and if space limits me to a single strong adjective, that should not be construed as a sneer." The complaint was slightly unfair in that many of the dismissive quotes reproduced had been qualified in the original piece with more positive statements – and, in fact, that particular edition actually featured far more favourable reviews than were usually present. Halliwell later explained, "I tried to be fair, but there were a great many bad films around, and some of the entries must have sounded malicious."

As well as providing a weekly forum to air his film-related opinions, 'Next Week's Films' gave Halliwell the added benefit of free entry to all the local cinemas, with the column taking on an importance undreamed of at its outset. It could "very easily make or break a programme at the box office, which made the managers cultivate me more assiduously than ever." It also marked the only time in his career when he could accurately be described as a film critic.

Luxury had never entered into its construction. It was simply a roof and four walls, three of them directly exposed to the elements, which could rage fiercely on the top of that single Cambridge hill.

A bizarre article appeared in *Varsity* in February 1951, under the headline 'Critic under Hypnotic Eye'. The report concerned a hypnotist called Roy Baker, who had been in residence at the New Theatre and who "hypnotised a member of the staff of *Varsity* last Tuesday morning. He was Leslie Halliwell, Literary Editor, who made a very good subject." A photograph was included, showing Halliwell's large frame sitting forward in a wicker chair. He has slicked-back hair; wears a thick striped scarf and sits with head bowed and eyes apparently closed. He holds his clenched hands between his knees and beside him stands a dark-suited gentleman with a Hitler moustache, leaning forward on one arm of the chair and apparently entreating his subject in some fashion. Halliwell added, "I made every effort to concentrate as he instructed … as soon as he made me row an imaginary boat and play an imaginary piano I realised that I was under his control… every time he snapped his fingers my feet would burn and I would take off my shoes at lightning speed, and that every time he spoke to me I would be very angry and shake him by the shoulders. I did all these things, although I had no desire to."

A rather more significant story appeared in this very same issue: "Rex Cinema sold – The owner of the Kinema, Mr. G. Webb, last week completed arrangements for purchasing the Rex, the town's third largest cinema, and its ballroom. Mr. Webb, garage-owner, sold his contracting business to buy the Kinema last summer and has been running it successfully ever since." Halliwell was not a frequent patron of the Rex. It was the only picture house which had never courted him in his role as University Film Critic. The cinema itself was situated on the northern outskirts of the city centre, on top of Cambridge's only real hill, and at the end of a row of gloomy-looking Victorian houses. It opened in 1932 as the Rendezvous, underwent a name change six years later and added a café and ballroom. The cinema seated eleven hundred but its remote location and poor management meant it had seen few full houses in recent years.

On his first visit, Halliwell found it to be "a vast, ugly, jerry-built barn of a building with the letters R*E*X stripped down its stucco in red neon." Passing the sign for the ballroom on his left he walked on toward the cinema entrance and found "the fake marble steps were cracked and the still display cases were falling apart with rot." The place seemed eerily deserted, with grass growing through gaps in the concrete and posters of former attractions on display. The only sign of life was an elderly lady in the pay box doing her knitting. Halliwell paid his fare and hurried into the one-and-nines "looking neither to right nor left, as though I were afraid of being spotted by the Proctors." Once inside he was able to appreciate fully the auditorium. The upstairs section was roped off, apparently whilst building work was taking place. The carpets were torn; many of the seats were broken and cobwebs hung visibly in corners. In short, it was a fleapit – apparently written off as a tax loss. Its manager had given up his losing battle with the ABC chain, who presumably could have bought the place for a song had they wished, so perhaps they had been put off by its location and its urgent need for costly renovations.

George Webb, on the other hand, did not mind how much the renovations cost... for the simple reason that he hadn't the slightest intention of making any. Ironically, the article announcing his ownership went on to say, "Immediate improvements at the Rex vary from better heating arrangements to the booking of first and second-run films. Other changes include extension of the café facilities and conversion of the ballroom floor into a roller-skating rink three days a week. Mr. Webb hopes to obtain Proctorial permission for the regular evening dances." Over the next few years those "better heating arrangements" would remain conspicuous by their absence, but under new management the tide was about to turn for the Rex.

George Webb was a large bald man who sported a 'toothbrush' moustache and wore a permanent grey suit. He was in his early thirties at the time but looked "a well-used fifty" on account of some hard living in his youth. He had recently sold his haulage business with an agreement not to be in competition for five years and so he was looking for another investment opportunity. He stumbled into the cinema business, purchasing first the Kinema and then the Rex – or possibly *winning* it in a poker game. He planned to "give ABC a run for its money by operating both halls in the way he would have operated a haulage business ... by native cunning and brute force." George was not a man to let lack of experience deter him – all he needed now was someone who knew something about the movies...

Halliwell, having been unable to obtain much in the way of accurate information from the Rex's previous manager, was surprised to hear a new voice when he made his weekly phone call from *Varsity*'s office, and felt the need to investigate further. He made his way out of town and up the hill to find George in his grey suit, on his knees fixing a broken chair with a giant-sized ratchet screwdriver which he boasted was the only one in Cambridge. The conversation may have gone something like this:

"Are you the new manager?"

"Yep, George Webb's the name. Used to be in the haulage business but I got bored with that. Now I run a couple of cinemas. Won this one in a card game!"

"So what's on next week?"

"Er... *Cairo Road* and *Tarzan and the Slave Girl*. Will we do any good?"

"I doubt it. *Cairo Road* died in London, and why play *Tarzan* when the kids are at school in the afternoon?"

"You're a bloody lot of comfort. What would you book in my place?"

"Something good that happened to run out of term, then you'll get the undergrads who missed it."

"Undergrads, eh? Won't they complain about the cold? I can't afford the bills yet."

"They won't mind; they'll bring their overcoats."

"What do they like to watch?"

"Get some Bob Hope comedies, and some early Marx Brothers. Danny Kaye in *Walter Mitty* and Gene Kelly in *On the Town*. That recent Launder and Gilliat one, *State Secret*..."

It is fair to say that this was a life changing moment for both of them. *State Secret* was duly booked and went down a storm with the undergraduate audience. George took Halliwell out for a curry supper to celebrate, and from then on probed him for tips on what titles to book. Over the next few months, significant changes occurred: roller skating became a regular feature at the Rex, but only "with Proctorial permission" as it went on until 11pm. A double advertisement for the Rex and the Kinema appeared in *Varsity*, "under the personal supervision of Mr. G. Webb (Owner)." This was eventually replaced with one which promoted only the Rex's offerings, as these were aimed primarily at the students. As for Halliwell's influence, a few Marx Brothers films did indeed find their way into the programmes throughout the next term, as did *The Secret Life of Walter Mitty* and *Road to Utopia*, but it would be another year before he truly made his mark on the place.

Halliwell's stage work continued with a Mummers' production of *1066 and All That*, billed as "The University's largest ever musical" and which ran for a whole week at the New Theatre. He played three barons and a magistrate, and had a similar number of roles in the Marlowe Society's staging of Shakespeare's *Coriolanus*. But the increase in parts must have dissipated his impact as in neither case did his performances rate a mention in the notices. In addition, he appeared in several college revues, on one occasion impersonating Groucho Marx – very effectively if the picture in his memoir is any indication – and on another singing 'Any old Iron', as well as supplying song lyrics to an Old Music Hall evening at the Amateur Dramatic Club. His friend Michael Wright summed up Halliwell's acting style, "Leslie was a 'natural' performer, but limited in his range – he was typecast usually in blustery, comic parts, at which he excelled." Eric Cross wrote, "I did not see him as a serious actor, and he was certainly not part of the Cambridge theatrical scene, but he acted, as he did everything else, with tremendous energy, with great *gusto*."

Halliwell somehow found time to pass the first part of his Tripos proper, achieving a 2:1 grade, before returning to Bolton to review his old school's production of *Edward the Second*. His hectic lifestyle had not gone unnoticed: in the 'Cambridge Letter' section of *The Boltonian*, a John F. Ryley observed, "R. J. L. Halliwell when sought is never to be found – he has just gone to rehearse this or review that; he is to be found in print, he can be seen in disguise, but it is impossible to find Halliwell *in vivo*."

It was in Bolton that his theatrical career reached its apogee. His beloved Little Theatre had begun a scheme to encourage young actors and actresses, called the Junior Little Theatre, and which was for under-30s only. Their first effort was a production of Thornton

Wilder's 1938 play *Our Town*, which Halliwell managed to persuade the company to let him produce, stage-manage and appear in. He even wrote to the twice Pulitzer Prize-winning author to ask him whether to retain certain references that a modern audience might not understand. Wilder responded philosophically from his home in Florida, "They are not the only things which already 'date' the play. Over here time has passed so rapidly that the whole tableau ... is now very nearly a superseded moment. All best wishes to you."

The play itself, in which small-town life is contrasted with the upheaval of world events, was performed on three successive evenings in January 1952. It featured a commentary delivered by Halliwell himself, leaning against the proscenium arch, smoking a pipe and expounding "crackerbarrel philosophy." He described the audience reaction as "thunderous" and a very favourable review appeared in the *Bolton Evening News* after the first night, under the headline, 'Charm of small town life captured at Little Theatre.'

"An unusually pleasant sensation began to steal over one soon after the curtain had risen," observed the reviewer, who felt that the various elements of the play were "all bound together with immense skill" by Halliwell's narration, achieved "without perceptibly raising his voice, and yet retaining a complete hold over the audience." The public and critical response led Halliwell to write, "I walked on air for days ... it was a perfect swan song." After that he never again seemed to find the time for stage work. He knew he would struggle to better the notices and maybe that was a contributing factor. Either way, *Our Town* was Halliwell's final theatrical performance.

> *Time is the scarcest commodity in Cambridge: we are all trying to cram a lifetime's experience into nine terms.*

Whether Halliwell actually invented 'Next Week's Films' is arguable. The first item to be so called appeared on October 29th, 1949, and was compiled by a 'G.H.N.', with later editions credited to a 'T.C.P'. Neither of these is likely to have been Halliwell: his pseudonyms tended to be more obvious. It might be significant that the item made its first appearance soon after he joined the University but he did not begin contributing to *Varsity* until the Lent term. What is clear, however, is how the item evolved once his name was attached to it, from January 1951 onwards. In terms of appearance, it gradually increased in size to a full column running prominently down the middle of the back page, with the advert for the Rex on one side and the ABC cinemas on the other. Further conspicuous changes occurred once its author began advising George Webb on which films he should show at his new cinema. The Arts had up until then maintained pride of place at the top of the list – it was clearly Halliwell's favourite picture house and received the largest write-up. However, in early 1952, when he became Assistant Editor, the Rex leapt up from its traditional position – about two-thirds down – to second in the list, and then overtook the Arts in terms of space allocated. Special recommendations to patronise George's cinema began to appear. On one occasion Halliwell wrote of "a brilliant programme at the Rex," and on another advised, "Go early." He said of one feature that it "cannot be too highly recommended," and even that bottom-of-the-barrel Marx Brothers film, *Love Happy*, was dealt with leniently: "It should be seen for purposes of comparison." In the February 23rd issue the Rex actually featured at the top of 'Next Week's Films' with a relatively enormous section. It *was* a particularly strong line up, though, with *Things to Come*, *Occupe Toi d'Amélie* and *The Man in the White Suit*, but Halliwell further says of the Rex Harrison film *The Rake's Progress*, "At least the first half bears seeing more than twice"! Summarising the forthcoming term's fare he complained, "Bookings so far suggest that the five circuit cinemas will this term tread their conventional way, with consistently dreary second features." By contrast, "The Rex plans an attractive series of English, American and French comedies…" In another edition, a separate advert appeared for the Rex saying "Watch out for the following outstanding programmes, all showing at the Rex this term," and proceeded to list the films on offer.

One might be reading too much into all of this but the term 'conflict of interest' does spring to mind. The counter argument would be that if he was picking the best films for George to show, then he was only giving honest assessments of them when it came to writing his column. In addition, there were still many examples where the 'Halliwell touch' brought Rex programmes back down to earth with a jolt, as in the case of *Forbidden Jungle*, which prompted, "Shoddy studio-made travellers tales, aimed at those with mental ages of three-and-a-half or thereabouts." Presumably George did not always take the advice he was given.

For the Easter term of 1952 – his last as an undergraduate – Halliwell finally became Editor of *Varsity*, and an announcement was duly printed, accompanied by a picture. Twenty-three at the time, he is shown in a dark suit holding his glasses in front of him, as if about to lean back in his chair in order to ponder some important editorial point. He has a full head of dark hair, a small moustache and a jutting chin, and looks every bit the scholarly critic. The article describes him as having "no political affiliations" and being determined to "continue the independent policy of the newspaper." Halliwell himself chipped in – as if under duress – "I refuse to hand over 'Next Week's Films' to any deputy." Possibly feeling the responsibility of his new position weighing upon him, the order in which the cinemas were listed in the column changed almost immediately to alphabetical... but the Rex still took the lion's share of the comment.

In the very week Halliwell became editor of *Varsity*, George Webb found himself in court. Two Downing undergraduates gave evidence against him on a charge of allowing unaccompanied children into a showing of *All Quiet on the Western Front*. The students were described as having "super-sensitive morals," and had reported the matter "to prevent such brutal films being shown to young children who could not understand them." The Magistrate, Mr. J. F. Ablett, said the case was "very, very serious indeed" and promptly fined George £30.

Halliwell went against convention by not setting down a clearly defined statement of policy in his opening editorial for *Varsity*, "for the editor *has no* clearly defined policy, and, if he had, would consider eight weeks an impracticably short time in which to demonstrate it." He pointed out that people were not slow to voice their criticisms of anything and everything that bothered them about University life, and those grievances would dictate the content of the newspaper since they were made by its customers. His first editorial highlighted the age old problem of the student: how to balance study and recreation. He seemed to be speaking from experience when he wrote, "The practising socialite can only hope at best to pacify his supervisor by occasional essays skimmed from the surface of an encyclopaedia." (Hopefully *his* supervisor did not read that part.) He argued that the social side of Cambridge might seem to some more profitable than a 1st in terms of life experience, but he cautioned against the undergraduate thinking it might bear any resemblance to *real* life. Cambridge revolved around the student, with shops, bars and restaurants all vying for his patronage – "almost everyone calls him sir [and] residents regard him as a playful kind of god." Some who had gone down from university found it a shock to be treated just like ordinary people again. Halliwell suggested that the undergraduate might receive better preparation for the real world in his two years spent in the army, rather than his three spent in Cambridge.

All his editorials contain the same well argued and thoughtful comment, and were not short on opinions – in fact, no-one in Cambridge seemed to be short on opinions. Each correspondent was utterly convinced that his particular grievance was of earth shattering importance, and that only he could express it in its purest form. And, like the internet today, *Varsity* provided him with the ideal forum in which to air it.

One of Halliwell's pieces concerned the poor quality of food offered in the Hall. "With the only known exception of Christ's, the catering story throughout the colleges is one of lack of imagination," he carped, "There is no excuse for black and soggy potatoes, for foul gritty cabbage, for Yorkshire pudding which tastes like fried Dunlopillo." He further complained of the serving of rabbit, which prompted one informative student to agree, "Rabbits are full of syphilis and are not fit food for man." An attack on the low standard of creative writing by undergraduates featured the observation, "Last term's poetry competition resulted in seven poems which it did not seem possible could be the best out of fifteen hundred largely appalling entries." This brought a heated response in the letters page, with one correspondent calling Halliwell's comments "peevish and cheap," and proceeding to charge, "You lower the tone of the paper with such arrogant remarks."

An editorial which railed against the Communist newspaper *Daily Worker* pointed out that its articles seemed incapable of reporting news "without subtly shifting its emphasis in such a way as to make it a piece of party propaganda." This resulted in a mixed bag of responses, with the negative ones accusing Halliwell of trying to incite "anti-Red hysteria." Another political piece dealt with the controversy surrounding an exposed plot by a so-called 'Fourth Party' to influence Student Union elections. Protracted correspondence had been received on the subject, including much criticism of the paper itself, to which Halliwell responded, "The story about the Union 'cabal' was not concocted in this office on a Friday afternoon when no other news was available." He proceeded to describe the assiduous information-gathering undertaken in pursuit of the story, affirming that he only published once "confirmatory evidence" had been received.

On one occasion he began, "It had to happen: this is about films. Not so much about films themselves, however, as about the people who go to them." He proceeded to decry incidents of barracking by students at recent showings, observing that when the audience was a mixture of "town and gown" they mostly behaved themselves. However, "when the irrepressible undergraduate finds himself among none but his own kind at cinemas such as the Arts and the Rex, which try to cater for his eccentric tastes, then the Mr Hyde in him is released."

The article was inspired by the reception at a Rex screening of the Spencer Tracy picture *State of the Union*, shown under its UK title *The World and His Wife*. The film's cynical jabs at political corruption were lapped up by the anti-establishment audience, but only jeers and taunts had greeted its pro-American sentiments. Halliwell called this "a short-sighted, intolerant and unpleasant attitude. There is no doubt that Americans are often silly, but so are Britons." The response to this duly arrived the following week, with a D. Harrison of Trinity initially choosing to highlight "the appalling grammar of the first four lines" of the editorial, but going on to agree largely with the opinions expressed, offering melodramatically, "If the world is to be torn apart by a Third War it will be because of the actions of people with minds such as those which jeered at Tracy's speeches."

As a frequent non-paying patron, I was surprised to find how easily the whole ambience of the Rex could be improved by a full house, despite George's antipathetic attitude to public relations.

Throughout 1951, Halliwell's influence on the Rex had been subtle but detectable – a 'Marx Brothers' here, a 'Bob Hope' there – but for the Lent and Easter terms of 1952 almost every programme has his personality written all over it. Double-bills were his speciality, pairing films with similar interest such as *It Happened One Night* with *On the Town*; *Green for Danger* with *The Lavender Hill Mob*; *Words and Music* with *The Philadelphia Story*, and *French without Tears* with *Trouble in Paradise*. However, by far and away Halliwell's biggest success in terms of recommendations was the film which had made a star of Marlene Dietrich: *The Blue Angel*, directed in 1930 by Josef von Sternberg. It was referred to in 'Next Week's Films' as "one of the few great movies which have also caused long queues in the suburbs. A fascinating film in the great German tradition, technically and aesthetically powerful."

George had his doubts about what was effectively a rather dour, moody German film, but fortunately an English language version had been made simultaneously, and he remembered it to have been a "bit saucy" so he booked it for a half-week. However, takings were poor and Halliwell, constrained by the burden of having to sit his Tripos exams, could not get up the hill until the Wednesday evening, whereupon he encountered an empty cinema and a bad tempered George stomping off to the pub to console himself. A rather poor effort called *The Saxon Charm* had been booked as the second feature but Halliwell was still puzzled by the lack of interest, as he had overheard students discussing *The Blue Angel*'s poster, which featured a sultry-looking Marlene. Furthermore, he knew that the film had been unseen for many years and was highly regarded among his contemporaries.

Feeling that he had let George down, Halliwell settled disconsolately into his seat in the circle to watch the opening feature – which was even "heavier and duller" than he had remembered – but about halfway through he was distracted by a shuffling in the one-and-nines. Peering over the rail he saw a group of gowned figures taking their seats, and became aware of more filling up the circle around him. He rushed out to find a large queue at the box office, with undergraduates continuing to arrive and bicycles being stacked six-deep by the wall. Clearly the other students had taken the same approach he had: to get the exams out of the way first and then to squeeze in a Rex visit at the last possible screening. The local was duly phoned and George came rushing in, grinning from ear to ear. Halliwell referred to the incident as being "like one of Hollywood's putting-on-a-show musicals, in which disaster is averted by the magical last-minute appearance of a society crowd including all the most influential Broadway critics and backers." By the time the main feature began the place was packed and Halliwell, deputising as an usher, finished up watching from the rear stalls gangway.

The film itself concerns an old college professor who clears his students out of a night club where a tawdry singer called Lola-Lola is entertaining them, only to fall in love with her himself and become self-destructively obsessed. Despite its slow start and heavy atmosphere, as well as the over-emotional acting of Emil Jannings as the professor, the student response was of hushed respect, and by the time Marlene sang her signature song, 'Falling in Love Again', they were hooked.

At the movie's tragic conclusion, the house lights came up and nobody moved. For fully ten seconds the undergraduates sat in silence before slowly filing out of the auditorium. They waited patiently for their cycles to come to the top of the pile and pedalled away into the night, gowns flapping in the breeze. After the last one disappeared round the corner of Magrath Avenue, George sidled up to Halliwell and said, "That stunned 'em, boy; I told you it would!" – and promptly took him out for a celebratory chicken biryani.

> *It is neither easy nor desirable to be serious about the end of one's Cambridge career: the fire of cynicism is as hard to avoid as the morass of sentimentality.*

An air of gloom permeates Halliwell's final editorial for *Varsity*, in which he highlights the sense of despondency felt by the undergraduate once the intense periods of study and examination were concluded. "Only the actors and the oarsmen are happy," he wrote, "for they have something to do ... the most sensible people are those who make a bolt for home as soon as they have kept their full term." In his conclusion, he took care to thank the staff, the readers and the advertisers, and rounded off, "Whether you approved of the results or not... it's been fun."

Halliwell's whole three years had been fun. His total immersion in the cultural miasma of Cambridge had not only been thoroughly rewarding in itself, but it had helped to shape opinions which he would hold for the rest of his life, especially those concerning the movies. His introduction to continental films had allowed him to appreciate fully the influence French, Russian and German film-makers had on the Hollywood pictures. But he had noticed in particular a worrying trend by more recent directors to be too obscure; to implant meanings more complex than the average filmgoer was prepared to accept, and which were consequently harming their chances at the box office. "*Avant-garde* films which make no concessions to popular taste can aspire only to an audience of connoisseurs," he cautioned, adding, "the work of Dulac and Dali is welcome at the Film Society but not at the Odeon." For the rest of his life, he would hold to the maxim that the best films were the ones which combined entertainment and art – or at least *craft*.

His knowledge of the industry made him well aware that it had been on a consistent downward spiral since the end of the war, despite such conspicuous blips as the Freed musicals and the Ealing comedies. His recommendations for the Rex had a distinct air of nostalgia about them: Halliwell was already a revivalist, at twenty-three. And with a 2:1 grade achieved in English Literature, he was faced with the time honoured graduate question: what was he going to do with the rest of his life? Ideally, he wanted to make use of his vast film knowledge in some literary capacity, and so he began sending clippings of 'Next Week's Films' to various publications to demonstrate his journalistic talent. Having no success on that front, he reluctantly signed up for a teacher training course which would at least have the benefit of keeping him in Cambridge for another year. However, a surprise offer then came in from *Picturegoer* magazine, his childhood moviegoing bible, and Halliwell suddenly found himself on his way to London.

He left Cambridge in the summer of 1952 for what he fully expected would be the last time...

But with George Webb making repeated offers for him to manage the Rex on a full-time basis, there might just be the possibility of a return...

4

A Dream Come True

- *Picturegoer* and the Rex, 1952-56 -

Perhaps the Freed Unit's finest musical for MGM was 1952's *Singin' in the Rain*, a film which centred on the greatest period of upheaval in Hollywood's history: the coming of sound. Leslie Halliwell's three years at Cambridge University coincided with its second great trauma: when the studio system was collapsing and television was beginning to keep the audience at home, where previously undreamed-of domestic comforts increased reluctance to venture out of an evening. 1950 had seen the emergence of the freelance actor, thanks to the seven year contract having been abolished. Stars and their agents were able to bargain for percentage points, and larger agencies like MCA took it a stage further. From their own roster of clients they could select a star, a director and a producer, and hire them out to the studios as a job lot. 'The Deal' had arrived, and is still to this day the way movies get made.

The power of the studios had been greatly diminished by the separation of distributors from exhibitors and the outlawing of the old block-booking system. Television took over the role previously occupied by the B-picture serials so *they* were no longer required, and falling attendances and rising production costs reduced film output still further. But the studios were not finished yet: with television seen as the ultimate enemy, over the next few years they would find more and varied ways of tempting people away from their new-found home comforts.

Meanwhile, Leslie Halliwell had moved in with his old school pal James Beattie, who was looking to make a career for himself on the stage. They dreamed together of someday opening their own theatre in the West End, which they intended mischievously to call the 'Macbeth'. Mr Beattie recalled to me:

> I had lived in Edgware Road; then this flat was going because some friends of mine were going on tour. Opposite Maida Vale tube station. Another friend was directing *Desire Caught by the Tail* and he took a room. There were three rooms and so there was a spare one – which wasn't very nice, next to this awful kitchen, and I said to Leslie, "Would you like to stay?"
> He stayed but it wasn't a very nice time for him. I was... down. And he wasn't very happy, of course, with the surroundings I suppose. I was used to that sort of life by then. It was just the top flat, with the bathroom down on the second floor.

It should have been a dream come true for Halliwell to write for the magazine he had pored over as a child, but *Picturegoer* had changed significantly over the years, adding a garish colourisation process to both its articles and photographs. "It was all brown blobs and squiggles," he wrote, "unreadable to anyone with a mental age higher than seven and a half" – which was just as well because it seems to have been aimed squarely at the younger market, and mostly female. Scattered among articles concerning Jane Wyman's legs and how the stars whiten their teeth, were copious advertisements for lipstick, hair conditioners, soap and chocolates.

Halliwell's appointment at the magazine's Shaftesbury Avenue office was due to veteran film reviewer Lionel Collier, then nearing retirement, having neither the time nor the inclination to assess the relentless stream of second features which poured out of the Hollywood studios at the time. Many of these had been made several years before but remained unseen in England due to quota restrictions. Halliwell, on meeting the man who had greatly influenced his own style of critiquing, found Collier to be "emaciated but sartorially elegant; always with a carnation in his buttonhole." Collier was still trying to bring a touch of class to his copy, which was clearly at odds with the house style. Any films of significance would receive evening press screenings at glamorous venues, with the added attraction of complimentary drinks, and as such were restricted to senior staff. The young deputy Halliwell subsequently found himself dispatched to a succession of underground Wardour Street mini-theatres, for 10am screenings of such soon forgotten efforts as *My Death is a Mockery* and *Captive Wild Woman*.

"I rather enjoyed setting my increasingly stern professional standards against such rubbish," he recalled, at the time finding free cinema passes and press screenings fresh and exciting. He was able to discover the museums and parks of the capital and to sample its more upmarket cinemas on his own time. In addition, he could act the proper sophisticate in Soho clip joints, holding critical discussions over an espresso, at the time the new height of metropolitan pretentiousness (now superseded by the 'skinny latté').

Picturegoer's gossipy jargon was anathema to Halliwell, who had recently found his own journalistic style at Cambridge. There, he had been his own boss but now he was finding his contributions rewritten by a sub-editor. An article about a new wave of horror films inspired by *The Thing from another World* contained some insightful comments, such as the observation that the film was at its best while the monster remained off screen. The piece typically delved into the history of the genre, referring to *House of Frankenstein* as "a surfeit of penny-dreadful clichés that invited more laughs than shudders." But it also contained this monstrous passage: "*The Thing* is getting into its stride and the pace was terrific. The film, as publicity proclaimed and viewers quickly realised, was horrific – with a capital 'X' that seems all set to clean up at Pudsey as it's cleaned up at the Pavilion."

The 'Halliwell touch' still shone through on occasion, though, as *Mother Riley Meets the Vampire* was reviewed as "a lumbering collection of badly timed chestnuts," and *Hidden Secret* was dismissed as "crude anti-Red propaganda masquerading as a jungle thriller." But, as the summer of 1952 wore on, Halliwell became more and more discontented. He felt sorry for his pal James who was struggling to land a decent part, and he found the quality of their lodgings a marked contrast to the comforts of his college accommodation. London, still bomb damaged from the war, ultimately failed to inspire him and the hot weather had produced an uncomfortably sticky atmosphere. The last straw came courtesy of an article he contributed about Ginger Rogers, specifically concerning the change in course her career had taken from dancer to serious actress. Halliwell was forced to rewrite the feature twice before it was accepted, and it eventually appeared in a much altered form under the headline 'Box Office Ginger'. As printed, it contains such clunkers as, "She's been assigned a long programme of films by Hollywood. What line will the new Ginger take?" as well as, "[*The Primrose Path*] didn't give us the Ginger some of us wanted. It was the Ginger that Ginger wanted." What really made Halliwell blench, though, was its concluding sentence which ran, "Her eyes are less mischievous – yet they're still on Ginger and that new line of box office ginger she's trying to put into her Paramount contract."

Halliwell promptly resigned and took a month off to consider his future. He spent two weeks in Paris and came to a life-changing conclusion at the top of the Eiffel Tower: if Bolton had been his Shangri-La then Cambridge was his Land of Oz, a magical world which he had "loved and lost" – and there remained just one chance to get it back…

George Webb was overjoyed when Halliwell shook his hand and agreed to become manager of both the Rex and the Kinema, in October 1952. He had finally got his man – courtesy of a few hastily made promises he would later fail to make good on, such as offering his young charge a share of the profits. From Halliwell's point of view it was a chance to return to the magical land of Cambridge, which had suited his sensibilities so perfectly. Furthermore, he could get paid for putting his movie knowledge to use while considering a permanent career more appropriate to his qualifications. He decided to give it two years.

Having never met anybody like George, I was fascinated to watch him operate. Even the original bull in the china shop can hardly have rubbed up so many people the wrong way in so short a time.

Still to this day on Chesterton Road, towards the bottom of the hill on which the Rex once stood, are a row of delightful white cottages with black doors and window frames. Each has a steep sided, almost vertical moss covered slate roof, with an upstairs window jutting out. In 1952, number six was owned by a Mrs W. Lavis and she rented a room to the new manager of the Rex Cinema. It was clean and quiet, conveniently situated for work and was a place in which he could "read and sleep and have breakfast, and do *The Times* crossword at night as I sipped my cocoa."

The cottages themselves back onto the River Cam at its widest point in the city, via a quaint sloping lawn. A little way along the road is a metal footbridge leading over to Jesus Green, or Midsummer Common as it was then called. This beautiful and relaxing park would have provided Halliwell with the perfect place for quiet contemplation, and the setting inspired him to write two plays and at least one novel during his tenure. From his front door he could cross Chesterton Road, walk up the slope of Hertford Street and turn left and then right into Magrath Avenue. As he rounded this last corner, the Rex would be visible at the far end of the street on the opposite side of the road. His total journey time to work would have been under three minutes.

As an occasional non-paying patron, Halliwell had been prepared to put up with the Rex's deficiencies, but with the building now to be his place of employment seven days a week he began trying to persuade its owner to spend some money on refurbishments. George was typically reluctant, responding curtly – and with some justification – "People go to the pictures to see the pictures!" Halliwell nevertheless conducted a thorough inspection of the premises and typed up his observations in an office he shared with the manager of the ballroom. His notes included, "Screen: damp patch in lower right hand corner near defective exit door ... main curtains: in desperate need of dry-cleaning; their smell fills the front half of the stalls ... auditorium walls: caked with nicotine grime and cobwebs ... carpets: badly worn, with some dangerous holes ... staff room: the broom cupboard under the stairs ... toilets: beyond comment..."

He distributed his typed observations around the venue, but although George never mentioned them they disappeared one by one and soon it became clear that Halliwell was fighting a losing battle. The Rex would remain what it had almost always been, a fleapit. Not that George was unwilling to help out, though: he worked longer hours than anyone else and was always on hand to fix broken seats and lights, and to repair electricals – anything that only cost time and effort. During busy sessions he could be seen selling tickets, restocking the sales desk or standing on the steps chatting to the queuing customers.

Halliwell's management duties were limited as George handled the staff, which consisted of a white-haired accounts clerk, "a gaunt ex-army doorman with a twisted leg and a curiously distorted face," and a rather camp usher. An ex-circus bareback rider named Rita ran the chocolate counter and Miss Cleaver sat perennially knitting in her box office kiosk. George's style was fairly confrontational: "When he had shouted at everybody on the cinema side," Halliwell wrote, "he would transfer his interest to the staff of the so-called ballroom." In addition, he had a habit of sacking someone on the spot, only to relent later and make amends by buying his poor victim a drink.

If he could not influence the comfort his patrons were expected to sit in, Halliwell could at least make sure they were provided with some solid entertainment. Since he knew that the Rex could not compete for the major titles, he had to content himself with reissues and the best of the ABC rejects. Most of the major distributors had offices in Wardour Street and he would peruse their latest offerings in trade papers such as *Kine Weekly*. If he sensed hesitancy on ABC's part over a particular title he would notify George, who would either harangue some poor executive over the phone or drive the two of them to London in his Bentley for a face-to-face. They became so well known that Wardour Street executives would take the day off if pre-warned of their arrival. Halliwell wrote, "I knew what I wanted and George made sure that I got it."

Commission-hungry travelling salesmen were another means by which the Rex acquired its fare. They often turned up unannounced, usually just after Halliwell had sat down after a long day dealing with administrative duties. He described them as "rogues, but genial ones," and he enjoyed skimming through their glossy brochures and conducting negotiations in his multi-functional office. Salesmen expecting an easy ride would be in for a shock when they came up against Halliwell's knowledge and experience.

"Here's a smashing little picture you ought to book while you can," one might say, "The circuits are crying out for it, but we're offering it to the independent exhibitors first. It's fast and funny and it's got sex appeal and..."

"I've seen it."

"I agree with you. It stinks. Now what about..?"

George often got involved in the discussions as the salesmen themselves were lively characters, which appealed to him. The whisky would flow and the boisterous conversation would continue into the night. Halliwell said he enjoyed these sessions but one can imagine him feeling slightly out of place. In terms of programming, he liked to pair big name oldies in double-bills, with three changes a week and with the last show commencing just after seven, so that his undergraduate patrons had time to cycle up the hill after "first Hall." He occasionally fell foul of the distributors for his coupling of big titles, though, even if the films themselves were many years old. "If you start doing this sort of thing you will make your public always want it," they objected.

Since the major releases were scarce, the distributors wanted them paired with second features, of which there were so many. But Halliwell was determined to maintain his standards and railed against Wardour Street's efforts to foist upon him "immense and appalling accumulations of cheap quickies." He wrote, "The most charming and the most exasperating aspect of the Wardour Street bureaucracy is its insane logic," after being refused a ten year old Rita Hayworth film for fear it would damage the takings for her latest release. At other times he was offered "fatherly advice" when attempting to book films which had done badly on their circuit release – but negotiations could get tricky when a distributor sensed Halliwell wanted something badly and would try to drive up the price. He was sometimes expected to pay as much as forty or fifty percent of the net takings as rental. Conversely, some films of genuine quality could be picked up for next to nothing simply because they were held in contempt by their owners, due to poor business on a previous run.

Halliwell was charge of publicity, and in that capacity he redesigned the advertisements printed in the *Cambridge Daily News* and *Varsity*. The former was more pronounced, and in addition to providing details for both the Kinema and the Rex it promoted the ballroom, which might feature 'Strict Tempo Dancing' on a Tuesday night, or jazz artists on a Friday such as Eddie 'Tash' Mendoza and his Crazy Orchestra. The *Varsity* advertisement featured a simpler design with only the Rex listed, as its fare was clearly aimed at the undergraduate market. Halliwell could not resist the occasional outburst, though, such as "The Rex will never show you a bad film!"

He printed up each term's forthcoming programmes in delightful A5-sized booklets, four of which survive at the Cambridge Central Library. Each comprises eight glossy cream-coloured pages with details in blue print for both the cinema and ballroom. The information is set out in a neat and symmetric way and includes a sprinkling of local advertisements to offset costs. The front page announces the venue as "The best value in show business!" and promises "continuous performance" at the cinema. The ballroom's attractions were provided with the bare minimum of information on a single page, whereas the cinema listings ran to three, with some typical Halliwell hyperbole. A re-run of *The Blue Angel* was trumpeted, "Last time it was here it broke all records! Don't miss it now!" *Bicycle Thieves* was "acclaimed among the ten best films ever made!" and *On the Town* featured the declaration, "You wanted it back, and here it is! That magical musical..." Halliwell distributed the booklets around the colleges and they became quite collectable. He would be cheered to see one displayed proudly on a friend's mantelpiece if he popped round for tea.

Surrounded by more than a thousand empty seats, on a cold afternoon in a half-derelict cinema ... I sat in my overcoat and came face to face with what, if there has to be one, is the best film of all.

That first Michaelmas term of Halliwell's management brought forth a strong line-up. Among the offerings were Powell and Pressburger's *A Matter of Life and Death*; Laurence Olivier in *Wuthering Heights*; the obligatory Marx Brothers films *Horse Feathers* and *Duck Soup*; a delightful Billy Wilder comedy called *A Foreign Affair* and a double-bill of horror: *House of Frankenstein* coupled with *The Invisible Man's Revenge*. Halliwell wrote of the response, "Partial success came our way almost at once: full houses did happen about once a fortnight, and there were always enough gowned customers who wanted to see *The Philadelphia Story*, *The Lavender Hill Mob*, *A Yank at Oxford* and anything with the Marx Brothers or Bob Hope in it."

In the first week of November, *King Kong* arrived at the Rex, and to publicise it Halliwell actually donned a gorilla suit and was driven around town in a specially painted van. A picture appeared in *Varsity* showing him in quite the most shoddy and dishevelled costume, with the comment, "What becomes of *Varsity* editors? Few would have guessed that only last term Halliwell was a nice unspoiled boy with a very pleasant manner, particularly when reviewing foreign films that he didn't understand…" A better picture appeared in the *Cambridge Daily News*, showing him striking an ape-like pose actually on top of the van, the side of which advertised the Rex Cinema & Ballroom as "Cambridge's Home of Super Entertainment!" The success of this exercise is difficult to assess, however. In his memoir, *Seats in all Parts*, Halliwell commented, "*King Kong* drew surprisingly few punters," yet elsewhere he wrote, "I believe my performance did several passing ladies no good at all, but it livened up the box office no end."

Another programme in that first term featured the film which became Halliwell's favourite of all: *Citizen Kane*. Directed in 1941 by Orson Welles, the film concerns a reporter's investigation into the meaning behind a newspaper magnate's dying word, "Rosebud". During the reporter's enquiries, episodes in the life of Charles Foster Kane are played out in flashback. The film was controversial in its day, as tycoon William Randolph Hearst thought it too closely based upon his own life and tried to have the negative destroyed. In addition, *Kane* proved unpopular with mainstream audiences who were unaccustomed to encountering such cerebral entertainments at their local Odeon. Having been quickly withdrawn after its initial failure, *Citizen Kane* surfaced again ten years later when a single print was struck from the British inter-positive – a direct copy of the original negative and the next best source material. Halliwell saw the new print advertised in *Kine Weekly* and snapped it up, doubling the film with the equally downbeat *The Ox-bow Incident*.

He managed to see *Kane* on the first afternoon it played, and the half-empty house seemed appropriate for such a solemn occasion. From the opening shot of a sign saying 'No Trespassing' followed by the sudden death of the main character, Halliwell knew that he was "in the presence of a master showman." He described the film as "an ingenious patchwork of conjuring tricks, patterns of sight and sound deftly blended and transformed by Hollywood expertise. It marks the coming together of every craft of studio film-making in its most advanced form." Typically, though, he had a few gripes, "It isn't a perfect film, certainly: one can point to the lack of real hard information about Kane's character, to the scant and unsatisfying mentions of his mother, to gaping lacunae in his biography…" In terms of its reception at the Rex, however, the evening attendance was good, "Friday showed a fall-off, and on Saturday we broke the house record."

In 1975, Orson Welles received a lifetime achievement award from the American Film Institute, and accepted it "in the name of all the mavericks." The term 'maverick director' surely dates from this moment, and would be applied to nearly all the American filmmakers of the seventies who regarded Welles as their hero and *Citizen Kane* as the ultimate maverick movie. Scorsese, Spielberg, Coppola, Bogdanovich, Friedkin, Rafelson, Schrader, Lucas and Hopper all learned their trade from the "master showman" himself, often demanding the same total control over their productions that Welles had enjoyed with *Kane*, but generally to much less effect. Indeed, Welles himself could never again repeat the trick, admitting, "I started at the top and worked my way down."

Citizen Kane is a remarkable film to behold even today, packed full of great performances and witty lines such as, "Old age: it's the only disease you don't look forward to being cured of." It positively abounds with tricks of cinematic technique and narrative: low-angle photography showing ceilings; shadows obscuring faces; composite shots of models and live action, and subjective camera. Most of these had been used before by directors such as Jean Renoir and F. W. Murnau, but never combined to such powerful effect. Arguments raged for years over exactly who wrote what in the screenplay but none of the controversy detracts from the actual experience of watching the film, and it is no surprise that *Citizen Kane* has topped all five of the BFI Critics' Top Ten lists since 1962. It will probably top the next five.

Personally I'd love to play nothing but classics ... but even in Cambridge, business is business and it's embarrassing to have to space out fifty people among eleven hundred seats.

After only a month in the job, Halliwell felt sufficiently experienced to write about his trials and tribulations, and an article duly turned up in *Varsity* entitled "Running the Rex: Revelations of a Cinema Manager". It included a caricature of him depicted as a 1930s-style frock-coated commissionaire, replete with epaulettes and cap, and with that famous chin well emphasised. A slightly rewritten version of the same piece appeared in the national periodical *The*

Spectator two months later, under the headline 'Continuous Performance'. He wrote of the difficulty of predicting the tastes of his undergraduate audience, who eschewed the sophisticated comedy of *To Be or Not to Be* but lapped up *Trouble in Paradise*. They delighted in larger-than-life personalities such as Marlene Dietrich, Katharine Hepburn and Groucho Marx, but, he complained, "One must rage with silent indignation when a French classic is greeted with empty houses, and smile with barely-suppressed contempt at the crowds which invariably flock to see the latest redskin epic in Supercinecolor." The regular local customers to whom he was forced to appeal during holiday periods, additionally refused to tolerate films which had "writing on the bottom."

Halliwell's knowledge of the changing industry made him well aware of the battle against television and he quoted producer Stanley Kramer, who had made a series of "critically acclaimed but modestly budgeted programme pictures." Kramer said, "The only way to beat television is to make films which cater for thinking people over twenty-five as well as for the retarded adolescents who now form two-thirds of the audience."

The studios did not agree: they felt the best approach was to come up with ever more imaginative innovations which they hoped would demonstrate the cinema's superiority over the little box in the corner. In January 1953, the Rex installed the Synchro-Screen, claimed to be the tenth in existence in Europe and designed to give the illusion of 3-D without glasses. The effect was achieved by the addition of four angular aprons around the screen, setting it back like a picture in a frame. Halliwell pointed out this innovation to George in a trade paper and they travelled to Bayswater to catch a demonstration. He recalled, "The dim reflection of the picture on the wings was certainly more restful to the eyes than the conventional sharp black edge." But he was not wholeheartedly convinced as to its effect – in contrast to George who was gripped, asking simply, "How much?"

The installation took place overnight and when it was ready they tried out various film clips, with mixed results. An observer for *Varsity* declared, "The sharp edge on a figure seen on a normal screen is less defined ... while the diffusing effect of the aprons makes colours more realistic." Halliwell put any improvement merely down to the benefit of having a brand new screen to replace the grimy old one. But despite his misgivings, and with a deft combination of advertising oversell and a few choice X-certificate films of "astounding ineptitude," the Synchro-Screen had paid for itself by the time the colleges reopened for the Lent term.

Indeed, Halliwell (or perhaps George) had become well aware of the effect an X-certificate could have on the box office. These films were mostly continental but re-titled to hide the fact, and were often accompanied by garish advertising which heavily hinted at the possibility of sexual content. Thus, *Dieu a Besoin des Hommes* played under the title *Isle of Sinners*, and *Altri Tempi* became *Infidelity*. One of Halliwell's biggest successes was René Clair's *Belles de Nuit*, which he thought "would scarcely have broken the house record had it not been rechristened *Night Beauties* and exploited with stills of Gina Lollobrigida getting out of her bath." Halliwell's friend Peter Hall observed, "Experience shows that undergraduates are suckers for the pornographic."It should be noted that despite the adult certification, these films were tame by any modern standards: the briefest flash of nudity was enough to provoke accusations of pornography in the 1950s. The showing of them might seem in contrast to Halliwell's attempts at promoting quality, but he would have argued that at least it got his audience used to foreign language films, even if they were mostly watching for the images rather than the dialogue. He wrote, "We are persevering in the hope of making subtitled films popular with the 'masses' but it is not easy."

One such attempt brought the Czech film *Extase* to the Rex, which featured a naked Hedy Lamarr before her Hollywood career began, and was booked by "popular request." In the programme booklet for that month, Halliwell had called it "the film that was banned and withdrawn so many times," adding the *nota bene*, "this film is not suitable for children." The showing caused an outrage – not because of any offence being taken but because of the sensational aspects having been cut! Peter Hall (now Sir Peter, "the academic one, not the actor" – his words) was at the screening and remembered the outcry among the audience, telling me they nearly had to call the police to calm the patrons down. Unfavourable comments in *Varsity* provoked Halliwell to respond, "Sir, your columnist last week was, as usual, both unkind and inaccurate. *Extase* was not 'hissed off the screen', except by the few who were disappointed to find it a work of art and not of pornography." He went on to explain that cuts had been made at the insistence of the censor, "and as for the implication that the film was of a low aesthetic 'calibre' I am sure that this would be refuted by any discerning film critic."

On another occasion, a reviewer wrote, "The Rex continues digging its way through the stock of American and British comedies ... but the supply is running out, and it is also re-showing its past successes such as *Fantasia* and *On the Town*." The same article referred to Halliwell's showing of more serious minded films like *Death of a Salesman* and *Bicycle Thieves* as a "dangerous practice."

So it seemed he could not win. If he tried to show continental films they had to be of the more controversial variety or the house would be empty, but if he stuck to the Rex's bread and butter policy of old American standards then he was criticised for repeating himself. It was all about maintaining the balance, which was the thrust of another article he wrote and which he managed to get published in *Sight & Sound*, no less. 'Strictly for Eggheads: Thoughts on Running a Specialised Hall' appeared in the April 1954 issue, and was not this time simply another rewrite of 'Running the Rex' – although it did contain similar gripes about the difficulty of obtaining specialist titles and the pitfalls of predicting audience taste. It was mainly concerned with the compromise the manager of an independent cinema had to make between art and box office.

"The 'discriminating' public is not nearly so large as *Sight & Sound*'s readers may think," he observed, "and the circuits naturally prefer to work for profit rather than for art." One *Varsity* observer was sympathetic, pointing out, "The Cambridge audience, which should be one of the liveliest in the country, is mentally lazy – it doesn't want to think. An article by Leslie Halliwell in this quarter's *Sight & Sound* illustrates this." Throughout his time managing the Rex, he would continue to book a mixture of sure-fire successes and experimental choices, to entice both his local and undergraduate audience. And it was in fact precisely *because* of the staple fare that Halliwell was able to experiment in the first place, since he knew he had them to fall back on if more intelligent or continental selections resulted in half-empty houses.

I was still, despite all the drawbacks, experiencing a dream come true, devising my own programmes from a choice of the best films in the world, and showing them to audiences which for seven months of the year at least were among the most appreciative one could find.

If the Synchro-Screen had been designed to mimic 3-D, then the real thing was not far behind. A whole clutch of films following on from *Bwana Devil* were reported as being produced in the new process, and Halliwell was consequently besieged by travelling salesmen hoping to tempt him to buy the necessary synchronised projectors, and to order boxes of the special glasses required to experience the effect. At a West End trade show, he and George were treated to a screening of the Vincent Price movie *House of Wax*, where "knives were brandished in our faces" and "a head was guillotined into our laps." George once again had his cheque book at the ready and the equipment was immediately installed, although neither he nor Halliwell were under any illusions about their prospects of actually obtaining *House of Wax*, on account of the ABC circuit. The best they could hope for would be a "range of barely tolerable (but profitable) westerns and crime thrillers, all apparently made in a matter of days and looking it." The new technology very much superseded the previous one, as the Synchro-Screen required repainting with a metallic sheen, thus removing whatever effect it had previously gained.

The *Cambridge Daily News* announced in August 1953 the "Biggest Film Sensation since Sound," and proceeded to report "thrills at Rex preview," where around fifty councillors and representatives of the film industry were guests at a morning screening of *Man in the Dark*, in which Edmond O'Brien played a gangster who loses his memory. The article continued, "In a short address of welcome, Mr. R. J. L. Halliwell, the Rex manager, who has made a special study of 3-D ... said that the expense was considerable and the extra charge for admission covered only the cost of hiring the Polaroid spectacles."

The audience allegedly sat "enrapt" throughout the screening as various objects were thrown or thrust at them, including knives, scalpels, hatchets and spiders. Columbia executive Jerry Wald said of the new innovation, "We'll throw things at the public until they start throwing them back." A picture of the audience all wearing their special glasses – and looking reasonably enrapt – was included with the report. One assumes it was taken at the Rex screening, and the fact that they are all in their overcoats would seem to confirm this. The caption ran, "How audiences will look in the future?" The question mark was a wise inclusion – although at the time of writing, a 3-D film has just become the most successful movie of all time.

Halliwell cheekily altered the Rex's advertisement to claim that *Man in the Dark* was "better than *House of Wax*!" which prompted a letter from ABC's solicitors asking as to how his patrons could make such a judgement since *Wax* was only on in London. Halliwell managed to get several friends to sign a petition stating that they had travelled to the capital to see the film – despite them having done no such thing – and ABC backed down. As he later recalled, "3-D came – and went – like a fever." Both *Man in the Dark* and *House of Wax* played for only a couple of weeks, and the expense of converting exhibitors' equipment – as well as the complications of the glasses – meant that only a handful of cinemas showed any interest in embracing the technology. Hollywood realised that the trend was not going to be the money-spinner they had hoped for, and subsequently most of the films which had begun shooting in 3-D were instead completed in traditional form.

That same summer the Rex was treated to the most successful week in its history... but Halliwell missed it. The coronation of Queen Elizabeth II at Westminster Abbey was broadcast live on British television, and as such provided a powerful stimulus to the sales of TV sets. But it was shown only in black and white, whereas soon after the event Rank released to cinemas an eighty minute colour production narrated by Laurence Olivier, entitled *A Queen is Crowned*. Since the ABC circuit was as ever the likely beneficiary, Halliwell had not paid much attention to the release, but Rank had struck so many prints that they were offering up to third and fourth runs at vastly reduced rates. He thought that many local people might be put off going during term time and so he booked it for a week-long run in July, after the undergraduates had gone home. His programme booklet for that month contained the claim, "Exclusive to the Rex Cinema!" and predicted "ninety minutes of glorious pageantry!" In the meantime, however, his old college friend Michael Wright had tempted him away for a week trekking in Scandinavia. "I had arranged for a holiday in Norway with a school friend," Wright told me, "who had to drop out at the last moment. I asked Leslie if he would like to go." Halliwell jumped at the chance, impressed that his usually more reserved friend was taking the lead for once. Wright tactfully withheld the fact that he was second choice and the two of them took in the sights and cinemas of Oslo, before nipping over to Stockholm where Wright was "violently sick" after some "Balkan-type paprika."

Upon his return, Halliwell discovered that George had been rushed off his feet – "alternating as usher, commissionaire and cashier" – and had even pressed his wife and two sons into active duty. They had averaged more than three full houses a day, with continuous queues, coach parties arriving and the telephone ringing off the hook. At the time, a good week at the Rex might have brought in around £900... *A Queen is Crowned* took £3,000. Halliwell was disappointed to have missed out on all the fun and wondered what he could ever do to top the figures.

These were indeed the golden years of the Rex, with the cinema achieving destination status among the undergraduate community thanks to the never-say-die attitude of its owner, the ingenuity and nous of its manager, and despite – or perhaps because of – the venue's faults. On one occasion a rope snapped and the curtains closed during a performance of *Kind Hearts and Coronets*. It took four of them to set things straight before emerging, covered in dirt, to a "rousing cheer."

'Dracula claims victims' was the headline following a double-bill of horror, with the old Count coupled with *Frankenstein*, both films having been unseen for many years. "A woman and a man fainted at the Rex this week," it was reported, and "many of the audience had to go out into the foyer for a breath of fresh air." Usherettes had to cover their ears during any performance of the Robert Taylor film *A Yank at Oxford*, for fear of being deafened by the roar which greeted the line, "I, sir – thank God – went to Cambridge!" A showing of *Mr Deeds Goes to Town* brought quizzical looks from the audience when reel eight turned out to be from *Lost Horizon*. This was due to Columbia having mixed up the cans of film, which no-one had checked prior to the screening. George refused to pay the rental and *Varsity* commented waggishly, but inaccurately, "Mr Deeds Goes to China!" – Shangri-La was in Tibet.

Alan Frank, who became a journalist and a governor of the BFI, was up at the University at this time and he told me, "I was studying medicine and I met Leslie whilst he was running the Rex. He introduced me to the Marx Brothers and I also remember their slightly saucy films. I spent all my spare time in the Rex... which is why I'm not a doctor."

As Halliwell described himself, he was "a square peg in a square hole," and he became a well known figure about town. During their traditional curry suppers, George used to enjoy watching his young charge field movie-related questions from other diners. The pair occasionally received invitations to premieres in London, with the Ealing comedy *The Titfield Thunderbolt* being a standout: "I remember the eager anticipation of the crowds which packed the Odeon Leicester Square for the press show," Halliwell wrote. A *Varsity* review of a book about the Marx Brothers featured the observation, "If undergraduates are prepared to spend half as much to *read* about the Marx Brothers as they are to see them, then Mr. Heffer [local bookshop owner] will be as happy as Mr. Halliwell."

His exuberant personality and "sharp, hammer-tap voice" made him ideal for public speaking. In addition to appearing once again at the annual Cambridge Old Boltonians' Dinner, where in 1954 he proposed the 'Toast of the School', Halliwell gave a talk for the Shirley Society at St. Catharine's, under the title 'The Perverted Art'. The art in question was of course the cinema, and the perversion that of money.

"The cinema is the only art to be controlled by businessmen," he explained, "The enormous expense of film production will ensure that box office takings remain the most potent factor. The film industry must pander to the 80% of the total audience which does not think about the films it sees, but goes to the cinema out of habit." He divided the remaining twenty percent into three groups: those who were pleased to see the cinema dying; cheerful optimists who hoped for better things, and "highbrows." It is not entirely clear from that list, however, into which category he placed himself. His conclusion was downbeat, "Films will never get better; present indications are that they will get rapidly worse."

He spoke again at a Cambridge Union debate on a similar motion: 'The Box Office is debasing the Film'. A Mr. M. W. Ballin of Selwyn College was the proposer, who opened proceedings with a story about the author who took the plot of his second novel from the film version of his first. Halliwell recounted some of his adventures at the Rex and pointed out that quota restrictions were "the main reason for so much trash today." According to one observer, though, he made the house "grow somnolent" when he displayed "his extensive knowledge of the film by reading out long lists" – an unfortunate tendency he would continue into his published works. Happily, though, he revived his audience by asking the president if he thought the Windmill Girls were debasing the ballet. Another speaker opposed the motion with the stance, "The film is not debased by the Box Office because the industry could not exist without it," and the proposer eventually lost by 135 votes to 123.

One way or another, therefore, my days were filled with excitement and my nights with conversation. I enjoyed as much university society as I wanted [and] had free passes to every show in town.

In 1954, a moment came which could perhaps be defined as the end of the Golden Age. MGM released Clark Gable, previously hailed by publicity as the 'King of Hollywood', from his contract. He wanted a share of the profits like everyone else and Metro simply could not afford him. There would be no more revivals after this: agents and deal-makers would run the business from then on. The moguls themselves, the pioneers of the industry, either retired or were squeezed out – or died – and their successors were not strong enough to prevent the shift of power from studios to actors. Halliwell commented, "Stars, producers and directors all helped to kill the system which had worked so well for so long." The lunatics had taken over the asylum.

Even the Film Society was doing badly. *Varsity* reported on its fall in membership and "desperate appeals for new members," but further complained that lately their programmes "lacked cohesion, having the air of being thrown together." One observer commented that the Society's problems were due to its "shocking publicity, which belongs to the pre-Halliwell age of Cambridge cinema." The decline in subscriptions led to the Society no longer being able to afford the Central Cinema for their Sunday morning screenings, but Halliwell stepped in and offered them use of the Rex. George was reported to have agreed "favourable terms" with the Chairman of the Society, who was pleased "to patronise a cinema whose programmes appeal to the more discriminating cinemagoer."

Halliwell had more literary success when a short story entitled 'Strangers in the Train' was published in the *Bolton Journal & Guardian*. The story itself was an unremarkable tale of confidence tricksters but it reveals his interest in the short story with a twist in the tail, a style he would later develop for his collections of ghost stories. *Varsity* still warmly received his contributions, which on one occasion publicised another continental film with a whiff of scandal about it. *The Sheep Has Five Legs*, a "sort of French reply to *Kind Hearts and Coronets*" was playing at the Rex for a run of six days and featured one Lina Lopez, "whose next-to-naked perambulating … has led to much speculation on the ways of the British censor."

On the same page as this review, a new name appeared under 'Next Week's Films': Michael Winner. A flamboyant character even then, he would go on to direct *Death Wish* and to appear in commercials, but at the time he was studying law at Downing College. In his reviews he was less punchy and more conversational than Halliwell, with whom he became friends and for years afterwards often met for lunch. I spoke to Mr. Winner half a century later, and he described his old pal as "tall, thin and very scholarly. He could be a bit arrogant and a pompous arse but I liked him immensely. Of course he believed there hadn't been any good films since about 1938!" Winner had fond memories of the time and spoke highly of George Webb, calling him "a rough diamond, a sweet fellow." On one occasion for *Varsity* he wrote, "There is only one source of entertainment in Cambridge film land more amusing than the films shown at the Rex, and that is the conversation of the man who owns it." He went on to describe how George had accosted him recently upon leaving the cinema –

"Look 'ere boy, I've got the film of the week next week: *Human Desire*…"

"But George, how do you know it's that good? No-one's seen it yet."

"I know, I know, but I can feel it… here!" said George, patting his chest (or perhaps his wallet), "Look at this poster: man and a woman kissing. She's taken her shoes off. See that? No shoes."

"I don't understand…"

"You're too young! Listen, I'll tell you what happened the other night. A couple of undergraduates were sitting in the two-and-threes with one-and-nine tickets. I said to Leslie 'Throw 'em out!' He said they wouldn't move. I went in there; I said if you don't get out of those ruddy seats I'll sit on top of you! They moved."

Just as Halliwell had been courted in his role as University Film Critic, Winner was also treated to chicken biryani at the Koh-i-noor, where on Sunday evenings the three of them would put the world to rights, an eclectic mix of characters. During one of these curry-fuelled discussions, the subject turned to the recent refusal by the British censor to grant a certificate to Stanley Kramer's *The Wild One*. The film starred Marlon Brando as a leather-jacketed, motorbike riding 'hoodlum' whose gang terrorise a small American town, but the censor was troubled by its lack of moral values. Halliwell knew someone who had seen the film in America under its original title, *The Cyclists' Raid*, and who had "given it the thumbs up," but Columbia had been unable to provide any further information when he called them, and later he read of the censor's decision.

Winner, doing his stint as editor of *Varsity* at the time, suggested they invite the local council to a special screening to see what they thought of it, as he recalled in his autobiography. However, Halliwell remembered it slightly differently, as he put it, "I had an idea. In such cases as this, local authorities may revoke the censor's decision ... I arranged for the Cambridge magistrates to see *The Wild One*." When I put this to Mr. Winner over the phone he almost exploded. His response was mostly unprintable but suffice it to say, he insisted most strenuously that it was *his* idea and not Halliwell's – which would make more sense, as Winner was a law student and so would be more likely to know the vagaries of council regulations.

Columbia duly sent a copy of the film and Cambridge Council dispatched either ten or twelve magistrates – depending on which source you take – to a Thursday morning screening. Halliwell handed out press books describing the work of Stanley Kramer and then stood at the back to watch the film, and to look for any audience reactions. After the performance, the magistrates were observed in conference and the following morning written approval arrived, permitting the Rex to show the film with an X-certificate, barring under-16s.

The Rex would be the only cinema in England to show *The Wild One*, and on 22nd March, 1955, the *Daily Express* ran the story with the headline, 'One City Will Show Wild One Brando'. A full column running down the length of the front page reported, "The British film censor refused to give any certificate because the film was too brutal and because it might have a bad effect on young people. But Cambridge will let the picture be shown." The release was still a month away but the newspaper helpfully provided train times and fares as a guide for cinemagoers who wanted to get to Cambridge. The reporter concluded, "I have seen the film. It is certainly tough but it is also good picture-making, with a fine performance from Brando."

The film opened on April 24th, just after the undergraduates had returned from their Easter holiday. Halliwell fielded enquiries from all over the country, and in addition to the usual student crowd the numbers were swollen by "teddy boys and a sprinkling of London sophisticates and actors," such as Beatrice Lillie, Jon Pertwee and Jackie Collins. He wrote that "hundreds of letters reached the cinema" and that several magazines had sent reporters. One of these, for *Picturegoer*, interviewed a Cambridge lady who said of her son, "If he were younger I wouldn't let him see a film declared unfit by the censor." A market seller commented, "These local magistrates would pass anything." Another resident said, "It's all right to show it in Cambridge: we have a low delinquency rate. But in some places it could be a harmful influence: I wouldn't show it in Liverpool, for instance."

The resulting article contained a sidebar: 'Why I fought for the film', in which Halliwell confessed to being an admirer of Stanley Kramer's "unusual, powerful pictures," and recounted the story of his booking the film, taking full credit. He is pictured in a bow tie with a beaming smile, and his moustache and prominent chin give him a likeness to Bruce Forsyth. "I am delighted to have shown the film," he announced proudly, "not because of its news value, but because it is good art."

Many cinemagoers arrived on motorbikes, giving Magrath Avenue a distinct similarity to the town invaded in the film. The presence of police on each corner further gave the impression that trouble was brewing, but they were in fact only there to stop people from parking in the street, as residents had complained. In fact, the local force had tied the film in with their advertisements for a motorcyclist training scheme, so they were clearly unconcerned about its moral effects. *Varsity* reported, 'Banned Brando film: Capacity business for Rex', in which George bubbled, "It's the first time that we have run a picture for two weeks and done capacity business all the time!" He went on to claim that most people who had seen the film declared it "the best they had seen for years." He may have been exaggerating, however, as *Picturegoer* reported takings in the first week were "not terrific." Halliwell himself later conceded, "Over the run we played to very average business," pointing up the lack of a constant queue and customers rarely finding any difficulty getting in. At the time, though, he was obviously swept along by it all, and may have let the excitement get the better of him, as he was quoted calling the film "a minor masterpiece."

The *Picturegoer* article was published under the headline 'The Fuss Fizzles Out', and the indefatigable Lionel Collier began his review, "I'm sorry to say it, but *The Wild One* bored me." He went on surprisingly to agree with the initial ban because "it could put wrong ideas into some juvenile minds." The editor added an admonishment to his young readership: "Don't use this film to criticise the censor. Remember he is the best and most enlightened in the world. Respect his decision."

That mythical character, the average picturegoer, has had many burdens to bear in the last few years ... wide screens have cut off the tops and bottoms of his films and put the rest out of focus ... and he is probably a chronic sufferer of CinemaScopus Horribilis.

A new weapon had emerged in the war against television, and this one would prove to be no fad. In 1953, 20th Century Fox patented CinemaScope, a wide screen process actually invented thirty years before, and the first film to be released utilising it was the biblical epic *The Robe*. Action was photographed onto the same four-by-three shaped 35mm film but a special lens squeezed a wider catchment area into the same space. The resulting image appeared squashed up on the actual film, but a corresponding lens in the projector stretched it out onto a screen with a ratio of approximately 2.35:1.

Halliwell had of course heard of the new development, and he and George were invited by Fox to the West End premiere of *The Robe*, even though they were pessimistic about their chances of securing such a prestigious picture. However, it turned out that ABC had balked at the cost of installing the new equipment and George was not about to pass up the opportunity of getting one over on his competition. Unfortunately, a mix-up during the delivery and installation resulted in him having a shouting match with the Fox representatives over the phone. As the confusion continued, ABC changed their minds and Fox seemed happy to pull out of the Rex deal. Halliwell kept their films out of his cinema for a whole year, until another dispute between the Hollywood giants and ABC resulted in a deal by which the Rex would get at least a share of the first-runs. By then their specialist house was one of the last in the county still to convert. "I was sad to see the monster screen go up in the Rex," he wrote, "but at least we were able to keep a good height, so that old films could be shown in their proper ratio in the middle of it."

CinemaScope spawned a swarm of imitators: Warnerscope, Metroscope, Vistavision, Panavision, Camerascope and Superscope – "everything but artistic scope," as Ezra Goodman put it in his book *The Fifty Year Decline and Fall of Hollywood*, going on to say, "What Hollywood desperately needed was not larger screens but greater vision." The new screens required different methods of projection and offered all kinds of ratios. 'Widescreen' itself was the process whereby all the action was grouped into the middle strip of the film, which was then magnified when projected, resulting in a loss of focus. Furthermore, the top and bottom of the image had to be 'masked', which meant that when an old four-by-three picture was shown, actors lost the tops of their heads and dancers lost their feet. Halliwell later wrote, "Four-by-three, which had been good enough for *Gone with the Wind* and *Citizen Kane* and *The Grapes of Wrath*, was officially labelled 'postage stamp' and condemned to instant extinction." The film-makers themselves were less than enthused by the new technology. Fritz Lang was quoted, "There was a time when all I looked for was a good story, but nowadays everything has to look the size of Mount Rushmore." That expert innovator Rouben Mamoulian called CinemaScope "the worst shape ever devised," and the inimitable Samuel Goldwyn observed, "A wide screen makes a bad film twice as bad." Another observer summed up the situation as "more a new kind of crutch than a fresh kind of wing."

CinemaScope led to the death of film technique. Longer scenes resulted because the director could not cut away and intimacy was lost. Watch any of the movies I have promoted in this book and observe how the director frames each scene, with actors and props distributed so as to keep the balance and to hold attention. How would a genre like *film noir* ever have come about in the widescreen era, where the characters – and indeed the audience – are required to be immersed in a claustrophobic world? The sharp angles and focused vision of *Citizen Kane* would have been utterly lost on a wider screen.

In October 1955, *Varsity* reviewer George Perry reported, "Despite Leslie Halliwell's frequent boast that the Rex would never have a wide screen, CinemaScope has at last been installed." Halliwell denied making any such claim. "What I have boasted," he responded, "and still boast – is that the Rex will never distort its pictures on a wide screen [and] non-CinemaScope films will continue to be shown at the Rex in their proper ratio, with nothing missing from the top or bottom. Viewers might like to consult the analysis I propose to display on the bulletin board in the Rex foyer." Despite his efforts, Perry was less than satisfied with the subsequent projection:

> Leslie Halliwell states publicly in *Varsity* that the Rex isn't going to spoil their presentation of ordinary films on their new screen. But if you have been there in the past few weeks you will have found that the screen shape remains unaltered regardless of the ratio of the film showing on it. Thus *Miss Julie* floats uneasily in the middle of a screen two-and-a-half times too big for it, an ugly grey margin on either side of the picture. Can't George Webb fit a motor to alter the black surround of the screen? This is a standard fitting in most cinemas. If the Rex has any conscience it should remember its boast, stop doing things on the cheap, and end this irritating and distracting malpractice.

There was no response from Halliwell the following week, perhaps indicating that he thought it fair criticism – after all, he had never wanted the new screen in the first place. Indeed, around this time he was growing increasingly disaffected with his lot in general. The 'riches' George had promised him failed to materialise; he never did receive that share of profits and only after a heated argument did he manage to secure a raise. It was now three years since he had told himself he would give it two, and he was thinking strongly about moving on to justify his mother's faith in him.

Halliwell's drive to find a job to suit both his qualifications and interests led him to apply for various opportunities in journalism, as well as a Commonwealth Fund Fellowship to study the art of the motion picture at the University of Southern California. Ultimately unsuccessful, he instead signed on for a three year executive trainee course with the Rank Organisation. George was disappointed to hear the news but had gained enough experience by that time to be able to continue, and so it seemed to be the best time for Halliwell to leave. He was a month short of his twenty-seventh birthday in January 1956 when *Varsity* reported, "The six thousand or so patrons of the Rex will be sorry to learn that Leslie Halliwell, Cath's man and cinema manager, is leaving for higher things." He was interviewed and spoke of his editorship at the paper, "In those days it used to be more like *The Observer* and less like the *Daily Mirror*. By the way, I hope I'm still on the free mailing list." (Probably not after that last remark.)

He vowed that the same booking policy would continue at the Rex but by then George obviously knew which side his bread was buttered, as over the next few months a significant number of X-rated films crept into the programmes, with titles like *An Artist with the Ladies* and *The Fruits of Summer*. Halliwell signed off with the comment, "I'll always keep a paternal eye on things. I've enjoyed being here very much." And with that, he left his Land of Oz behind him and promptly took his mother on holiday to the Isle of Man. Back in Bolton, they went to see *The Blackboard Jungle* and were disappointed, as "authority was shown with its back to the wall, and nobody wore pearls or dinner jackets or set his face against the stars."

The Golden Age was truly over, and almost poetically this proved to be the last film they ever saw together...

Two months later, Lily Halliwell died of pneumonia at her Bradford Road home. She was seventy-one.

5

Just like Ealing Broadway

- Marriage and Granada, 1956-67 -

Ruth Turner was born in 1922. She was the daughter of a Nottinghamshire minister and in her early twenties she married Edward Porter, a mechanical engineer. They settled in Slough, a few miles west of London, and had two children, Denise and Stewart, but the marriage was later dissolved. While Stewart was away convalescing after a bout of asthma, Ruth let his room to Leslie Halliwell, who, as part of his executive training course for the Rank Organisation, was acting as a relief manager at the local Ambassador Cinema. Ruth was seven years Leslie's senior and with him having lost his mother only a few months before, it would seem reasonable to assume that she may have partially occupied that role. Indeed, Denise confirmed as much to me when I spoke to her over fifty years later, saying "My mother offered him comfort and support during a difficult period. He was very close to his mother. Ruth was kind and supportive, which is why he felt so welcome in our home. All I really remember was this gentleman in a business suit, coming and going to his room."

During the three months of his tenure, Leslie and Ruth became good friends and in the ensuing period their relationship developed further. Sir Peter Hall, who knew him at Cambridge and afterwards, told me, "Leslie was living in digs in Slough and he fell in love with his landlady." Sir Peter was Best Man at the subsequent wedding, which occurred on July 18th, 1959, at the Kingston Registry Office in

Surrey. Halliwell was thirty years old at the time and the whole family, including boxer dog Sooty, had already moved into a terraced house in Kew. Another family friend recalled that Ruth appreciated more than anything else Leslie's kindness, evident in his being prepared to take a ready-made family under his wing. There was no official honeymoon but the happy couple did undertake a coach tour of European capitals soon after.

Two years later a son, Clive, was born, although this blessing presented particular challenges as the boy had Down's syndrome. Halliwell's friend Michael Wright observed, "Despite his disability, he was much loved by both of them and looked after with great care." Leslie became an active member of the Richmond Society for the Mentally Handicapped, where it was reported that his bookstall "was a popular feature at local fundraising fairs and events." TV writer Philip Purser remembered, "He had a handicapped son and my wife and I went to the splendid concerts that Leslie arranged to raise funds for his son's special school."

The Halliwells would remain in Kew for the next thirty years – on one occasion moving house but only a few streets away, just as Leslie had done many years before in Bolton. Michael Wright remembered, "I think both children by her first husband got on well with their stepfather. Ruth and Leslie were a happy pair and well suited to each other. The only minor bone of contention between them seemed to be the huge accumulation of books that Leslie made, spilling over the whole house."

Ruth seemed to play the role of the dutiful wife to perfection, saying in an interview, "I was content in his contentment; his job was his hobby and his hobby was his work. I looked after him. I preferred it that way. His love of films continued throughout his life." Kew provided her husband with easy access to the cinemas of the capital, as well as to the more local houses such as the Kingston Granada. In addition, Halliwell began a lifelong acquaintance with the National Film Theatre, where he was often seen attending performances of films from the Golden Age. He was a regular attendee at the annual dinner of the London branch of the Old Boltonians' Association – as he had been its Cambridge equivalent during his time there. They held their event at the Criterion Restaurant in Piccadilly Circus, and in early 1961 experienced a record turnout.

That same year, Wright and Halliwell holidayed in Wales and the

West Country, where they caught up with Canon Stanley Leatherbarrow, the ex-vicar of St. Mark's Church, then living in Malvern. Wright recalled, "We sat in an enormous room with a wide timber staircase leading up to a gallery on the first floor. Leatherbarrow was a fan of the ghost stories of M. R. James, which held a fascination for Leslie." That fascination would ultimately result in Halliwell himself writing supernatural tales, but it would be many years before he did so. In the meantime, he had obligations to his new family and needed to concentrate on his career, which at that time was – surprisingly enough – in television.

As for me, just let me hear Laurel and Hardy's 'cuckoo' signature tune and I'm happy. I whistle it loudly every evening when I near my front door, as a signal to my wife to put the kettle on.

After Oscar Deutsch died in 1941, his chain of Odeon cinemas was sold to the Rank Organisation, which consequently became both a producer and an exhibitor of films. Halliwell was required to work as a relief manager in several of their picture houses during 1956 and 1957, as part of his traineeship, but he found it a very different experience from the Rex. There, he had been able to pick and choose from twenty-five years' worth of product, but the Odeons were the largest chain in the country and as such demanded only the most prestigious releases. Given the desperately poor quality of that period's output, though, it is no surprise that even they were struggling to fill seats.

After a brief stint in Ipswich, Halliwell was moved to Radcliffe, only few miles from his hometown. The unique atmosphere of the Robert Mitchum thriller *Night of the Hunter* was never likely to pull in many punters, as he observed, "It turned up on my beat in Radcliffe, Lancashire, and serve me right. That cinema may have been on its uppers, but seventeen pounds in three days was a low broken only by Laurence Olivier in *Richard III*." He rounded off the year at the aforementioned Slough Ambassador, which for some reason had never changed its name despite being owned by the Odeon chain. He, at least, seemed eager to promote the association as the advertisements in the local paper began featuring the slogan, "See all the best films in 'Ambassador' comfort! This is an Odeon Theatre!"

Other similar Halliwellian outbursts included, "For comfort, courtesy, the best films and the best presentation – visit the Ambassador!" and "Come once to the Ambassador – and you'll come again! Free car park."

Rock Around the Clock, featuring Bill Haley and the Comets, had reportedly caused 'riots' at showings in some towns. It arrived in Slough in December with the local paper announcing, "Dig that crazy music! We'll all get hep at the Ambassador Cinema, for the film that hit the headlines a few months ago – and was banned across the border in Windsor – is at last coming to Slough." Halliwell was interviewed and responded rather ominously, "We don't expect any trouble here. A large number of people want to see the film and anyone who interferes with their entertainment will be dealt with in the usual way."

One of the most highly regarded films to come out of this period was Sidney Lumet's classic jury room drama *Twelve Angry Men*, but even that failed to bring in any great numbers. Halliwell recalled, "I played it from Monday to Wednesday, one cold week in February. We did moderately with it, but we trebled the daily income at the end of the week with a double-bill of Audie Murphy and Abbott & Costello."

There were still, however, occasional aspects of the industry which he could get excited about. One of his favourite genres was about to undergo revivification, as a small British company called Hammer produced *The Curse of Frankenstein*, with Peter Cushing as the creator and Christopher Lee as the monster. Halliwell remembered "all too vividly the unease with which I sat through [it] in a suburban cinema during the cold first month of 1957." Whereas Universal had achieved its horror through the skilful use of shadows and camera tricks, combined with imaginative sets and clever editing, Hammer's approach was simply to push the boundaries of gruesomeness to new levels. The charmless monster looked every bit the rotting corpse he was, and with severed eyeballs and other gory details included, not to mention the revealing décolletage of the ladies, the studio was breaking new ground in a genre it would become forever associated with.

The Curse of Frankenstein was a huge success and Hammer duly announced a follow-up. Halliwell actually attended the pre-production press conference at which Sir James Carreras, the head of the studio, announced that he was "going to make a sexy *Dracula*," which apparently had Peter Cushing looking rather worried. "Not you, Peter," said Sir James, "We'll leave that to Chris Lee." Halliwell was further invited to the subsequent West End press show and found the film to be "a whirl of nightmarish sensation." Of Lee's performance as the immortal Count he observed, "Although he never showed much in the way of acting talent, he had undoubted star appeal of a rather cold variety." Halliwell regarded the film's first sequel, *Brides of Dracula*, as being the highpoint of Hammer's efforts but the series quickly tailed off. The subsequent productions suffered from a tendency towards repetition, and were further hampered by the increasingly contrived manner in which the Count was revived at the beginning of each episode. In addition, Hammer began to shoot in CinemaScope, which Halliwell felt "totally robbed [the films] of any opportunity for suspense."

Not only was there very little film quality in general for him to appreciate but there were also an increasing number of 'lemons' – films which were so bad as to be almost enjoyable for it. One such was *The Story of Mankind*, Irwin Allen's fantasy about the human race being put on trial. It was mostly told through the use of clips from much better movies and was packed with guest stars such as the Marx Brothers and Ronald Colman. Halliwell found it to be "so replete with personages usually welcome that it would have been impossible in 1957 for me to stay away from the Hammersmith Commodore, whatever the critical reports." The film was further replete with a succession of embarrassing performances and poorly staged scenes, and he later called it a "gloriously bad movie."

The Golden Age this was not. Cinema attendance had fallen steadily since the war, and the subsequent closure of picture houses did not encourage people to seek out the remaining ones further afield – they simply stopped going. The major chains could diversify into bingo and bowling but many of the independents folded. At the end of the fifties, cinema admissions were nearly half the level of twenty years before.

After finishing his training course, Halliwell was appointed to the Publicity Division of the Rank Organisation, where he helped to publicise the likes of John Mills and Norman Wisdom. Michael Wright recalled of this period, "I only had a hazy idea of what he actually did. He seemed to go to a lot of film showings and premieres.

When Leslie and I did meet, it was most likely to enjoy the odd film or play, and we usually ended up in a pub or restaurant. This was a time, also, when we were both mainly focused on our first serious attempts to earn a living."

The novel Halliwell had written whilst managing the Rex, *Portion for Foxes*, unfortunately never found a publisher, but in the late 1950s he was having modest success as a playwright. The Bolton Hippodrome put on one of his creations, *Make Your Own Bed*, in April 1957. It was described by publicity as "A Continuous Uproar of Laughter!" but by its own author as "completely low-brow." Halliwell had clearly drawn on his extensive stage experience for the plot, as he elaborated, "This one has a Lancashire background and is a melodrama set in amateur theatrical circles."

Two years later, the Rapier Players Company at the Bristol Little Theatre performed *A Night on the Island*. The play featured character names borrowed from *Lost Horizon* and *Sherlock Holmes*, and a plot containing elements of *Rebecca*, *The Old Dark House* and *The Cat and the Canary*. Richard Conway and his manservant Watson arrive at a "gaunt and eerie dwelling-place" on a remote island off the coast of Devon, where they are due to take possession of Conway's inheritance following his uncle's death. They find the place occupied by a sinister housekeeper and butler, and apparently endure some "hair-raising experiences" before the story's end. The play was produced in Bristol by Peggy Ann Wood and ran for two weeks. Halliwell took his family to see it and stepdaughter Denise remembered it being "a bit like Agatha Christie." The local paper carried the headline, 'New farce-thriller skips along', and proceeded to give a generally favourable notice:

> The premiere of this play was punctuated by weird noises offstage, shouts and cries from the players and much laughter from the audience. [It moves] so fast that one hardly has time to detect the script's improbabilities. Sliding panels, secret hide-outs… all the paraphernalia of a whodunit is here. The author works hard to put the onlooker off the scent and to a large extent succeeds. The denouement, although stretching credibility to breaking point, is fast and furious by way of compensation [and] the farcical situations are well timed and so is the dialogue.

Over one million television licences were issued in 1953 and 1954, with the Coronation of Queen Elizabeth II credited as a major influence. Such interest in the new entertainment medium had made entrepreneurs well aware of its potential for profit making, but the BBC still held a monopoly over the airwaves, supported by the post-war Labour government. Pressure grew for the introduction of commercial television, and when the Conservatives came to power they promised to break the BBC's stranglehold. A scheme was introduced whereby a corporation would own transmitters and hire them out to commercial companies, who would bid for licences on a regional basis. The type and length of advertisements was to be regulated but there was still much opposition to the idea of television for profit. Many felt that rivalry over the airwaves would result in a general lowering of standards and a reduction in impartiality. Some feared the 'Americanisation' of British society, and others even predicted a television-induced increase in the crime rate.

Nevertheless, the Television Act was passed in 1954 and the ITA, later the IBA (Independent Broadcasting Authority) was appointed to take charge of the transmitters and to become watchdog of commercial television – to ensure that nothing offended the delicate sensibilities of the British viewing public. The whole affair resulted in the strange situation whereby the corporation funded by public money was allowed to govern itself, whereas the commercial company had to be overseen by an independent body.

ITV went on the air in September 1955, with fourteen separate regional companies contributing programmes. They initially reached just 3% of the total audience but within three years this figure grew to over 80%. Many viewers deserted the BBC's stuffy, paternalistic approach to broadcasting, instead preferring the lighter entertainment offered by ITV's quiz shows, westerns and comedies. The Rank Organisation was part of the consortium that bid successfully for the ITV South franchise, which became Southern Television in 1958. As a result, Leslie Halliwell, who had previously been working for a film company, found himself with a "staff appointment" at a television company, the dreaded enemy of the cinema. The opening night of the new station occurred on the 30th August and featured a variety show called *Southern Rhapsody* starring Halliwell's old favourite, Gracie Fields.

One of the ironies of the emergence of independent television was that two of its founders, brothers Sidney and Cecil Bernstein, initially opposed it. They had established Granada Cinemas in the 1930s, a major chain of picture houses in the South, and they were as wary as any exhibitors about the success of television. Sidney, however, was entrepreneurial enough to see things philosophically: if there *was* to be commercial television in the UK, he felt they "should be in." With the Granada name already established in the entertainment business and with significant resources at their disposal, the Bernsteins' application for a commercial television licence was described as "uncontentious." Granada Television would become one of the biggest of the independent companies, with the contract for the north of England. However, they retained an office in London's Golden Square, and it was there in 1959 that Halliwell began a career with the company that would last for nearly three decades. He had been interviewed for a job at Granada three years before by Sidney Bernstein himself, on the recommendation of another major player at the company, Denis Forman. I contacted Sir Denis – ninety-two at the time of writing – and he was kind enough to respond:

> I knew Leslie Halliwell long before I joined Granada. He ran an art cinema, as they were called in those days, in Cambridge, the Rex, and I was Director of the British Film Institute. We frequently discussed his booking policy and the Institute would often help him to get a rare film.

When the Bernsteins were looking for an assistant to help with the previewing of films, Sir Denis knew just the man. Despite tripping over the office doormat on the way in, Halliwell made enough of an impression to be offered a position, but they "dilly-dallied" over a starting date and so he instead took the Rank trainee course. Three years later he had come full circle: with his reputation for extensive film knowledge preceding him, he was sent to Granada on secondment from Southern Television, to work as a researcher on a proposed new film programme called *Flashback*. Once again, Denis Forman was the instigator, as he had formulated the idea for the programme when he was at the BFI, observing, "There's some marvellous stuff in the archive – we must find a way of using it." Halliwell proposed a season of British silent films but they could not find enough good ones, and so instead they settled on the idea of a half-hour retrospective programme. He was dispatched to the BFI to meet with archivist Ernest Lindgren, who apparently demanded "some absurd figure" for the use of their material. Halliwell asked him why it was so expensive and Lindgren replied, "When Denis Forman was here he used to say that we were sitting on a gold mine, and as soon as commercial television came in, we'd make a fortune."

Not surprisingly, the programme was never made, but Halliwell's services were retained by Granada and he would remain at their Golden Square office for the rest of his working life. They seemed not to know quite what to do with him at first, though, as he found himself sent to work at Granada's Zoo Unit. Sidney Bernstein had the idea of establishing an outside broadcasting team permanently stationed "in a small disused office above the Reptile House" in Regent's Park. *Zoo Time*, the resulting natural history series, eventually ran for five hundred episodes and was hosted live by Desmond Morris. One wonders exactly what use Halliwell might have been to such a venture, but he seems not to have been there for very long as he later recalled working only briefly with Morris at the zoo.

He was certainly attending programme meetings at the time as he remembered one in 1960, during which the Bernsteins were considering what course of action to take following the wave of criticism surrounding Alfred Hitchcock's *Psycho*. They were old friends of the legendary director and Halliwell valiantly suggested that they try to run a season of his older work. However, his programme controller felt that it was time to dissociate themselves completely and instructed him to cancel the TV series *Alfred Hitchcock Presents*, saying the director had "gone too far." Halliwell caught up with *Psycho* on his regular Monday visit to the Kingston Granada, although he went alone as Ruth had read the reviews and refused to accompany him. He found the film to be a disappointment, as it lacked the humour and lightness of touch which were so prevalent in the director's earlier work.

He was next seconded by Cecil Bernstein, then head of Granada, to be his personal assistant. Cecil was impressed that Halliwell knew as much about box office films as *he* did, and he further bestowed upon his new charge "special responsibility for buying series." *I Love Lucy* and *Wagon Train* were two of Halliwell's early successes, although it has to be said that he only negotiated the buying of subsequent series, as both shows were already being broadcast by the network. One show he did purchase brand new, though, was *The Beverly Hillbillies*, which he described as "corny but amusing" and which ran for several seasons.

Many second feature producers were able to get large sums of money for not offering for sale downright awful films which television would not have touched.

The showing of films on television had been a contentious subject for several years. The Cinemas Exhibitors' Association (CEA) had formed with the express purpose of preventing such activity, and as early as July 1952 it had passed the Llandudno Resolution. This rule, actually motioned by Cecil Bernstein, advised its members to discontinue trading "with any renter or producer making or handling entertainment films for both television and cinema exhibition." The Film Industry Defence Organisation (FIDO) was set up in 1958 – with Cecil again involved – to buy up films so that they could not be sold to television. It raised funds by placing a levy on all cinema admissions, and it was notably successful in imposing a five year ban on new films being televised. However, FIDO could only buy titles which were at least ten years old, and then only from independent producers. The bigger studios were apparently supposed to "hold back without subsidy for the good of the industry." But with various mergers and acquisitions occurring, back catalogues were changing ownership many times over. Paramount's went to Universal, Warner's went to United Artists – and since the studios had only promised not to sell their own films to television, they felt perfectly free to sell those they had *acquired*.

In addition to various deals being struck in the United States, the BBC bought a hundred RKO films for £215,000, including the Astaire/Rogers musical *Top Hat*. Michael Balcon sold his Ealing Studios to the Corporation, along with its back catalogue – which brought threats of boycotts from the CEA, who further censured David O. Selznick for selling twenty-four of his films including *The Prisoner of Zenda*, *Spellbound* and *Intermezzo*. By August 1959, FIDO had obtained "the covenants of 57 feature films," though they admitted that this was "a drop in the celluloid ocean." Many low-rent producers willingly sold films to FIDO, since they could get better value for their substandard product than they ever would from the TV companies. By the early sixties, however, the Bernsteins' position on the issue had changed, as Sidney said, they were now "wearing two hats." The weekly trade magazine *Television Mail* reported on the increasing interest in old films on television, with BBC2 having achieved their highest ever ratings, for a John Wayne film called *Reap the Wild Wind*, shown in a season entitled 'The Vintage Years of Hollywood'. The magazine additionally pointed out that the Oscar-winning *Room at the Top* had gained an audience of around 8.3 million, topping the weekly chart and making it the most successful TV showing of a movie. With the popularity of the medium increasing all the time, there were high ratings to be gained from the showing of feature films: the war between television and the cinema was entering a new phase.

By December 1963, Halliwell, then thirty-four, was being described as "Head of the Film Department of Granada Television." He was still involved only in the buying of TV series, though, as film acquisition was handled at the time by a triumvirate of Cecil Bernstein, John McMillan of Associated-Rediffusion, and a TV legend in the making: Lew Grade. It was Grade who, in August 1964, negotiated the purchase of fifty films owned by the independent Hollywood producer Samuel Goldwyn. FIDO was incensed and threatened legal action but Grade was unapologetic when he announced his coup to the press, saying, "If we have to upset the film industry, we upset the film industry." Halliwell visited Grade's office at the time and remembered him exclaiming, "Isn't it great? It'll last us for the next two years!" He cast his expert critical eye over the titles and was not quite as enthused. "I'm not so sure about Colman in *The Unholy Garden* and *One Heavenly Night*," Halliwell commented, "but at least you've got Danny Kaye in *The Secret Life of Walter Mitty*." However, when the Kaye film was due for broadcast, he happened to notice in the *TV Times* that Grade had scheduled the film in a ninety-minute slot. Knowing it ran fully 108 minutes, Halliwell called to enquire and Grade replied, "Oh I looked at it and thought *seven* dreams? We don't need *seven* dreams... start at number four!"

Halliwell was further present at the conception of a famous television show, as he recalled, "*University Challenge* was thought up by Granada, and as Cecil Bernstein's assistant I well remember his gleaming eye as he envisaged a long-running, easily-produced combination of instruction and entertainment which would please the public and satisfy the IBA." Bamber Gascoigne became famous as the show's quizmaster, and he briefly presented another new programme which Halliwell was personally involved with for many years. *Cinema*, a half-hour weekly, went out initially on Tuesday evenings and offered "a fresh look at today's releases and a look back to the films of yesterday." The show began in July 1964, with each edition being themed and often designed to coincide with a new release. In addition to showing clips they managed to secure interviews with many major stars and directors, such as Gene Kelly, Danny Kaye, Burt Lancaster, Howard Hawks and – in the very first month – Alfred Hitchcock, who was back in favour with the channel after receiving more positive notices for *The Birds*. Halliwell's precise role on the programme seems to have been somewhat exaggerated in later years, with book covers proclaiming that he "devised" the show. Whether he suggested it as an idea is not known but I contacted Bamber Gascoigne to see if he could elucidate:

> I only did *Cinema* for its first three months, and my memory is only of working with the producer, Mike Wooller, viewing the selected films together and then working on my presentation. I am sure Leslie must have been involved from the start, since he was Granada's film guru, but I imagine only in the sense of planning the structure of the programme and then recommending to Mike which films to concentrate on each week. I knew Leslie a little later, but purely socially, meeting in the Granada canteen or at events.

Sir Michael Parkinson, who presented show in the late sixties, was also kind enough to respond to my email enquiry, and said of Halliwell:

> He was a large, methodical and sometimes irascible man. He worked on *Cinema* from its inception to about the time when the film research was taken over by Peter Matthews. I doubt if Leslie 'devised the show.' It was such a simple format it almost devised itself.

Film author David Shipman remembered having coffee with Halliwell at press screenings around this time and wrote, "I found him delightfully obsessed by films and as self-effacing as the description of him, on a jacket blurb, as 'the man behind' Granada Television's long-running *Cinema* series (he was in fact its researcher)." In the *TV Times* listings, Halliwell was credited quite clearly as the show's Film Adviser, and a Granada memo of the time explains that he was responsible for selecting which film clips were to be shown. One episode concerned those "wide wide screens" which had been one of the cinema's attempts at fighting television. The *TV Times* said, "In 1952 a competitor to the film star as an audience winner arrived…" Halliwell would have had no trouble selecting clips for that edition, having had personal experience of the arrival of wide screens at the Rex.

The show was an instant success. In December 1964, *Television Mail* reported, "Another example of the interest in films on TV is the high placing of Granada's *Cinema* in [the] top twenty. Although it is not shown over the whole network, and in spite of its somewhat early timing (19.00-19.30), *Cinema* has been regularly attracting audiences of more than 6,000,000 homes." The show remained consistently in the top twenty highest rated programmes for the rest of the decade and was easily the most popular arts programme on television at the time. Its regular audiences of around six million were not far behind *Coronation Street*, another Granada production, and in one week in June 1968 *Cinema* actually topped the weekly ratings.

The show's team additionally presented live coverage of the British Academy Awards ceremony in three consecutive years, and Halliwell recalled "helping to organise" the events at the Grosvenor House Hotel. He was further required to act as a "special adviser" to a spin-off show called *Clapperboard*, aimed at youngsters, and for which he made the occasional onscreen appearance. Presented by Chris Kelly, the show began in 1971 and ran for seven years.

Whilst working on *Cinema*, Halliwell gained first hand experience of the conspicuous greed of movie stars. Charlie Chaplin, the worldwide phenomenon of the silent era, had arranged through United Artists a reissue of three early shorts under the title *The Chaplin Revue*, and Halliwell, despite never having developed much affection for the screen legend, recognised the potential of a tribute show devoted to him. However, he discovered that Chaplin's publicists were preventing any clips or trailers from being shown, as they felt his name would be enough to sell the film. Since *Cinema* depended largely on film clips, Halliwell thought he was out of luck until an "influential friend" encouraged him to approach Chaplin personally. He recalled, "In those days I was game for anything," and he tracked the star down to the Savoy Hotel whose switchboard surprisingly connected him straight away: "An unmistakable high-pitched voice said 'Hello' and took my breath away for a moment. I babbled my story about a tribute programme, and mentioned our mutual friend."

"Oh dear," said Chaplin, "I hope you weren't expecting me to appear." Halliwell admitted that he would have been keen but instead would settle for the use of some clips. Chaplin seemed amenable enough and instructed him to speak to his publicist. "I rang off with profuse thanks," Halliwell wrote, "Puffed with pride, I dined out on the conversation that evening." However, the following day he called the publicist who stated, "Oh yes, you can have any three clips you like… and his fee will be twenty thousand pounds…"

One can imagine Halliwell gulping before politely concluding the conversation. Suffice it to say, the tribute programme was not made.

The backlots were more or less intact; on many corners one could recognise locations from famous films, and when one lunched at The Brown Derby or Chasen's, one did so cheek by jowl with such stars as Groucho Marx, Ingrid Bergman, Fred MacMurray and Cary Grant.

As a result of the huge success of *Cinema*, in March 1967 Halliwell found himself undertaking his first trip to the United States. He was required to stay firstly in New York, followed by a journey to Hollywood, the place which had provided so much of the movie magic which had cast a spell over his childhood. He was to travel with the film crew and the current presenter, Michael Scott, and the whole excursion was planned for the purpose of obtaining film star interviews.

The team arrived at Kennedy airport during a snowstorm and the weather proceeded to be variable for the next week. Halliwell seemed to spend the entire New York phase of the trip constantly comparing the city to its myriad celluloid depictions. Naturally, the place could not fail to disappoint. Instead of finding it characterised by the "admirable resilience and bonhomie" of the people in films such as *Dead End* and *On the Waterfront*, he instead encountered the squalor of alcoholics, pimps and prostitutes. The streets were nowhere near as exciting as they had appeared in *The Naked City* and *The Lost Weekend*, and there were many areas in desperate need of redevelopment. Furthermore, the city did not revolve around its theatre district in the way Hollywood had shown it... and the policemen were actually carrying guns. On his second evening, with jet lag still bothering him, Halliwell took a "stayawake" tablet in order to watch the Bette Davis Broadway satire *All About Eve* on the late show. "To enjoy it here," he wrote, "within a stone's throw of Sardi's and Shubert Alley, surrounded by the theatre folk it treated so vividly, was a temptation I simply couldn't resist."

American television was another new experience. Apart from the picture quality being poor there were of course commercial breaks every ten minutes, and films sometimes had their opening credits moved to the end out of fear that the audience might get bored. He additionally experienced a case of creative scheduling of which Lew Grade would have been proud, as one announcer said, "We join *The Magnificent Ambersons* already in progress..." But Halliwell did admit that television could provide the tourist with the most accurate depiction of the country: what could be more telling than the announcement, "Two American soldiers were killed today in Vietnam. That story after these words..."?

He took in the standard tourist attractions such as the Statue of Liberty, which reminded him of its appearance in the Hitchcock thriller *Saboteur*. The 'El' train "splendidly torn up by King Kong" had by then actually been removed by more conventional means, and he felt cheated by the inaccurate depiction of the Empire State Building painted by *On the Town*: "You have to take not one but three lifts and often queue for an hour." He cursed cinematographers for daring to film the view from the top in precisely the most romantic light, which the average tourist was unlikely to experience. However, Halliwell "discovered" the city in its uptown area, just south of Central Park, where "here at last, in the district of big business and expensive shops, the pavements are clean and the air bracing." He was especially enamoured by the Rockerfeller Centre, with its sunken ice rink, golden statue of Prometheus and towering skyscrapers, and he likened it to "an oasis in the concrete jungle, an outpost of civilisation in the crassness of commercialism." He grudgingly admitted that New York was a wonderful town but he had found it to be more like the city of *Sweet Smell of Success* or *The Blackboard Jungle* than the lyrical, poetic metropolis conjured up by the likes of Neil Simon, Leonard Bernstein and Gene Kelly. "I wouldn't have missed seeing it," he wrote, "but it must be the worst city in the world to be lonely in."

And so, with most of his New York illusions shattered, Halliwell headed for the West Coast, where he found the vast urban sprawl of Los Angeles overwhelming; the heat stifling and the lack of public transport frustrating. He later recalled, "When I first went to Hollywood in 1967, I took one disappointed look at the famous boulevard and remarked to the taxi driver: 'It looks just like Ealing Broadway'." If the hot dog stands and cheap bookshops of Hollywood Boulevard were not as glamorous as he was expecting, then he found the atmosphere surrounding the boutiques and nightclubs of the Sunset Strip much more to his taste. Halliwell further noted the exclusivity of Beverly Hills, where "lone pedestrians are likely to be questioned by police." He traversed Sunset Boulevard in a hired car, following its winding way up into the hills whilst imagining bodies floating face down in swimming pools, and shady characters involved in Chandler-esque plots à la *Double Indemnity*.

During his stay he met Mae West, who actually used her famous movie catchphrase, inviting him to "come up and see me sometime" at her ranch. Halliwell called the number she gave him but there was no answer and so he assumed he had been duped. Being married at the time, one hopes he was simply angling for an interview with the controversial septuagenarian. He did manage to secure one with Rock Hudson, however, who recalled an occasion when he ventured along Hollywood Boulevard and was accosted by out-of-towners. One of them looked directly at Hudson and asked, "Hey buddy, where do we go to see all them movie stars?"

Hollywood itself had changed immeasurably from the days of the movie factories. The studios themselves were mostly understated, either located down deserted streets or hidden behind anonymous grey walls. The only one within walking distance of Hollywood and Vine was Columbia, which Halliwell found to be a rather cramped collection of buildings, with narrow corridors and the only place of any comfort being Jerry Lewis's ostentatious suite. There was no room for a backlot among the crowded streets and so Columbia kept its permanent sets on a ranch out in the San Fernando Valley, where Halliwell and his camera crew observed a petrol commercial being shot.

Paramount's famous Spanish gates opened onto a side street but they did have room for a backlot. The obligatory Old West street was being used to shoot the TV show *Bonanza*, and provided the *Cinema* team with a useful location in which to interview James Coburn. Only Universal called attention to itself. The studio was already cashing in on its legacy at the time, with a "mountain-high" sign inviting tourists in to marvel at the sets and props from dozens of movies, and to watch stuntmen displays and to take a mini-train tour of the studio, all for three dollars.

Warner Brothers' "pale brown hangar-like buildings" were to be found over in Burbank, where the studio promoted a businesslike atmosphere beneath its famous water tower. Here, two historic streets were in evidence, one for the Old West and one for Old Chicago, where Halliwell pictured Cagney, Bogart and Robinson striding along with their machine guns. Additionally at Warners, Halliwell visited his second major movie set – the first having been at Ealing when he was in the Army. Here, he saw the impressive castle of Camelot, constructed for the movie of the same name. The team were treated to the filming of a scene in the throne room, with Franco Nero on a horse and Vanessa Redgrave in a rather cumbersome dress. They ended up spending the whole day watching the activity – or lack of it, as director Josh Logan managed to capture only two full shots in the entire period.

At RKO, whose space had been taken over by Paramount, Halliwell's keen eye recognised one of the original models used in *King Kong*. Thirty-four years sitting on a dusty shelf had taken its toll, with some of its leather split and the stuffing visible but the fact that nobody quite had the heart to throw it out cheered him. On a subsequent trip, Halliwell actually rescued the very last surviving model, one of six originally made. He was allowed to take it with him provided he willed it to the Hollywood Museum, and he later lent the model for use in a Granada Schools programme called *Horrorstruck*, which looked at monster movies and trick photography. He was pictured holding the 18-inch-high model for a publicity shot for *Cinema*: Halliwell wears a suit and tie, dark-rimmed spectacles and has neat parted hair. He has no beard but sports a moustache which appears to traverse all the way to his sideburns, and his face has filled out a bit, making that famous chin less prominent. Kong, it has to be said, had seen better days: much of his fur is damaged and completely missing from one hand, displaying instead a metal frame underneath. In an accompanying memo, Halliwell commented, "My model is the one used for middle distance shots, the most famous being the scene where he is climbing up the Empire State Building. Other different sized models were used for long shots and big close-ups." Ron Edge, an Old Boltonian, recalled to me that he had seen the model on a visit to Halliwell's Golden Square office in the eighties, and Sir Michael Parkinson remembered it sitting on Halliwell's desk. He obviously took good care of it, as Nancy Banks-Smith wrote several years later in *The Guardian*, "I am comforted that neither moth nor rust doth corrupt this loveable creature."

After RKO, Halliwell made for Culver City, the home of MGM, the grandest of all the Golden Age dream factories. The studio was going through a lull in TV production and so there was very little activity occurring on the day. Tours were being encouraged there at the time, as the famous backlots were still more or less intact – but they would not be so for long. Metro would soon take a leaf out of 20th Century Fox's book and start to sell property for real estate. The difference being that they would go the whole hog, whereas Fox would only sell half and continue to make movies and TV series. Halliwell found Fox to be "one of the most friendly and spacious studios to stroll around" and the place was buzzing with activity. He recognised sets for *Peyton Place*, a big television hit at the time, and the Gotham City Police Department from the *Batman* show. He further observed two major movies being produced there, *Star!* and *Doctor Dolittle*, but the team were unsuccessful in obtaining any interviews.

If the studios had largely been a disappointment to him, Halliwell at least enjoyed the social aspects of the trip. He was able to sip vodka with George Cukor by his swimming pool, whose house overlooked that of Spencer Tracy. Bob Hope mixed him a drink at his home in Palm Springs, complete with miniature golf course, and Halliwell especially enjoyed a low-key cocktail party in Bel-Air with a group consisting mostly of TV people whom he respected. Paul Stewart, who played the butler in *Citizen Kane*, was perhaps the most famous name present, and while the event may have been just a routine Saturday night get-together for the other guests, it became a treasured memory for Halliwell. The following day he was even treated to lunch at the famous Chasen's restaurant:

> *This was the Hollywood I could enjoy, as would anyone with half an interest in movies; but then, for one night only I was moving as a friend among rich and successful people, and they, even in Hollywood, are in a minority.*

The highlight of Halliwell's first visit to America was undoubtedly the Academy Awards ceremony, which the *Cinema* team were invited to attend, albeit only in the press room. The event was held at the seafront Santa Monica Civic Auditorium, fully eight traffic-congested miles from Hollywood itself. The publicists who were the team's hosts were rushed off their feet all week in preparation, with personalities arriving on domestic and international flights, and administrative meetings and lunches being organised.

Come Tinseltown's most glamorous night, as searchlights splashed the sky and red coated ushers raced each other to open limousine doors, the film crew took their places behind the rope line on the auditorium forecourt, with camera bulbs flashing around them. Halliwell seems to have been swept up by the occasion, taking it upon himself to do a bit of frock watching as the great and the good arrived to be interviewed by an official TV commentator. Inger Stevens was wearing a "silver-sequined drum majorette creation barely longer than a bathing suit," while Julie Christie wore an "excruciating spotted, frilly mini-dress… to her discredit." Vanessa and Lynn Redgrave were "respectively in unbecoming spectacles and a strange piled up hairdo," but classy 1930s comic actress Irene Dunne was "exquisitely gowned." Halliwell was surprised by the appearance of the older generation of stars, "who looked astonishingly young and healthy" and he debated whether the Californian sunshine held magical restorative qualities, or merely that he should instead admire the "supreme skill of cosmeticians and toupee-makers."

This was the ceremony for the 1966 Academy Awards, held on April 10th, 1967, and hosted – as so many had been before – by Bob Hope. The event nearly did not take place at all due to a strike by a theatrical union which threatened to prevent the live broadcast of the show. The ban was lifted with hours to spare but resulted in a vastly reduced TV audience to watch Fred Zinneman's captivating *A Man for All Seasons* become the triumphant picture of the evening. The film was characterised by a masterful performance from Paul Scofield, who was not present to pick up his Best Actor award as he thought Richard Burton was going to win. Similarly absent was the Best Actress winner, Elizabeth Taylor, who won for *Who's Afraid of Virginia Woolf?*, a film which marked a watershed in the history of the cinema, with the first appearance of four-letter words on screen.

As the show got underway, Halliwell and crew settled down in the press room with typewriters clacking all around them on some fifty desks, and with several TV monitors and a buffet table present. After each award was handed out, the recipient would make his or her way to the press room to be interviewed on a specially constructed dais, flanked by giant Oscar statues. Interviews were conducted in strict hierarchical order: newspapers, then radio, TV and finally newsreel, the category Halliwell's team belonged to. They had mixed success: Dean Martin apparently gave them the slip and the camera actually jammed on Audrey Hepburn, but they scored big with James Stewart, Fred MacMurray, Omar Sharif and Charlton Heston. Halliwell was bubbling over, "The sheer proximity to such a throng of these long-familiar big screen people proved almost overwhelming."

The highlight of the evening was what turned out to be the final appearance in public of Fred Astaire and Ginger Rogers, that dancing duo who had written their names across the 1930s. They were due to present the award for Best Song and even danced a few steps together when they made their entrance, to a rapturous response from the audience. The ovation was such that the pair struggled to read out the list of nominees. Halliwell was similarly affected, writing, "We too were speechless, content simply to gaze at them and remember with gratitude the enjoyment they have given us over the years."

After the show, there was just time for a quick word with Bob Hope, who expressed his disappointment that neither of the main acting winners had been present. Halliwell mused that it would never have happened in the Golden Age, when the stars were tied so obediently to their contracts. The camera crew managed to capture some parting shots of the auditorium and forecourt – rapidly emptying due to the onset of rain – before the equipment was loaded into the van. On the drive back to the hotel, Halliwell observed that the streets were almost deserted despite it being only around 11 o'clock. The whole town had seemingly stayed in to watch Hollywood's most glamorous evening, "and for everyone in the American film industry, tomorrow could only be an anticlimax."

Halliwell's career, indeed his life, was far from an anticlimax. Over the previous decade he had got married and started a family; moved into a new home and seen his career take off in ways he could never have imagined. He was putting his vast film knowledge to good use and he was getting paid for doing so, which had been his ambition since leaving school. But the industry he so adored was changing rapidly, and in different ways. In an interview several years later, Halliwell said of *Who's Afraid of Virginia Woolf?*, "It cut off one entire kind of audience from another. Until about 1965, there was a sort of winding down from the great period of the thirties and forties... I think you'll find it was around then that a lot of people stopped going to the cinema." He had experienced for himself the falling attendances at the Odeons, as well as the quality of the films being so markedly poorer than twenty years before.

But somehow he still retained a childlike affection for the medium, and the desire to celebrate it...

Another career development would give him the ideal opportunity to do just that...

6

For People who like the Movies

- The Filmgoer's Companion -

In the early sixties, books about the cinema tended to be of the dry, academic variety – more for the film student or the art critic than the average moviegoer. There were in addition the popular magazines but these tended to focus on the cult of celebrity, and were more interested in displaying exotic pictures on glossy pages than in delivering solid information to the curious fan. As Alfred Hitchcock put it, "Nobody wrote for the sensible middlebrow picturegoer who was keenly interested in the craft of cinema without wanting to make a religion of it." At a cocktail party in London in 1964, Sidney Bernstein introduced Leslie Halliwell to Reginald Davis-Poynter, a publisher for the Granada-owned company MacGibbon and Kee. Davis-Poynter had a reputation as a shrewd judge of potential literary talent and during the conversation asked Halliwell what kind of a film book he thought would sell. He replied that there was no one-volume encyclopaedia aimed squarely at the common movie fan, who wanted something handy to check a few quick facts.

"Grand," said Davis-Poynter, "Do it."

Halliwell suggested that a committee be formed to tackle the job, later saying, "In my innocence I was thinking of 10 or 12 paid volunteers to help me, but it turned out to be impossible to corral them." His efforts ultimately resulted in the recruitment of only one other contributor: John Cutts, a journalist for *Films and Filming* magazine, but he left during the project – or "defected to Hollywood," as Halliwell put it. Pressing on alone, he gathered information from back issues of periodicals like the *Monthly Film Bulletin*, *Bioscope* and *Film Weekly*, as well as scouring the British Film Institute Library for old fan magazines and publicity handouts, and stacking his own dining room table with books and manuscripts. He still had those exercise books he had used in his younger days to record his trips to the cinema, as well as a growing movie library of his own. And, of course, he was able to utilise his almost photographic memory of all the thousands of films he had seen by this point in his life.

Ruth helped with the administration and proof reading, and her husband would reserve his chief gratitude for her, as she "suffered the domestic accumulation of mountains of paper and publications, and allowed me to live a hermit-like nocturnal existence." As work progressed, Davis-Poynter still had doubts about the book's commercial value and set a 400-page limit, which his author duly broke by sixty-odd pages. Nevertheless, in December 1965 *The Filmgoer's Companion* was published, with Leslie Halliwell, then thirty-six, ascribed its sole author – but with an acknowledgement to John Cutts for collaborating on the selection of entries and for "researching letters M, Q, Y and Z." Halliwell once said of the *Companion*, "It started because I felt the need for a reference book, and a great deal of it came straight out of my head. Then, having produced it, I found I didn't really need a reference work because it was all still in my head."

The British issue came in a light blue book jacket with occasional red and black diagonals, and featured small pictures of Laurel & Hardy, Hitchcock, Boris Karloff and – quite out of place – Claudia Cardinale, a recent Bond girl at the time. It is interesting to note that although listed as its author, Halliwell was yet to receive the accolade of having his name form part of the title, *à la* old Moore and Whitaker. The flyleaf stated that the book was "for the comparatively new audience for old movies on TV, for the student of film art and for the enthusiastic regular cinemagoer of general tastes." Halliwell added in his introduction, "This book is for people who like the movies," and went on to describe his intended audience as "the general filmgoer, not the egghead student of film culture who shuns commercial entertainments in favour of middle-European or Oriental master-pieces, which never get further than the National Film Theatre or a very few art houses." He cautioned that no attempt had been made to be comprehensive in the selection of subjects, as this would have resulted in a work the size of the *Encyclopaedia Britannica*.

So what did the "general filmgoer" get for his 45 shillings in 1965? An alphabetical list of stars, directors, writers, composers and other film notables, with brief filmographies – rarely complete – and with further entries for film series and a few scattered techniques such as "library shot" and "post-synchronisation." There were in addition separate entries for several hundred film titles "which seem in one way or another important, influential, or simply excellent of their kind." Surprising inclusions were foreign language films such as *Les Enfants du Paradis* and *La Règle du Jeu*, and silents like *Intolerance* and *The Cabinet of Dr Caligari*, all of which would be absent from the first edition of his *Film Guide*, published twelve years later. The list ran from Bud Abbott to Adolph Zukor, taking in around 4,000 entries along the way. There were no essays on studios or genres and *Sing as we Go* was not counted among the most important or influential films of the century. The entries were brief, with major names like Chaplin and Bogart never running to more than half a page – the longest in fact being for Sherlock Holmes, at just over a page, with Tarzan second.

The first edition was a little larger than pocket-sized but handy for quick reference and pleasingly set out in single columns. The emphasis, as with all of Halliwell's work, was on British and American movies, for the simple reason that these were the ones with which his intended audience was most familiar. The author admitted that many readers would disagree with the selections, "which must remain their privilege until a second edition, if called for, comes out, amended and improved according to comment received." The other hint at subjectivity came in the last line of the introduction: "This is a collection of facts rather than opinions; if a few of the latter have crept in, they are usually the ones most generally held." Despite the disclaimer, more than a few opinions did creep in, whether they were the most generally held or not. For example, the entry on Cleopatra lists the significant filmings of the story, starring Claudette Colbert, Vivien Leigh and Elizabeth Taylor, but Halliwell could not resist adding, "She seems to encourage expense, for the Leigh version was Britain's most expensive film, and the Taylor version the world's; in neither case did the money show on the screen." In later editions the word "expense" was changed to "waste." René Clair's 1930 film *Le*

Million was described as a "brilliant early sound comedy with music ... probably his best film and certainly his most engaging," and *The Grapes of Wrath* was "one of the most moving and beautiful films to come out of America."

There is a wealth of information contained within the pages of *The Filmgoer's Companion* and it is a delight even now to skim through, but when compared with its subsequent editions – and indeed with the *Film Guide* – it looks as though Halliwell could have knocked it out on a wet Wednesday afternoon, as it includes none of the pictures, quotes – or indeed the fun – of its descendents. In fact, the only concession to humour in the first edition at all is in its dedication "with affection" to several movie characters the author had encountered over the years, including C. K. Dexter Haven (*The Philadelphia Story*), Walter Parks Thatcher (*Citizen Kane*) and Saul Femm (*The Old Dark House*), "...wherever they may be." The films they had appeared in were not listed in the book, however: the reader was expected to identify them. The dedication would vary in subsequent editions, sometimes being a list of screen villains, sometimes eccentric characters. He eventually bowed to pressure, though, from correspondents who were "driving themselves mad tracking down the references," and included a key.

The *Companion* also featured an affectionate foreword by Sidney Bernstein's friend Alfred Hitchcock, who appreciated the book's stated objectives to appeal to the average film fan. He wrote, "The volume you hold in your hand aims to be the first comprehensive reference book in English for that numerous but neglected audience," adding, "The author has done his homework rather better than the villains in my films, who always seem to get found out sooner or later."

One other aspect of the *Companion* present in that first edition was its compiler's brilliant style of summation: the terse assessment, the succinct dismissal – the 'Halliwell touch'. It had begun with those exercise books he carried with him on cinema trips during the Golden Age and developed through 'Next Week's Films' at Cambridge, where in both cases limited space had necessitated brevity. It was a style which would characterise his encyclopaedias for the next quarter of a century, bringing him both praise and criticism. Leslie Howard's entry read, "Distinguished British leading man, the 'romantic intellectual.' Former bank clerk; turned to stage 1918; later filmed in

Britain and Hollywood." That's it – plus some selected titles but effectively a whole career summed up in twenty words. Robert Bresson was assessed even more economically as, "French writer-director of austere, almost mystical films." Character actor Elisha Cook Jnr was described as, "Slightly-built American stage actor, in films since 1936. Adept at neurotics." Tippi Hedren, then a big name on account of starring in a couple of Hitchcocks, rated dismissively as, "American leading lady, former socialite," and Kenneth More was a "British leading man with a tendency to breezy roles."

The Times Literary Supplement reviewed the *Companion* as "not so much for people who go out to films as for those who sit at home and wait for television to bring them in." The choice of significant titles was described as "a trifle capricious" but the book was felt to be a "thoroughly useful volume [which] fills a want admirably." It is interesting to note that in this very first review of a 'Halliwell', the writer points out one or two mistakes. Almost every reviewer over the next twenty years would delight in spotting the slightest of errors in his encyclopaedias – among literally thousands of accurate facts – with all the relish of a good dog expecting a pat on the head. Either that or they would with unabashed horror announce to the world that they had discovered the most glaring of omissions, such as Dwight MacDonald of *Esquire*, who exclaimed in 1966: "Unbelievable! – no Andy Warhol."

The first edition of *The Filmgoer's Companion* sold ten thousand copies, including four thousand in the United States. The American release came a few months after the British one, published there by Hill & Wang in a maroon hardcover with discreet gold lettering on the spine, and somewhat misleadingly advertised as "an international encyclopaedia." *Antiquarian Bookman* called it, "Overly adjectival for our taste," but recognising the audience it was aimed at they concluded, "Lots of people will like it. No pix."

So was it really the first of its kind? In 1933, the year Leslie Halliwell actually began his cinemagoing, Clarence Winchester published *The World Film Encyclopaedia: a Universal Screen Guide*, with the stated aim, "To fill a long-felt need of a really comprehensive and universal film guide." Could there really have been a *long-felt* need in 1933? Either way this was no one-man effort, as the introduction admits, "A large and loyal staff of experts has worked incessantly to make *The World Film Encyclopaedia* as comprehensive and accurate as it is possible to be." 'Winchester's' featured among other things over a thousand biographies of stars and directors, plus a few other important personalities but no writers, composers or cinematographers. Whilst going so far as to give a director or player's *height and weight* – Capra 5ft 5½in, 9st 9lb; Colman 5ft 11in, 11st 4lb! – it scandalously failed to provide dates for any of the films listed. It did include five hundred separate movie titles under the heading 'Famous film casts' but listed them by year, making quick reference impossible. Several splendid essays were included on different aspects of film-making and the financial structure of the major studios, as well as many black and white portraits and stills. A rather strange addition, very much of its time, was 'Players' Addresses at a Glance'. Most of the major stars were listed as c/o their studio but you could find out that Elsa Lanchester lived at Stapledown, East Clandon, Surrey, and that Lillian Gish and her sister Dorothy resided at 132, East 19th Street, New York City.

The World Film Encyclopaedia was not followed up with a second edition until fifteen years after the first. The 1948 volume added some essays by film notables such as Adolph Zukor and Sir Alexander Korda, with additional pieces concerning the Quota legislation and the Production Code. '500 Famous films' again appeared but with an updated list covering the years between editions – resulting in many of the entries from the first edition being simply left out. Having said all that, 'Winchester's' is a hugely entertaining and informative work, which Halliwell himself recommended in a section on movie books in the *Companion*. The 'general filmgoer' would have been more than well served by it, whether in 1933 or 1948 – but by 1965 he would have been left wanting. Even taken in isolation, though, Winchester's does not rank alongside the first edition of *The Filmgoer's Companion* because it is not sufficiently comprehensive, and does not lend itself to quick reference. A whole team of collaborators could not deliver the same breadth of conveniently retrievable information that Halliwell managed almost on his own.

There was one other who *nearly* competed. Paul Rotha, a documentary film-maker and critic, who in 1930 had written a seminal work, *The Film Till Now*, appeared in the letters column of *Films and Filming* magazine in January 1965 writing, "Your readers may like to know that I am editing a World Encyclopaedia of the

Screen which is about to be published... we have an editorial board consisting of Michael Balcon, Carl Foreman..." adding *nine* other names, and going on to proclaim, "So far as I know, no such ambitious project has been undertaken in any country." Once again, a group of collaborators the size of a football team was employed to produce a film book, but alas, Rotha's effort never even made it to the book shelves – perhaps on account of Halliwell beating him to it?

David Quinlan, who later compiled masterful reference books on *Film Stars*, *Character Actors* and *Film Directors*, was kind enough to respond to my enquiry about Halliwell's influence:

> His *Filmgoer's Companion* – I do have the first edition, though it is alas tatty and scribbled in – was certainly a trailblazer and paved the way for a whole slew of film reference books for more than 30 years, until the market dived with the arrival of the Internet Movie Database.
>
> The fact remains that *The Filmgoer's Companion* was the first one-volume encyclopaedia devoted to *all aspects* of the cinema, and its subsequent editions, all being the work of only one man, would further enshrine its uniqueness – despite some stiff competition in later years.

I have a terribly good memory. Wrong dates glare out at me from the proofs, and I don't have to check spellings.

Halliwell said of updating and correcting subsequent editions, "I start off with the best will in the world and try to improve every entry in the book, but the publisher's deadline catches up with you, and you finish up with everything after M being left!" On another occasion he was asked how he went about the task and replied, "Copious notes and lots of correspondence ... there's a Latin teacher in Tashkent who's a trove of facts – writes me all the time." He took care to thank those who had pointed out mistakes and omissions, and continued to encourage them in future editions, often listing contributors by name on the Acknowledgements page.

The 2nd edition of *The Filmgoer's Companion* obligingly appeared in 1967 and was twice the size of the first. With a book jacket decorated with quotes from enraptured critics, the intention with this volume was to cast a considerably wider net. Halliwell claimed to have brought up to date all the existing information; he had made extensive additions to the filmographies and added over two thousand entirely new entries, but admitted to these being of lesser interest – "half-forgotten stars and small-part actors." A sense of fun was injected courtesy of selected 'themes', short essays on the cinematic use of such subjects as bathtubs, custard pies, Eskimos and monks. Halliwell offered these "light-heartedly, in the hope of amusing cineastes." They added an extra dimension to the book, for the average referrer was not likely to have deliberately looked up 'leprechauns' or 'drunk scenes', but having stumbled upon them would not be able to resist sampling the information therein.

The other major inclusion was an essay on 'Title changes' which the author had previously written for *Films and Filming* magazine, a publication to which John Cutts was a contributor. The essay, running to several pages, originally appeared in the main body of the book, where it looked out of place among so many terse entries. Halliwell confessed it to have been "rather amorphous" and sensibly moved it to the appendices, where it was subsequently reduced down to what it effectively was to begin with, a list. Anthony Quinton in *The Times Literary Supplement* called this very act a "nobly self-denying display of the lapidary concision which is his most striking gift as a stylist." However, Halliwell received so many requests for it that he was forced to put the essay back in.

Otherwise, though, the 2nd edition was just much more of the same, retaining the single column design on the same sized pages. Charles Champlin of the *Los Angeles Times*, who would become one of Halliwell's most faithful champions in print, pointed out, "Claude Lelouch isn't included, but there are notably few other lapses." Jack Conroy of *American Book Collector* was more positive, if mistaken about the author's background: "Halliwell, a Londoner, has a gift for capsulated characterisations, frequently enlivened with shrewd and puckish humour." Clifford Terry of the *Chicago Tribune* had picked up on those small slivers of subjectivity, calling the book, "An ambitious, comprehensive, frequently witty, and occasionally maddening volume."

For the 3rd edition, published in 1970, the author could finally boast complete filmographies of the major stars, while still resisting the many requests he had received from correspondents to make *every* listing complete, because "the least important people would have the longest list of credits." Present on the book jacket was a picture of Halliwell, then forty-one, sporting dark-rimmed spectacles and a moustache – looking a dead ringer for TV presenter Alan Whicker. Charles Champlin was by then hooked, reviewing the 3rd edition somewhat poetically: "I have been wandering barefoot through one of the brightest browses I know of, a work whose many splendoured pages are as restorative as warm cocoa or cold martinis in these frazzling times... a source of delight, zesty outrage and memory-flogging." Richard Schickel was more down to earth with his comments for *Harper's*, stating that the *Companion* was "*the* place to begin research, assuage idle curiosity and settle bets."

The first signs of Halliwell's disillusionment with the current state of the cinema crept into the introduction, where he cautions that if the *Companion* "still seems nostalgic rather than forward-looking that is probably because I personally, working every day among films as buyer for a television station and as adviser to a weekly programme about the movies, find that I still get more genuine pleasure from the old ones than I do from the new." He went on to say, "Despite the immense technical advances shown by the latter, they have lost a few essential ingredients: simplicity, innocence, and optimism being among them." That sentiment would grow over the next few years until it found its ultimate expression in an essay for his *Film Guide* entitled 'The Decline and Fall of the Movie', a hatchet job on an industry which by then had dismayed him completely.

Halliwell's commitments as a TV buyer took up more and more of his time in the early seventies, and so it was fully four years before the 4th edition of the *Companion* appeared, by which time the book had undergone a complete overhaul, being reset in a larger page size and using a two-column style with new fonts. During its production, Ruth had banished her husband to a "room at the top of the house" rather than have him clutter up her dining room table once again. He set everything in his new study on casters: file cabinets, chair, typewriter stand etc., saying, "When I need something I can wheel over to it without having to stand up. I spend my weekends propelling myself around the study furiously, like Monty Woolley in *The Man Who Came to Dinner*." However, this meant that he saw very little of Ruth over the course of the year but he promised to make amends, writing, "I shall take her to the pictures at least once a week."

Halliwell's stepdaughter Denise had long since moved out of their Kew home by this time, but I asked her what she remembered about the place:

> He had boxes and boxes of magazines, and the bookshelves were filled. His desk was in the corner of his study and you could hear him typing away. He had a bed in there because he sometimes worked into the night. His habit would be to come home from the office, take off his business suit and have a shower; put on his towelling bath robe and spend the evening in his study. Anyone calling at the house would be greeted by the sight of Les in his slippers with his bare calves showing!

Halliwell was once asked if the book had made him rich, and he replied, "No. You could say that it has enabled me to add two or three rooms onto my house, but that's all. Still, I'm not complaining – I'd do the work even if the publishers didn't pay me." I asked Denise if success changed him at all:

> It totally didn't affect him. He still used to check the price of a bottle of sauce, whether it was a ha'penny here or there. His background formed his spending and clothing habits. It was my mother who encouraged him to spend more and to buy more clothes.

Denise actually gave me one of her stepfather's very own interleaved copies of *The Filmgoer's Companion*, from around 1969, with every other page blank to enable the author to make notes – and what a profusion there is! On almost every page, whether blank or printed, are scribbles, squiggles and scrawls, written with a succession of different pens and pencils. The book overflows with ideas for new sections, items circled or crossed out, mistakes corrected and even whole new entries written out for future inclusion. The handwriting is tiny, and sometimes jotted down at such a pace as to be illegible to anyone but the author himself. Halliwell has pencilled in a new entry for Joey Bishop: "American TV comedian who has made a few film appearances." A selection of Bishop's film titles follow and at a later date he has added the star's real name, Joseph Abraham Gottlieb. Above this proposed entry the author has begun one for Jacqueline Bisset, but obviously changed his mind as he has struck it through.

Additions to filmographies seem to have been written down as fast as they sprang to his agile mind. Next to John Barrymore he has jotted a further seven titles for inclusion, added at different times, and around brother Lionel's already impressive list another *twenty-one* films are proposed. Ideas for future subjects include baseball, under which Halliwell has dashed off – seemingly in one go – seventeen films featuring the sport, then added several more at another attempt. A similar number of films featuring hospitals were intended, as well as for card games... the industry and dedication required in all this is simply mind boggling.

When it was finally released, the 4th edition's jacket boasted ten thousand individual entries, and with the addition of hundreds of stills and poster reproductions the encyclopaedia then assumed the form in which it would become most familiar to movie fans over the next fifteen years. Russell Davies of *The Observer* commented that the new-look larger version ironically meant "you can't actually film-go with it any more" but that was never actually the intention, despite its title. The introduction contained a neat little nugget of Halliwellian insight, in which he commented on the career progression of the average star, which generally consisted of "the gradual climb, the good cameo role, the star period, the two or three 'dogs' in a row, the gradual decline, the cheap horror burlesque." In an interview he commented on the ephemeral nature of stardom, "I'm always noticing how short the careers were of some of the famous stars. Clark Gable only made about four or five good films and the rest were padding."

A section which had been introduced in the 3rd edition as 'boobs' underwent a name change to 'boo-boos', and was concerned with mistakes in movies, such as a cast member wearing a wristwatch in the Dark Ages-set drama *The Viking Queen*, or the Invisible Man's footprints in the snow having clearly been made by shoes rather than feet. Benny Green in *The Spectator* commented, "The entry is so enjoyable that I am willing to forgive him for using so wretchedly provincial a phrase as 'boo-boos' to define his theme."

The many stills and publicity materials used for this edition were deliberately off-beat. Halliwell had personally selected them as "lively, entertaining and mainly unfamiliar [images] which sharply point up the personality of an actor, a film-making trend, or a striking set." Indeed, the set pictured for Warner's 1967 production of *Camelot* – which Halliwell had actually visited during filming – was obviously still standing several years later, when it was re-modelled to serve as Shangri-La for a musical remake of *Lost Horizon*, as the two printed stills clearly show. Russell Davies of *The Observer* was not impressed, however, feeling that the "many rare stills and appalling posters ... tend to get out of sync with the text, making the book faintly irritating as a browsery."

Another new and subjective feature which would cause much discussion was Halliwell's use of italics to denote a person's "most significant films." The reader was intended to interpret significance as "commercially, artistically, critically, or simply as indicating a film in which the subject gave a good typical account of himself." This he added as a service to younger readers who might not be very well acquainted with their subjects. An interviewer asked Halliwell about this practice, saying, "In the case of the *Companion* where you can't have seen all of the films of all of the people, to italicise something... to give it extra stature, there's always a danger that you're recommending something that isn't very good."

"The other way would be not to italicise anything or recommend anything at all," he responded, with typical gusto, "I thought it was a way of helping people coming to it completely fresh. I'm really looking for historical significance, if that isn't too pretentious, rather than a judgement of a film in particular."

Two other additions to the *Companion* came in the form of whole books. In 1973, Halliwell published *The Filmgoer's Book of Quotes*, advertised as "Hollywood wisdom in barbs of pure gold" and consisting of hundreds of categorised quips, quotes and one-liners from the cinema. The book was intended to be light hearted but not "entirely frivolous" as the author stressed, "It should also provide a useful source for those who need to know about movies, to write about them, or simply to be well-informed." It was dedicated to Ruth, "whose pithy quotes about my addiction to old movies are mainly unprintable." Interspersed among sections devoted to such outspoken movie personalities as Bette Davis, W. C. Fields and, of course, the Marx Brothers, were several quizzes. The reader was faced with a list of film titles and asked to name the literary sources from which they were taken; to supply the original films to a list of remakes, or to identify several film posters with the titles removed.

Halliwell relished the role of quizmaster and four years later a whole book of similar material appeared. 1977 was additionally the year of the 6th edition of the *Companion*, the 1st edition of the *Film Guide* and the year in which the author saw his name at last incorporated into the titles of his books. Thus, *Halliwell's Movie Quiz* duly appeared – in paperback only – consisting of 3,571 teasers. There were questions on particular themes such as opening scenes, silent movies, films about Christmas, relations appearing together, as well as some fiendish 'laddergrams' and more posters with the titles removed. The quizzes were graded as easy, medium and difficult, although Ernest Callenbach of *Film Quarterly* rated them as "some easy, some hard, some impossible." The introduction hinted at what was in store for the unsuspecting contestant: "Movie quizzes come and go, but the complaint of real buffs is always that they're too easy. Well, here's one that isn't; and it's a big one." He goes on, "If you get a thousand correct answers you're doing pretty well and can count yourself a fan of some dedication. Two thousand, and you ought to win an Oscar ... two thousand five hundred and you should have written the book yourself." Halliwell predicted he could probably have got a score of 2,250 himself but thought he would not be alone in attaining such a figure. He was constantly amazed at the breadth of movie knowledge possessed by young people who wrote to him, "who must have relied entirely on television for their movie education." Several years later, he incorporated the entire contents of both the *Book of Quotes* and the *Movie Quiz* into the *Companion*, thus expanding its already bulging covers even further, but adding immeasurably to its entertainment value.

> *Before my next edition comes out you may be able to buy a pocket cassette of* The Maltese Falcon *and play it back on your television set.*

Halliwell admitted to having succeeded far better than he ever imagined with the *Companion*. Benny Green was similarly surprised in *The Spectator*, referring to him as a "publishing phenomenon, that is, the producer of a work whose success and staying power has surpassed the expectations of every expert who originally shook his head." Green highlighted the other major delight which the book provided: the ability to hold the referrer's interest long after the initial item of research had been sought and obtained. He challenged, "If like the present writer you belong to the generation which went to the local cinema as the Victorians went to church, then pick up Halliwell and see how long it takes you to put it down. The perusal of one entry leads to five others." Richard Schickel agreed, "Mr. Halliwell is almost as dangerous as he is useful; I'm always grabbing his book to check a quick fact and looking up a half-hour later to find I've read all the Qs and not a few of the S, T and W entries." Charles Champlin added, "The referrer needs an iron will to look up only one fact," and further contended, "You can no more look up one item than you can eat one potato chip."

The 6th edition received a dedication from British film producer Herbert Wilcox, who died shortly before publication. He praised the author for maintaining "an unswerving affection for films," and commended the book to "all serious film lovers … I cannot fault it myself and doubt whether you will. It is to be read for reference or at leisure, to be believed and to be enjoyed." Incidentally, the 5th edition had simply been the paperback version of the 4th, cheekily renamed by Halliwell's publishers, to his embarrassment.

Towards the end of the decade, Halliwell was sensing change: he had written of a nostalgia craze being at its height in the mid-seventies but he had observed a drop off in the correspondence he was receiving. "I know that there aren't many more names missing," he told an interviewer in 1979, "But I am nevertheless also frightened that it has to do with a reduced affection for film." However, by this time *Halliwell's Filmgoer's Companion* had attained almost legendary status among the movie watching *cognoscenti*. Gene Siskel, writing for the *Chicago Tribune*, said it was becoming "the single most valuable reference book on film," adding of Halliwell's famous style, "His brief assessments of talent are gems of economical writing and well-considered opinion." Anthony Quinton in *The Times Literary Supplement* wrote that it was hard to imagine life, "and in particular, the part of life spent watching old films on television, without it," and further praised the author, "His really special gift, which turns the *Companion* from a marvellously comprehensive and reliable collection of facts into a distinctive literary experience, is his power of compressing detailed description into the smallest conceivable number of words."

Philip French was less kind in the *New Statesman*. Despite confessing that out of the 500-odd film books he personally owned the *Companion* was the one he consulted most often, he said of

Halliwell himself, "He isn't a scholar, critic or cineaste, but rather a movie buff, a man who knows the credits of everything but the value of very little. His only intellectually demanding work is the paperback *Halliwell's Movie Quiz*." The argument being that the *Companion*'s author could not possibly be able to assess critically films and film-makers, being only a humble fan.

There were other negative reactions from the stars themselves, as Halliwell observed, "Douglas Fairbanks Jnr. wrote to argue about something I'd written about his father, and Joan Crawford blistered me for having her age wrong, so she said ... but people have told me she always lies about that anyway." Ever willing to react to complaints, however, he shaved a couple of years off Crawford's age in the 4th edition and amended the tailing-off of Fairbanks's career from, "Was forced to retire because his romantic zestful image could not fight middle-aged spread" to, "Sound did not suit him, and his thirties films showed a marked decline."

George C. Scott was similarly unhappy with his entry, which read, "Distinguished but taciturn American actor; usually plays tough or sardonic characters and was the first actor to refuse an Oscar."

"I don't get it," puzzled Scott, "Distinguished *but* taciturn? Why 'but'? That's like saying 'poor but honest.' There should be a comma in there instead of the 'but'" ...and another thing, "I never *refused* an Oscar. Marlon Brando refused an Oscar. I have asked to be withdrawn from the list of nominations – that's quite different. I am against anything that places actors in competition with each other."

Halliwell noticed that film encyclopaedias themselves were increasingly in competition with each other, writing of a deluge of books which had emerged in recent years, "As one might expect, ten per cent are informative and provocative, the rest are quickly remaindered and forgotten." He admitted, though, that at least two of the recent reference books were "very learned, well-researched and sumptuously produced," making him wonder whether *his* book might no longer be necessary, but he was encouraged to continue.

It is likely that one of the books Halliwell refers to as being solid competition was *The International Encyclopaedia of Film* by Dr. Roger Manvell and Prof. Lewis Jacobs, published in 1972. This featured several contributors including Margaret Hinxman, who had worked at *Picturegoer* with Halliwell in the fifties. The introduction stated that the book attempted "to cover the international history of the film, mainly as an art, but also as an industry." It was heavy on photos, including some splendid colour stills, and covered foreign language movies in far greater depth than the *Companion*, but there were no individual film entries and no subsequent editions. Philip French claimed rather unfairly that Halliwell "scarcely invites comparison with large-scale reference works like Manvell and Jacobs." Whether one is better than the other is another matter, but neither deserved to be dismissed out of hand. George Perry, the film editor for *The Sunday Times*, said of Halliwell, "What gives him the edge over the others is his reliability and the fact that you get more than just the facts, even if you don't agree with his opinions.

With so many reference books emerging, critics began comparing them in their reviews, with Halliwell often cited as the benchmark. *The Oxford Companion to Film* appeared in 1976 and measured up poorly. Mark Crispin Miller of the *New York Review* declared that its errors invalidated it as a reference work and were "particularly destructive when they bear a distant relation to the truth." He concluded that Halliwell's *Companion* was "a friend worth having" whereas *The Oxford Companion* was "like a friend whom we never ask out to the movies for fear that his comments afterward will take all the joy out of the experience." Stanley Kauffmann wrote of the Oxford book in *The New Republic*, "I recently looked up the entry for *Citizen Kane*, read the first line: Press magnate Kane dies in his west-coast palace of Xanadu, and shut the book." Xanadu was in Florida.

The only publication which seriously challenged Halliwell was Ephraim Katz's *The International Film Encyclopaedia*, which came out in 1979, was the work of one man, and covered all aspects of the cinema. In his introduction – in what might be a thinly-veiled jibe at his main rival – Katz stated that his desire was to include "as much information that can be found elsewhere only in a wide variety of sources, or that is *treated sketchily* in other works" – emphasis mine. Katz's book was simply enormous, but with very little space on the page its two-column design was harder on the eye than Halliwell's. It ran to 1,270 pages and boasted complete filmographies of major stars and directors. There were no entries for individual films, no photographs and, it has to be said, no fun. The entry on Orson Welles spread across seven columns, whereas the section for the United States stretched to thirteen *pages*. The film student seeking dry facts would not have been let down, but might have been left wanting for a little entertainment along the way. Philip French loved it –

> Ephraim Katz's *International Film Encyclopaedia* ... strikes me as the best, most useful single-volume reference book currently available. It's half as long again as [Halliwell]. Compare any entry and Katz is far superior. He shrewdly characterises the actors in his lists and provides neat career summaries, where Halliwell just says 'director' or 'actor with stage experience.' If you look up Katz's half-column on 'The Auteur Theory' (an objective history of the term) and then Halliwell's four lines on 'Auteur' (blustering philistinism posing as Johnsonian robustness) you'll appreciate the difference.

The general filmgoer might well appreciate the difference but perhaps not in the way French intended, and it is ironic that he picked that particular slice of film student vernacular for his example. Does it really take a philistine to show disdain for the idea that directors are the sole creative force behind films? Either way, Ephraim Katz's *International Film Encyclopaedia* is a seriously impressive work. Fred Zentner of the Cinema Bookshop in London said of it, "I never thought I'd see Halliwell replaced," and even Charles Champlin announced gravely in the *Los Angeles Times*, "I never imagined it would happen but Leslie Halliwell has a rival for my reference shelf affection." Champlin also did a side by side comparison for his review, going so far as to calculate a value *coefficient* based on price per page. Halliwell won that particular contest but lost out in the comparison of continental film coverage, predictably enough. However, Champlin – like most observers – ultimately could not pick a favourite, ending his review with an introduction, "Mr. Katz meet Mr. Halliwell: you're permanently partnered beside my typewriter and I need you both."

Time would decide the eventual winner. Katz failed to publish a follow-up edition of his book until 1990, eleven years after the first – which was so often the case with Halliwell's competition. With dozens of new movies coming out every year and many new stars emerging, no matter how comprehensive or insightful an encyclopaedia was at its outset, the absence of regular additions and revisions would inevitably lead to a decline in its usefulness.

Even I ... find many of the original entries fresh to read, and my tired eyes are led gently from one fact I had almost forgotten to a quote that makes me smile all over again.

The last major subjective inclusion in the later editions of the *Companion* was the awarding of rosettes, lightly sprinkled throughout the book and bestowed "as a token of respect and gratitude for significant work in a particular field over a sizeable period of film history." The author conceded, "These are purely personal judgements" – and as such are further examples of Halliwell's talent for summation, with the best of them being little gems of affectionate endearment, such as the dedication to director René Clair, "For creating films in which, by a dexterous combination of sound and picture, the feet of the characters appeared never to touch the ground." Fred Astaire received a similarly gravity-defying commendation, "For his apparently lighter-than-air constitution, his brilliantly inventive dancing, his breezy elegance, his unlikely but effective voice, and his pleasing longevity."

Jean Harlow had made a devastating impact before her shockingly early death in the thirties, but was remembered for "combining a sophistication which she acted with an innocence which was her own." The enigma that was Garbo gained her rosette for "stretching a mystery over twelve splendid years and for knowing when to quit." That other European siren, Marlene Dietrich, received hers simply for "enjoying being a legend," whilst her long-time director Josef von Sternberg was acclaimed, "For being the kind of director who, if he didn't exist, publicists would have to invent."

The Marx Brothers received praise, "For shattering all our illusions, and making us love it," whilst their constant foil, Margaret Dumont, was consoled, "For suffering beyond the call of comic duty." The King himself, Clark Gable, was acclaimed, "For effortlessly maintaining a Hollywood legend, and for doing so with cheerful impudence," and Errol Flynn's wicked wicked ways prompted, "For living several lives in half of one, and almost getting away with it." Elegant William Powell was celebrated, "For spreading his cheerful suavity over 30s Hollywood; and for being so much at home in a dinner jacket," while Ronald Colman's dedication ran, "For conquering world audiences by steadfastly playing the old-fashioned British gentleman adventurer in a number of elegant guises."

The final edition of the *Companion* edited by Halliwell himself was the 9th, published in 1988. It ran to 786 pages – with *three* columns per page – and supposedly comprised almost a million and a half words. However, although this edition was the fullest on facts, it left out literally hundreds of the wonderful stills and posters which had brought the 4th edition so splendidly to life. Halliwell had by then for many years been regularly updating not only this book but the *Film Guide* and *Teleguide* as well, referring to them collectively as "the astonishingly weighty results of a casual conversation at a 1964 cocktail party." *The Filmgoer's Companion* remained his personal favourite, however, his "first love." By that time, each edition was selling more than 30,000 copies worldwide in hardback, and between 25,000 and 30,000 in paperback. And he had seen off the competition: those which had not been remaindered had failed to follow up with new editions quickly enough to retain their relevance. By contrast, Halliwell's work had evolved and improved over the years, adding many wonderful facets which are a joy to discover even today, and which put *his* book in a class of its own. Entertainment as well as craft... now where have I heard that before?

Although by the sixties a selection of major films had become available to British television, the majority remained undiscovered...

The Film Industry Defence Organisation came under increasing pressure in the mid-sixties. The BBC had introduced its second channel in 1964 and was keen to satisfy the subsequent extra demand for programming with feature films, both recent and vintage. The American studios, for their part, were tempted by the large sums of money being offered for their properties, which in the case of Paramount's pre-1948 back catalogue, then owned by MCA, was enough to offset the effects of any blacklist in the UK – if the exhibitors still had the power to enforce one. In the end, FIDO had to compromise, and whilst it was able to retain the five year ban on new films being shown on TV, the organisation stopped buying in 1965, causing a flood of films to become available to the TV networks and creating a buyer's market that would last for the next ten years. Ever the keen industry observer, when FIDO collapsed Halliwell made his pitch to the Granada controllers to be in charge of buying films for the channel. Since the job had not existed as a dedicated position before, their response was a simple, "OK, you do it." He would never actually be given an official job title but would hold this position more or less for the next twenty years. At first he felt like a square peg in a round hole, as he was neither a businessman nor a politician: he was just a film buff who had once again found himself in a situation where he could put his vast knowledge of the medium to work.

Most of the major film companies had offices in the centre of London and in 1967, at the age of thirty-eight, Halliwell wound up securing his first deal on a Sunday morning in a back street in Clapham, halfway between his home and that of the Paramount executive he was to deal with. The somewhat haphazard nature of the arrangement indicates how new the whole process was and conjures in the mind a clandestine meeting between two suspicious looking individuals, checking over their shoulders as one of them opens a briefcase. As for the deal itself, the BBC might have already snapped up those pre-1948 properties but Halliwell was able to secure another 100 films at $3,000 each, including Cecil B. DeMille's Oscar-winning *The Greatest Show on Earth*.

Movies would be sold in packages like that for the next few years, with the quality of the titles varying considerably. It was reminiscent of the old block-booking system of the thirties, when cinemas were forced to take a whole clutch of films they did not want in order to get at the few choice titles they did. Thirty years on and the studios had found a new lease of life for their dusty old properties, and given the falling attendances in cinemas – coupled with the escalating cost of making movies – they needed the injection of cash.

The network may have wanted a cheap and easy way of filling airtime, but the sheer influx of titles was so great that many of them would languish in ITV's vaults for years to come. Until, that is, a new channel came along in the 1980s which was designed to cater for more specialist audience tastes – Halliwell would find himself perfectly positioned to take advantage of *that* situation, also. Many films did get broadcast, however. In one week alone in August 1968, ITV had four in the top 20 ratings list: *The Malta Story*, *Cargo to Capetown*, *Black Narcissus* and *When Worlds Collide*, all of them being watched in over 4 million homes (*Coronation Street* was seen in 6.4 million in the same week). *Black Narcissus* was the only work of any great quality among them and so it would seem that people were just enjoying the fact that they *could* watch a movie in their own home, preferring it to venturing out to the decaying cinemas.

Halliwell continued to work out of the same office in Golden Square, the walls of which were predictably covered with posters and stills of old movies, including that signed photo of Laurel & Hardy. One observer remarked upon it being a "poky second floor office dominated by piles of paper," and a journalist interviewing him some years later observed on the wall a series of Chinese prints depicting stylised images of people being tortured.

Over some of them Halliwell had pasted the names of studio executives and others in the business who had especially riled him over the years…

It is a safe bet that the name Gunnar Rugheimer would one day be added to them…

7

Things became Fraught

- Buying films and shows for ITV, 1968-81 -

By the late 1960s, the era of the big Hollywood studios had come to an end. One by one they were taken over by conglomerates who bought them as brand names, to make money out of their back catalogues and to hire out their sound stages to independent producers. The bosses were no longer 'movie men', and they were prescient enough to see that the future mass entertainment medium was not the big screen but the small. The programme makers were lured over from New York and soon the factory floors of Columbia, Fox, Warners, Paramount and Universal were filled with TV crews making sitcoms and cop shows. MGM, by contrast, had become more interested in the hotel and casino business, and began to sell their decaying Culver City backlots for real estate. Ex-contract player Debbie Reynolds was horrified, "They should have put up turnstiles!" she protested.

Halliwell had begun travelling to New York regularly to scout for new TV shows, but the subsequent shift in emphasis from east coast to west rendered these trips obsolete, and so instead he began a routine of twice-yearly visits to Hollywood, usually in May and October, which he would maintain for nearly twenty years. In 1968, he became chief buyer for the whole ITV network, but that did not mean he had total control over acquisitions. Since he was representing some fifteen separate companies a committee was formed, known as the Film Purchase Group, which handled the buying of both movies and shows. It was made up of programme controllers for the 'big five': Granada, Yorkshire, Central, London Weekend and Thames, as well as a single representative for the smaller regions and an elected chairman. It was Halliwell's job to liaise with the studios and production companies to decide which titles would be put forward to the Group. All the separate companies contributed to the cost on a pro-rata basis according to the size of each, hence the big five's larger presence. As he put it, "Attempts by any one member to buy a network series unilaterally are akin to the Governor of Texas declaring war on Russia and sending [the President] a copy of the message." In the beginning, Halliwell was the sole overseas representative, but as time went by more of the group began accompanying him, until finally the entire team was going on the trips.

Paul Fox, now Sir Paul, was Chairman of the Purchase Group for many years, and he was kind enough to invite me to his home for an interview. A large, affable man with a sonorous voice, eighty-five at the time but seemingly thirty years younger, Sir Paul spoke with much affection for his old colleague and indeed those days in general:

> We bought films as a group. It was one of the few occasions when ITV actually came together. And Leslie was – whatever his title was – the chief film negotiator for the network. He didn't schedule the films – he bought; he was a buyer. Don't forget it wasn't just films – it was also series, hour-long series. The programme controllers met every Monday morning at 10am and Leslie would come and report to that group. He was the guy who did all the dealing. And the great thing about Leslie was that everybody trusted him 100%. Now, this was a business where millions of pounds were spent on a handshake in Los Angeles. In an industry which is tricky at the best of times, his ethics were above reproach. And he had good *taste* also: he knew what the ITV audience wanted.
>
> I was his chairman but I never got involved in the grubby commercial dealings. Leslie would always come to me and say, "This is the deal: we're paying this much, which is the average price of the series, and we're going to buy these number of films for this amount of money. Is that OK?" And I would say OK or not OK. I mean, we didn't have a budget as such, so it was pretty free and easy in those days. We could spend money.

Sir Denis Forman recalled that Granada capitalised on the fact that they were purchasing on behalf of ITV. He told me in a letter:

> For many years Granada bought all the films and television series for the Network. They insisted that the companies paid up on the date of purchase. But they also arranged with the film companies that payment should only by made on the date of transmission, and sometimes the gap was up to a year or so. Thus Granada sat on huge sums of money earning interest every day. It was some years before they were rumbled.

The price for the hottest film properties was going up all the time and Halliwell managed to bag the last of the great bargains, in the shape of the hugely successful James Bond films. He bought the first six from United Artists for just under two million dollars, which would prove to be remarkably good value. The latest of them, *On Her Majesty's Secret Service*, was made in 1969 and with the five year ban still in operation, ITV decided to sit on all six so that they could be shown in a consecutive sequence over several months. The BBC had dropped out of the bidding and it was perhaps because of this that they appointed a new man to purchase their films and shows. His name was Gunnar Rugheimer, and he was described variously as "a giant of a Swede, a little like Ernest Borgnine," as well as "bold and courageous" and "splenetic but canny." Michael Winner, however, told me he was "highly untalented" and – inevitably – "a pompous arse." Rugheimer liked the idea of spending large sums of money in Hollywood, and his profligacy would later land him in trouble with the Corporation over his hiring of an entire suite at the Hotel Bel-Air for negotiations. Even Parliament got involved when he was found to be advancing thousands of pounds to production companies to guarantee early viewings of material. Rugheimer's approach may not have sat all that comfortably with the BBC's reputation as a public service broadcaster, but if they were going to compete with ITV they had to get realistic about the prices they were prepared to pay. His appointment began a rivalry with Halliwell that would last for over a decade.

Things became fraught when Gunnar Rugheimer came to the BBC in 1970. I used to enjoy going off for a recce to

Hollywood occasionally. Now we have to dash off all the time with a battalion of buyers... everyone gets tense, expecting Gunnar to pounce.

With *The Streets of San Francisco* and *Hawaii Five-O* both doing well for ITV, Halliwell made an attempt to buy two other major American cop shows: *Kojak* and *Starsky and Hutch*. He was not especially fond of *Starsky* for the rather obscure reason that he did not like their habit of eating hot dogs and throwing away the wrappers, but he negotiated a firm option anyway and was about to go for *Kojak* when the IBA stepped in, claiming that ITV already showed too much crime. He was forced to back down; Rugheimer pounced, and the two shows became a major part of the BBC's Saturday night line-up. Halliwell was bitter, and regretted not going ahead and buying them anyway, reasoning that ITV could have just sat on them for a while. This put him under extra pressure: from then on he knew if he turned down a show there was always the risk that Rugheimer would snap it up and have a hit with it. That pressure would lead to the occasional hasty decision, such as the Robert Blake cop show *Beretta*, which one reviewer described as the worst American show he'd ever seen.

Buying decisions were often based purely on pilots, with no guarantee of the resulting show lasting so much as a season. Halliwell said of the studios, "They have as their image of the typical American viewer a fat little guy in Milwaukee, slouched in an armchair, with an empty can of beer in one hand and a 'zapper' button in the other." Halliwell would not only have to judge whether the British public would like a show but also if that guy in Milwaukee would like it, because if it did not appeal to *him* then it would get cancelled, and ITV would have made an expensive mistake.

The loss of *Kojak* may have been a blow but Halliwell could console himself with the sci-fi drama *The Six Million Dollar Man*, which he described as an "all-stops-out hokum show," and which began its British run on January 14th, 1975. It was viewed in over seven million homes and continued to be popular throughout that year. He would later buy the spin-off series *The Bionic Woman*, which proved a modest success before both shows fizzled out towards the end of the decade. Further consolation came in the shape of his biggest ratings success ever. On a Tuesday evening in October 1975, the first James Bond movie, *Dr No*, was shown by the entire ITV network and watched in an estimated 10.5 million homes. The broadcast itself was marred in some areas by a transmission error blamed on "tropospheric scatter" – supposedly freak conditions in the "aether" which produced substantial interference and caused pictures from European channels to appear on some people's television sets. The ratings did not suffer, though: even the BBC estimated that an impressive *27 million* people had watched the film. Alasdair Milne, who later became managing director of the Corporation, said, "It is the rare film which will gather in more viewers than *The Generation Game* or *Morecambe and Wise* or *Match of the Day*." *Dr No* was one such rarity.

From Russia with Love followed in May of 1976 and obligingly hit the top spot – although it has to be said that if the Cup Final that week had been shown on one channel instead of two, the football would have won out. *Goldfinger* was either just ahead or just behind the Miss World competition in November 1976, depending on whose figures you go by, and *Thunderball*, the most popular of the six films at the cinema, was bizarrely ranked in only 7th position in the weekly listings by Jictar. However, it turned up in 25th place in the BBC's own ratings list for the whole year, a list in which *You Only Live Twice* was crowned top film of 1977 with 24.5 million viewers. To complete the set, *On Her Majesty's Secret Service* followed in September 1978 and duly achieved the highest ratings for that month. All the films would continue to draw audiences of several million when re-run over the next few years, and it is fair to say that this single purchase secured Halliwell's reputation as an expert buyer. Paul Fox called it "one of the shrewdest deals ever made."

By the mid-seventies, however, the number of movies being sold to television had dwindled to almost nothing. A few years before, Halliwell had been buying them in batches of a hundred; then thirty-odd and latterly in tens or even singly. The rivalry over the remaining hot properties increased accordingly, and consequently so did the prices. The BBC purchased *Butch Cassidy and the Sundance Kid* and *Oliver!* but had to agree to show the latter on Christmas Day so as not to take away any potential business from the cinemas. Rugheimer was coy about the amount they had paid but just under $200,000 was rumoured. Jeremy Isaacs, then at Thames, said, "We would have bought *Oliver!* for $450,000 but not when we're told what day we can show it." The audiences were there to be had, though, as *Spartacus* topped the weekly charts for ITV with 15 million viewers, and the *Planet of the Apes* films were another major success for them. *Broadcast* magazine announced that the Purchase Group had secured the multi-Oscar winning *Ben Hur* for $800,000, for two showings, and proceeded to lay down the challenge, "Can Rugheimer top that?"

To the buyers these amounts seemed like a lot but to some it was not enough. Distributors were keen to exploit the fact that each new box office success now had an added sell-on value, but felt they were getting short changed in the UK on account of there being only two bidders, and one of *them* represented several different companies, which in a truly free market would have been allowed to bid separately. In America, by contrast, the prices were much higher: CBS paid MGM *$5million* for *Network* in 1976. The Association of Independent Producers even presented a report to the Government calling for an increase in the prices TV companies should pay for films.

And they were not the only complaints. At the time there was a quota imposed by the IBA of 14% of broadcast material allowed to be imported, but they were threatening to reduce this further, and programme makers were protesting that the networks should spend more on homemade drama. Some felt that money was being lost to "people who own casinos and hotels in California" when it could have been injected into the British film industry. But the film-makers themselves were generally more annoyed about the prices being kept artificially low by Halliwell and Rugheimer. Indeed, Michael Winner was still furious about this state of affairs when I spoke to him thirty years later: "They were price-fixing, the pair of them, for *ten years*. It was outrageous!" he thundered. The accusation is not without foundation, as Halliwell himself once admitted, "If we clash over one film, the only people who profit are the distributors ... we're happiest when the BBC goes for one film and we go for another. That way the price stays low."

With television shows it was even more blatant. There was much talk of an unwritten agreement between the BBC and ITV that neither would attempt to 'poach' a show from the other when a new season became available, but it turns out in fact to have been a *written* agreement. Paul Bonner, in his book *Independent Television in Britain: Volume 5*, quotes from a document registered by the Independent Television Companies Association with the Office of

Fair Trading: "The only understanding we have with the BBC is that once a series has been acquired by one organisation, that organisation is offered the first option for renewal." This agreement would be tested to breaking point in the 1980s.

Other complaints centred on those packages Halliwell had been buying up in the late sixties, which led to a great deal of airtime being filled with average or worse movies. At an NFT-hosted book launch in 1973 for Elkan Allan's *A Guide to Movies on Television*, Halliwell himself came under fire. Allan accused him and the other buyers of accepting too much "bad and mediocre" in the packages they bought, in order to get a "few starry crowd-pullers." Halliwell explained that films may have previously come in job lots but now the packages had to be negotiated to fill lesser slots in the schedule, such as family viewing for Saturdays or horror films for late nights. The counter argument ran that these 75 or 80 minute slots were actually being created for the specific purpose of being filled by forgettable oldies because they were cheap to acquire.

In addition to complaints about quality there were complaints about content. In the late sixties, a spate of movies following on from *Who's Afraid of Virginia Woolf?* had made a mockery of the old Production Code, which was subsequently abandoned. But television was yet to catch up, and the new permissiveness was rendering many modern films unsuitable for broadcasting without major cuts for the unholy trinity of sex, violence and bad language. But, whenever an edited version was broadcast it resulted in opposing calls, from movie purists and film-makers alike, for television to screen films uncut or just to leave them alone. Halliwell received criticism for ITV's presentation of Sam Peckinpah's *The Wild Bunch* – a movie which positively revels in its own violence – but he had actually gone to great lengths to ensure that the company acquired the fullest version available, saying, "Only about a minute and a quarter was cut, yet people accused us of being butchers." He further pointed out that Peckinpah himself had cut ten minutes after it was released because *he* thought it too long.

According to Halliwell, cuts for content were only made after a full assessment had been made of current attitudes, which might have changed since the movie in question had been released. For example, ITV actually screened a fuller version of *The Killing of Sister George* than any UK cinema had, although there were still cuts made for broadcast. Some ITV companies chose to run films earlier in the evening, ignoring recommended viewing times laid down by the Purchase Group, which occasionally led to the necessity of two separate prints being struck. Unless, that was, an American TV version could be sourced, since their rules about acceptable television entertainment were even stricter than the UK's. Indeed, on one of his Hollywood trips Halliwell met Francis Ford Coppola, who told him he was preparing a TV version of *The Godfather* with the violent moments replaced by "looser shots from stock." Halliwell made a point of inspecting such versions as and when they were acquired, to make sure the films were not, in his words, "artistically mangled."

On the issue of cuts for the purposes of *timing*, however, the purists were beside themselves. The IBA's yearly report asserted that "such editing was done with restraint and with skill" – so gone, it would seem, were the days of Lew Grade cutting the first three dreams out of *Walter Mitty*. But there was still much controversy around the subject, leading one reporter to counter, "*Hamlet* regularly loses half an hour without loss, and if you turned over five pages of *Wuthering Heights* you wouldn't notice the difference."

The five year ban on screening recent movies meant that Halliwell could buy a film like *Dog Day Afternoon* and hope that the language would be permissible by the time it came to broadcast the film. Indeed, when he had seen *Virginia Woolf* in the sixties he thought it would *never* be shown on television, but it played uncut only a few years later. Television was slowly catching up with modern attitudes but in the meantime Halliwell had schedules to fill: "What everyone's scraping around for are films to play at seven or seven-thirty and they're just not making them any more," he complained.

The American TV networks were facing the same problem, and since it was they who dictated what Americans – and by extension the rest of the world – saw, a change was inevitable. Some years before, a number of mediocre movies had been sold directly to television, and the studios realised that they could make them specifically for the small screen if they kept the costs down. The TV movie was born, and for several years into the 1970s brought with it an ever-so-slight return to the old studio days. Productions were typically completed in only eleven working days and with "laughably low" budgets. Even some of the old stars were dusted off and given a new airing: Barbara

Stanwyck, Bette Davis, Ray Milland, Edward G. Robinson and Myrna Loy all appeared in made-for-TV productions. Universal bought into the idea in a big way, not least because they still held the largest backlot, allowing them to produce some ninety such entertainments during the 1973-74 season. Their *Mystery Movie* series was perhaps the most successful, especially when running at around 73 minutes in order to fill a 90-minute slot. Crime was the most popular element and *Columbo* the most famous example, but some telemovies were so highly acclaimed that they received theatrical outings, such as Steven Spielberg's *Duel*.

Halliwell found the whole concept an unexpected and welcome delight, and started buying them for ITV, saying they offered "perfectly adequate and satisfying entertainment of the kind most people used to enjoy in cinemas twenty years ago." He felt that their low budgets "brought a welcome new discipline to Hollywood," adding that they were "briskly narrated, good to look at and easy to understand, something a visit to the movies would no longer guarantee." Typically, though, the phase was short lived. Producers got more money if they filled a 2-hour slot rather than a 90-minute one and so the stories became interminably padded out. The subject matter switched from punchy, incisive crime films to overwrought family dramas of which Halliwell wrote, "Medical dictionaries have plainly been ransacked for diseases of which the actors can die beautifully (and very slowly)."

Another problem with television was shape. Audiences at the time were viewing films on a screen that was roughly four units across to three down, the same ratio as cinema screens up until about 1953 and known as 'academy frame.' After that – and due ironically to the emergence of television – films began appearing in various widescreen processes. When these productions were transmitted on television the optimum framing had to be decided upon for each individual scene, a process that became known as 'panning and scanning'. As a result, no film made after the early fifties looked entirely satisfactory on television, leading one observer to remark, "losing a third of the image is losing a third of the story." Halliwell himself approached the problem in typical fashion: he would rather just buy the older movies that were the *right* shape, but he still complained, "More and more producers have come to rely on a high-priced television sale as part of the process of paying off overheads.

Yet never is television able to transmit a post-1953 film in the version originally intended."

Television – ever the scapegoat for the ills of the world – was being blamed on all sides. The exhibitors still held the small screen responsible for the general decline of the cinema – conveniently forgetting the consistent drop in attendance that had occurred well before the mid-sixties, when films first began to be shown on TV in any great number. Their other complaint was that television sales precluded any possibility of re-releasing films to the theatres. But this was no longer the Golden Age, when re-releases were a familiar and lucrative part of the business. There was a much greater demand back then to see films that people had perhaps missed on their first or second runs, but in the 1970s *Gone with the Wind* and *The Sound of Music* were rare examples of films which could be profitably revived. The vast majority would be languishing in the vaults of the major studios had it not been for television giving them a sudden new value. Halliwell summed up the paradox:

> *How would feature films ever be preserved if it weren't for television? They'd have been thrown away and we wouldn't have them any more. I regard television as the saviour of feature films and what I don't understand is why people go on making films which are unsuitable for television, when it's so important to them to get television money in order to make more films.*

With the buying of movies and shows big business in Europe, the American TV bosses were tempted to visit from time to time, and profit-seeking entrepreneurs hit upon the idea of organising events at which the television companies could display their wares to prospective buyers. One such was the Marché Internationale des Programmes Télévision, or MIP, established by Bernard Chevry and held at the Palais des Festivals in Cannes – on La Croisette, *naturellement*. MIP was held in April so as not to clash with the famous film festival and to take advantage of the hotels being off-peak. Needless to say, Halliwell added it to his growing roster of overseas trips. The event itself had been running since the mid-sixties and ten years on had become *the* premiere European television market. It was held in a huge convention centre on a specially constructed part of the harbour, jutting out into the Mediterranean. Four separate levels were required to host the hundreds of stands of eager distributors from all over the world, hoping to tempt buyers like Halliwell and Rugheimer, who, it has to be said, were almost exclusively interested in the American market. *Broadcast* magazine reported that executives and distributors alike "slumped around the hot, sweaty corridors of the *Palais*," and that the event was "as much about cementing relationships" as it was about viewing products. At one MIP festival, Halliwell was spotted taking his morning dip in the sea by a film producer, who saw Rugheimer swimming nearby at the same moment – they appeared to be circling each other like sharks…

On another occasion, Halliwell's temper got the better of him. He was apparently indulging in his "stylish custom of holding court around the [Hotel] Majestic pool," surrounded by cocktail-sipping industry execs. An unfortunate representative of the IBA, doing no more than looking for a quiet drink, happened unsuspectingly upon the scene and found himself on the receiving end of a "tirade of monumental proportions" from Halliwell. Among his complaints were apparently the IBA's restrictions on foreign imports – the loss of those cop shows must have still rankled.

At another MIP, Elkan Allan recalled attending a dinner given by a distributor at which several industry execs and journalists were present, including Halliwell. They were all driven round the bay to a three star Michelin restaurant, but the food was "over-fussy" and the distributor a little embarrassed. Halliwell saved the occasion by asking which of his favourite movies would appear in everyone else's list. The choice fell on *The Philadelphia Story* and he proceeded to recite any section of it his audience requested, to their delight and astonishment. Apparently he went on "until the sorbets arrived."

Aside from overcrowding, the other downside of MIP was that the event itself occurred towards the end of the 'TV year', when the producers were waiting nervously to find out if their shows would get the go-ahead for another season. For them it provided a welcome opportunity to sit in the Riviera sunshine and to socialise, knowing the axe might fall a few days later back home. Halliwell wrote, "Cannes now attracts so many thousands of buyers and sellers that it is impossible to get anything done in the appalling hubbub which results … [it is] a good place to go if you do *not* want to buy or sell any programmes."

MIP itself spawned a swarm of imitators in places such as Curaçao, Hong Kong, Helsinki and Prague, but it was not quite the first of its kind. In 1961, Prince Rainier of Monaco had organised the Festival de Télévision de Monte-Carlo, held at the Loews Hotel. Unlike MIP, where the stalls were displayed on the dedicated floors of an exhibition centre, the Monte Carlo festival was held at the hotel itself, with rooms converted into offices where viewings and negotiations could take place in comfort. The festival was arranged for February, which made it more suitable to the sellers, as MCA executive Colin Davis observed, "Monte Carlo is the most important market; [it] follows directly our mid-season L.A. screenings, whereas MIP is now too early for the May/June screenings." Halliwell found this event created "a more sensible and pleasant atmosphere than is possible in MIP's great underground bunker," but with waiting lists for viewings it did lead to a lot of waylaying in hotel corridors, which *Broadcast* reported as being filled with "zombie-like execs shuffling along to their next viewing in a room or a suite." On one occasion Halliwell himself was described as "stalking the corridors ... telling all who spoke to him that he was too busy to speak to them," leading one exasperated American to ask, "If he's always too busy to speak to anyone, who the hell does he ever speak to?"

The crowded corridors of Monte Carlo led to an industry joke in the 1980s about an unshaven executive apparently still trying to *leave* the 1978 festival.

> *There is little love here for the film as a medium. It is more a case of, "Oh, we have no programmes there? Let's show a film" ... ITV has the better films but the BBC schedules them better.*

The scheduling of films on ITV was becoming a source of frustration for Halliwell. Unlike the BBC, they did not have a second channel on which to show films of a more specialist interest, i.e. old ones. BBC2, however, could present them in dedicated seasons, and Halliwell further observed in France that television there treated vintage movies with significantly more respect, each presentation being "exhaustively introduced" and followed by discussions and appreciation. At ITV he was struggling to get his golden oldies onto the screen: colleagues would say to him, "Don't you know everything is in colour now?" In 1976, however, he actually got the chance to schedule some films himself, for both Granada and Yorkshire, and an interviewer noted that his eyes lit up as he told her about it. Indeed, he was pictured in *Screen International* at the time, sporting spectacles and a full beard, and smiling sweetly for the camera. "I acquired all the Humphrey Jennings war documentaries," he explained, "and we decided to present them as second features." The season was entitled 'Saturday night at the Odeon' and the idea was to recreate the experience of going to the cinema in the good old days. Firstly, there would be a trailer and a newsreel, followed by a Jennings picture and then the main feature, "That way we'll have a whole evening at the movies," he enthused.

In addition to scheduling, which he continued to do for Granada over the next few years – though never to his complete satisfaction – Halliwell made a number of appearances in front of the camera. His first was in 1974 as a guest on the nostalgia programme *Looks Familiar*, hosted by Denis Norden and which involved guests *of a certain age* reminiscing about years gone by. Norden described the show as "an amiable meander around the thirties and forties" – which inevitably featured the cinema. Halliwell, a couple of months short of his forty-fifth birthday, appeared in the second half of a show alongside ex-music hall comedian Tommy Trinder, Jack Warner from *Dixon of Dock Green*, and *The Forsyte Saga*'s Lana Morris. Norden introduced him by saying that *The Filmgoer's Companion* "is to films what Wisden is to cricket," and called it "the most comprehensive and charming of all cine-encyclopaedias."

Halliwell duly arrives in a smart suit, with slicked back hair and a beard. He is shown a clip of *To Have and Have Not* and asked to complete Lauren Bacall's famous 'whistle' line, which he slightly misquotes but the others are astonished he gets close. Norden then proceeds to test him on a few other quotations from movies such as *Now Voyager* and *I am a Fugitive from a Chain Gang*, which Halliwell breezes through. "I think he knows his stuff, this guy," remarks the host. The other guests then take their turn, followed by a clip of George Formby in *Let George Do It*, after which Halliwell is asked to name six other Formby films. He races past seven before Norden stops him. Despite answering well enough, though, Halliwell is rather stoical throughout, and does not register much of a smile at any of Norden's jokes – perhaps he was nervous.

He gave a much more engaging – indeed ebullient – performance four years later in *Clapperboard North West*, a special edition of the film show aimed at youngsters and presented by Chris Kelly, which covered movie locations used in Bolton and Blackpool. Kelly opens the show with his hands in the pockets of his casual jacket, standing in front of the Bolton mill factory used in the Gracie Fields film *Sing as we Go*. He introduces a beardless Halliwell, who wears a dark jacket and a white shirt with an enormously wide collar. A silver medallion on a black lace string hangs down his front, and his long sideburns and stocky build make him the spitting image of football manager Don Revie. Halliwell proceeds to recount some of the tales of his own childhood in the area, interspersed with long clips from the Fields film. He recalls taking his father's lunch to the mill and seeing all the unemployed workers sitting on doorsteps. He describes the film as propaganda, just like the later wartime documentaries, as Gracie's screen persona "enabled people to overcome their difficulties and see the brighter side of things." The pair then appear outside the old Queen's cinema, where forty years before Halliwell had taken his first trip to the movies, which he proceeds to recall with childlike enthusiasm. They then venture up to Churchgate where he describes queuing for films at the Capitol and nipping round to the pastie shop.

Throughout, he appears authoritative but amiable; his voice is clear and commanding, with the merest hint of a lisp but no trace of a northern accent. That is, until the pair of them are standing across the road from Blackpool Tower eating ice cream cones, and Kelly asks him to recite a few lines of Marriott Edgar's poem *The Lion and Albert*. Halliwell does so with relish, prompting Kelly to remark, "We'll pass the cap round." They end the show sitting astride donkeys on the pleasure beach. Halliwell has clearly enjoyed himself and grins throughout Kelly's final address, whereupon they share a joke before the credits roll.

Halliwell was less enthused about his hometown in an interview for the *Bolton Evening News*, apparently conducted during the *Clapperboard* shoot. He expressed his sorrow at the number of cinemas having by then been reduced to just two, and further changes led him to comment, "All my familiar landmarks have disappeared."

He next appeared in 1980 on a programme about television called *Look Here*, in a segment dealing with audience complaints. ITV had received letters from viewers who were annoyed about the regional scheduling of their movies. One pointed out that Granada had recently shown a season of "vintage favourites," whilst Londoners had been treated to "bland TV movies" in the same time slots. Halliwell is interviewed sitting at his desk and wearing a dark suit. The beard is back, with a trace of grey visible but no moustache, giving him a curiously Amish appearance. He has a copy of his own *Teleguide* among his papers and responds, "There aren't too many people in ITV whom I would call classic film buffs" – going on to say that film seasons were difficult to schedule because you needed to fill particular time frames – the implication being that expert knowledge was required to do it. He says most of the scheduling is done at the local level because the stations "like their independence," adding, "I schedule for Granada [and] I always have in mind to do seasons of vintage films."

Thames and LWT responded that such seasons were not important to them and that Londoners had the advantage of specialist cinemas. Halliwell wrote that this was the reason he had failed to see the Gene Kelly musical *On the Town* at home, despite having purchased it for his own network. He lived in the London area and the local companies would not show the film because they thought musicals were bad for ratings.

> *Early evening action series are one of the areas British TV is weakest in, so these are what I buy. They get the ratings because the box is on and the kids want to watch and Dad, just back from work, lets them.*

By the late seventies, Halliwell had written off feature films as a regular source of programming material. With so few acceptable movies on the market, he came to rely more and more on the American television product, and hoping against hope that the quality of it would be good enough. He had a big hit with *Charlie's Angels*, which he recalled winning after "a tremendous battle" with the BBC. The show did well on its first British run in 1977, achieving audiences of around 9 million, rising to 13 million the following season when another of Halliwell's purchases proved to be a success: *The Incredible Hulk*. Both were regularly in the top ten most watched programmes in the summer of 1978, and later that year Halliwell was asked about them in an interview for *The Sunday Times Magazine*. He was pictured apparently in a screening room, with the Amish beard and medallion both present. The reporter alleged that his "purist devotion to Hollywood's golden era is constantly compromised by his job as chief film buyer for the ITV network." He responded to the suggestion that there was any contradiction between the two by saying, "I'm buying for an audience of millions, not a few hundred buffs at the National Film Theatre ... I don't have to like everything I buy, any more than the manager of the Odeon, Leicester Square, has to like everything he shows."

Of his talent for spotting potential ratings winners he said, "I can see a few minutes of a series and feel a tingle that tells me it's going to be a success. It doesn't necessarily mean *I* like it, of course, but my instinct is rarely wrong. After 20 years in this business, you simply get a feeling for what will play in Oswaldtwistle." Unfortunately, his feeling was wrong about the private eye series *Vega$*, starring Robert Urich, and which Halliwell bought on the strength of a two hour TV movie because he thought it had a nice 1930s feeling – and because he knew the BBC were interested. The resultant series, though, was a disappointment to him: "It was supposed to be sparkling champagne but it was not the best quality champagne I'm afraid."

The type of shows he was looking to purchase can be summed up in one of his most oft-used adjectives: hokum. Because he felt that Britain made its own drama series, and did them rather well, what he was after were cop shows and westerns; supernatural stories and science fiction. But he wanted *quality* hokum, like *Dragnet* and *Have Gun, Will Travel*, which was not easy to find in those days. American shows were cheaper to acquire than commissioning homemade dramas, and they were generally slickly produced and popular – in just the same way that American movies were more appealing than British ones to those Bolton filmgoers in the Golden Age. Asked what the qualities that made a good buyer were, Halliwell answered, "Being in the right place at the right time; reading *Variety*; being one step ahead of the BBC and one step ahead of the seller." Of *The Incredible Hulk* specifically, he said, "I was dubious about [it] at first because I thought it might be too scary for children... but actually I'm quite pleased with it in a funny sort of way. It's watchable, well-made, and the producers reveal a nice sense of humour." And when people asked him how he could show "such rubbish," he simply pointed them toward the ratings.

In the mid-seventies, Universal began producing television 'novelisations' under the umbrella title of 'Best Sellers', with the unique approach of scheduling them on consecutive Monday nights over several weeks. The instant success of *Rich Man, Poor Man* inspired other studios to imitate the formula and the phenomenally popular slave drama *Roots* followed in 1977. Its twelve episodes were broadcast even more economically, going out on eight consecutive evenings to massive critical and public acclaim... the mini-series was born.

Halliwell was not particularly thrilled by their quality but he recognised their ratings value, and over the next few years he would buy a clutch of similar productions for ITV. Mini-series were still cheaper than home produced drama, but more expensive than standard shows since they were generally epic in scale, and usually featured several big name stars. He bought the Dashiell Hammett private eye thriller *The Dain Curse*, describing it as, "Impeccably done, the best mini-series I've ever seen." However, he turned down *Holocaust*, a controversial nine-part story featuring Tom Bell and Meryl Streep, saying, "We had a firm option on it. We only let it go finally on grounds of taste: you couldn't suddenly interrupt it with ads." The show had been a ratings topper in the states but had provoked some criticism, with accusations that it "reduced the sufferings of millions of people to a mere soap opera." The BBC took it instead, with Rugheimer declaring that ITV had simply not bid enough money, adding, "It is typical of them to turn a financial decision into a theological virtue."

In addition, the BBC bought the Nixon exposé *Washington: behind Closed Doors*, which was less successful. Halliwell said that although it was "a marvellous entertainment" it was "morally challengeable" due to its blurring of fact and fiction. The BBC never quite bought into the idea of mini-series, though, only occasionally dipping their toes, and so Halliwell would generally have the pick of the crop, which he would eagerly harvest over the next few years.

I have been known to conclude deals worth millions of dollars over a McDonald's hamburger, in a hospital sick-room and in the middle of Death Valley, for as Hollywood always knew, an interesting location can add zest to a tired old plot.

Since Halliwell and Rugheimer concentrated their overseas efforts almost exclusively on American product, what Britons were viewing on their screens was determined by the American studios, and *their* choices about what to make depended upon what their audience (that fat guy in Milwaukee) liked or disliked, which is why the Los Angeles trips became so important to Halliwell. They were not only useful for viewing and purchasing product, but over the years he had built up relationships with many key executives, and it was only in the heart of the industry that he could take the temperature of the studios, and find out what the latest trends were. Paul Fox later wrote of him –

> The best time to watch him in action is in Los Angeles. When he steps out of the Beverly Wilshire Hotel, silver cane in hand, medallion round his neck, this tall, bearded figure is an impressive sight. The Hollywood film community has real respect for his encyclopaedic knowledge of feature films and his energetic negotiating skills. In the darkness of the studio viewing room his acerbic comments on the shows before him make salesmen cringe.

The scheduling of the trips was arranged with the BBC in advance, in one of the rare occasions when the two organisations actively consulted. The BBC usually sent only two representatives, Rugheimer and a deputy, whereas in the late seventies the entire ITV Purchase Group would go. Both teams took separate first class flights and stayed in separate five-star hotels: ITV at the Beverly Wilshire – where incoming guests received a complimentary half-bottle of champagne – and the BBC three miles away along Sunset Boulevard, at the Bel-Air. They would arrive in Los Angeles on a Sunday and spend the next four and a half days viewing product and making deals, before catching Friday afternoon flights home. The rival teams would view the same material but usually at different times, and the logistics of getting them around all the studios led Halliwell to remark that the trips were "a miracle of timing and transportation."

A typical day would begin with a 7 o'clock wake-up call, and after breakfast the Purchase Group would assemble on the paved and covered drive which separates the two halves of the Wilshire. At 8.30 they would be on the way to their first screening, at either a major studio like Columbia or MCA-Universal, or at an independent such as

MTM or Norman Lear's Tandem. With destinations separated by as much as forty minutes' drive, days would be allocated to groups of studios situated relatively close to one another. At any given location they would view a mixture of pilot films and movies, and watch five-minute presentations. In between, they would chat to producers and studio executives, and sip coffee and sample the complementary nibbles. They would occasionally mill around with other buyers, the conversations being cordial but guarded, with everyone keeping his cards close to his chest.

More screenings would be squeezed in at the next studio before a quick lunch in the commissary; then back into the cars to journey on to the afternoon's viewing, lasting until about 4pm. But nothing too heavy, as all the buyers would now be suitably sedated by the lunch and intervening drive. Back at the hotel, Halliwell would take a quick bath, put on a change of clothes and make a few phone calls before the cars would arrive again, this time for the evening screenings, which might last until 10 o'clock. A running buffet would be put on to save time and finally they would repair to the Wilshire bar for a late night discussion about the material on offer, and possible strategies to take.

The deals themselves could end up being made either the following day before breakfast or at 2am over a "bottle of Perrier," but there was an agreement not to express any interest in a particular product until both ITV and the BBC had viewed it (in addition to the agreement about not poaching series from each other). Sir Paul Fox remembered the experience well:

> You would go and sit there in a darkened theatre and see all this stuff – and I have to say I was impatient and I would say after twenty minutes, "Right cut this. We're not buying this rubbish." Or, we'd go to the end. And we had coffee and doughnuts and a decent buffet lunch in the commissary, and you met various executives. And the presence of Leslie ensured that the top brass from MCA and Columbia always turned up to lunch. [They] would wheel out the producers and we would hear what the storylines were like and what they were planning to do … and one came back much better informed. Whereas MIP was just a straightforward trade fair, you know, everybody had their stall out there. It was like going to a market, and I didn't care for that.

To go to Hollywood when you are a buyer is wonderful. Don't go there as a salesman. Fortunately, I never had the need to go there to sell something – I always went there as a buyer, and as a buyer you were treated extremely well.

Halliwell wrote that on one L.A. trip he watched 55 shows and wrote a 46-page report. The studios took good care of their visiting customers, inviting them to social events where famous names would be trooped out for meet-and-greets. Ron Edge, an old school pal of Halliwell's, recalled to me that Leslie had told him they even offered entertainments of a certain female variety, if such were desired. He said his old friend had politely declined.

The May trips involved buying shows on the strength of pilots of series which would not begin shooting until the summer, and might well have changed in emphasis and appearance by the time their October premieres rolled around. From that point on they could be shot down by critics and public alike, potentially disappearing within a few weeks. Because so many of them did fail, new series had to be commissioned mid-season, and consequently January trips became necessary, either to view shows which were already established or those just about to take the plunge. The real hunt was always to find the 'big one' – another *Kojak* – a show that would be popular with critics and public alike and would run for several seasons. In January 1979, all the talk was about *Supertrain*, NBC's $10million series about a giant-sized atomic powered train crossing the States at high speed, and characterised by the intrigues of its passengers. Some called it *Love Boat* on rails; Halliwell instinctively likened it to films such as *Strangers on a Train*, *Murder on the Orient Express* and *Death on the Nile*, and it was clear early on in the trip that both the BBC and ITV were interested.

The problem was that neither team could get to see any of it. NBC apparently had very little to show them even though its American premiere was imminent. A party was held on the MGM lot featuring the enormous constructed set, with a backdrop so convincing they had to put a barrier in front of it. But it was all starting to look like smoke and mirrors. One journalist interviewing a special effects man was told that the reason he had been hired was because the doors on the train would not open properly, and that the model train to be used for long shots moved so slowly as to be a joke.

Later that week, Halliwell did manage to view a few scenes and thought it slightly better than he had feared. He indicated his interest but on the Friday morning Rugheimer sewed up the deal for the BBC, over breakfast at the Bel-Air. Halliwell consoled himself with a mini-series version of *From Here to Eternity*, with an option on its sequel which Rugheimer disparagingly referred to as *From Here to Eternity and Back*. The joke was on him, however, as *Supertrain* was later reported to have been "laughed off the screen for its unconvincing train models and the banality of the plots." It never even reached British screens and was written off by an embarrassed BBC. Halliwell said that the show lost out "by casting a set as its hero." Another reason for him not to be too disheartened was a surprise meeting with one of his childhood idols. On this very trip, in January 1979, in the lift of the Beverly Wilshire Hotel, Leslie Halliwell found himself standing next to none other than Gracie Fields, and could not resist informing her, "I was born twelve miles from where you were."

"Oh? Where were that, love?" she enquired.

"Bolton."

"Ee, they said it were a gradely place, that. I only went there once or twice. They used to say they were a snotty lot that came from Bolton."

"Do you still sing *Sally*?"

"Aye, they won't let me stop. Isn't that daft? All me life I've been singing a song written for a chap."

Gracie even hummed a few bars before giving him a cheery wave goodbye as the lift doors opened. Later that year she died, on the island of Capri, at the age of eighty-one.

Two months after the *Supertrain* trip, Halliwell wrote a very entertaining piece for *Variety* in which he bemoaned the lack of acceptable material available for purchase. Once again that fat little guy in Milwaukee with the can of beer and the 'zapper' was mentioned (although by then he had moved to Minnesota). Halliwell remarked that "even he, in 1979, must be sorely tempted to throw his empties at the set." He likened the old days of buying to Roman orgies, where he and Rugheimer would order the "immediate and painful execution of impertinent salesmen" who tried to sell them inferior product, and with the pair "occasionally condescending to buy a small package, and yawning as [they] did so." This is the only time he spoke of his opposite number with anything bordering on affection, although elsewhere he said, "There was no relationship really. We met occasionally and very occasionally we exchanged gossip. You have to acknowledge that you're playing a game and you have to play to win."

June Dromgoole was Halliwell's assistant at Granada in the early 1970s. She later worked for a distribution company handling major American shows such as *Starsky and Hutch* and *Dynasty*. As a result, she found herself on the other side of the purchasing fence: trying to sell programmes to both ITV and the BBC. One of them was *Dusty's Trail*, a show she had previously viewed for Halliwell at Granada, and written a report dismissing it as "ghastly." June told me:

> About a year or so later I was on the other side, and we had the distribution rights and I was trying to sell it to Leslie. He wrote one of his caustic replies, saying they weren't going to buy it and quoting everything I had said about it! He could be wicked in his sense of humour, you know, with people, but there was never any malice in it. If people needed help, Leslie was there. He was very much a mentor to me.

I asked her what he was like to work for and she responded, "He was a fantastic boss; I mean he was totally eccentric in many ways, but under that sort of gruff exterior he was very kind, very kind to a lot of people along the way." I then asked her what Rugheimer was like to deal with and she replied, "Er… I wouldn't be quite as kind in my description of him as I am with Leslie, let's put it that way. He was a much more tricky character; more difficult to deal with."

Alan Frank was another colleague of Halliwell's at the time, having previously met him back in the days of the Cambridge Rex. He spoke to me on the phone:

> Twenty years later Leslie gave me a job handling certification – i.e. deciding which films were allowed to be shown at which times. I lived in Richmond and we travelled into work in his car every morning. We used to argue a lot but it was a great pleasure to drive in with him. His northern background had given him a very acute awareness of what the ITV public wanted to see. He was mainly in conflict with Gunnar Rugheimer, who apparently got paid more than him.

There was growing criticism about the quality of TV shows on British television, primarily regarding acquisitions. The *Daily Mail* ran an article about the buying process with the headline, 'Why you have to put up with this TV trash'. They claimed that British TV schedules had become a "dumping ground for flat, unadventurous and boring American television programmes." The reason was that the studios had begun packaging their properties – just as they had done with movies when they sold them to television in the sixties, and before that with cinemas during the Golden Age. Halliwell wrote, "I suppose the only neat trick … is to wrap up the property which both buyers want in an overall deal of irresistible size, including the series which the distributor has been aching to dispose of for a year." Once again, inferior product was being sold alongside a few choice items, with the prices inflated accordingly so that the bad eggs did not lose too much money – it had been going on for nearly half a century. The *Mail* asked, "Is there any other consumer industry where it is openly admitted that the public are expected to accept inferior goods just in order to sample one worthwhile product?" The same article mentions a new show the BBC had just purchased, and which was due to appear imminently on British screens… *Supertrain*.

Gunnar dealt a stunning blow … when he agreed to pay $4,250,000 for The Sound of Music *in 1978 … he distorted the whole market.*

In 1978, the BBC purchased *The Sound of Music* from 20th Century Fox for ten showings, in a reportedly "frantic" auction. Halliwell and the Purchase Group had dropped out of the bidding but Brian Cowgill of Thames had launched his own separate bid, eventually losing out. The Group were not best pleased and it was suggested that this rogue bid hastened Jeremy Isaacs's departure from Granada, as he left soon after. Cowgill would try the same trick a few years later with the TV soap *Dallas*.

Smarting from the defeat, Halliwell insisted that the BBC were reckless in their spending and that the top price should have been no more than a million – despite ITV having clearly taken part in the auction. Rugheimer commented, "Typical Leslie, when things reach the bitter end he dons what I call clerical garb and begins to go on about the awful spending at the BBC." Other complaints followed, especially from TV producers who were being constrained by tightening budgets on account of the Corporation's claims of hardship. Eyebrows were raised on hearing the news that they had forked out four million dollars for one film. Rugheimer went on the defensive, stating, "It need not be paid in a lump sum but will be spread over a number of years," and further asserted that it would come out of the normal yearly budget for film expenditure, so the money would have otherwise been spent on films "almost inevitably of lesser quality." Alasdair Milne, the director of the BBC, defended the decision with the argument that the cost per hour for the ten showings worked out roughly the same as it would cost to produce new TV dramas covering equivalent running times. But this did not take into account re-runs, and the question remained whether the BBC was serving its licence fee payers better by repeating an old movie ten times over instead of making ten new dramas, each of which would have an added sell-on value to foreign networks.

With so much claim and counter claim going on in the press, coupled with the suppliers themselves playing a game of cat and mouse in the hope of driving up prices, the truth is somewhat difficult to get at. Both Rugheimer and Halliwell seem to have been genuinely convinced that the prices for the bigger films were too high, but both appear also to have been fairly easily tempted into an auction if the property was hot enough, during which one of them would eventually back down and then accuse the other of overspending. Given that the big titles were running out, though, it was clear from this example that when the two networks did lock horns, all gentlemen's agreements were quickly discarded. And the distributors knew it, so when they had an important product to sell they could milk it for all it was worth... and that is precisely what MGM did next.

Gone with the Wind, made in 1939 – the Golden Age's Golden Year – remained the most successful movie ever until the mid-sixties, when it was usurped by *The Sound of Music*. At MIP in 1980, Halliwell asked a representative of the studio when it would finally become available to television, and he replied that they were just giving it "another little brush around the theatres where it is picking up some nice dollars." However, the rumour persisted that the film was about to come on the market, and later that year a package deal was indeed announced. The BBC was involved in initial talks but did not like what was on offer and so the deal went silent for a few months. Then, in December, Rugheimer announced that the BBC had tabled a bid of $8.7 million for an improved package totalling 56 films. Halliwell had not heard from Metro that the film was available again and was irked that Rugheimer should make this announcement. He was further annoyed at an article in the *Financial Times* which stated that ITV had countered with a bid of $10m. Halliwell denied making any such offer and claimed he was less interested in buying movies since they did not have the week on week appeal of a series. This may have been generally true but *Gone with the Wind* was the best of the remaining unsold movies from the Golden Age, and Halliwell wanted it just as badly as Rugheimer. Apart from anything else, since the IBA was becoming concerned about the low quality of feature films on ITV, the Purchase Group were keen to go after a film of such high standing. But to buy better meant to spend more — something the IBA were equally concerned about.

While MGM was rubbing its hands at the thought of the two British giants slugging it out for their classic movie, MCA-Universal had other ideas. They had heard about the imminent sale of *Gone with the Wind* and thought they would throw a spanner in the works, in the form of *their* hottest property of the time: *Jaws*. The box office record breaker had been offered for sale to ITV for $3m the year before, but in a package they had not found particularly tempting. The BBC then offered $4m but asked for a moratorium because they were going through a series of cutbacks and did not want the bad publicity the announcement would inevitably bring. Since some of the films in the package were still tied up in legal wrangles, ITV were happy to wait. However, with fears growing that available spending cash would dry up as a result of any deal for *Gone with the Wind*, MCA felt they had to act quickly. They improved their package by throwing in *Jaws 2*, all the *Airports*, *The Birds* and *High Plains Drifter*, and offered it for sale during the January 1981 L.A. trip. Some might comment cruelly that including *Jaws 2* should have *reduced* the value rather than increased it, but nevertheless both sides were back on board and a bidding war began.

With the rival teams ensconced in their usual hotels, negotiations for the *Jaws* package continued right through Thursday night and into Friday afternoon, with the price climbing to nearly $10million. ITV were just shading it when MCA decided to check with Rugheimer one last time. He said he would get back to them, but with the group needing to catch a flight home the deadline for the deal was 4pm. Halliwell once said, "I take a bath twice a day to relax, and while I am not a drinking man, if things get tense I take a *crème de menthe frappé.*" As the deadline passed there was still no response from Rugheimer, and so MCA knocked the hammer down and ITV walked off with the package, sharks and all. Halliwell later credited Paul Fox with the buy, saying, "He got it finally in the middle of packing his suitcase... he stood there, thumbs up and beaming."

With the ITV team ready to leave and feeling satisfied that they had done some pretty good business, they then heard the strangest news from London. Rugheimer had telephoned a statement from his Bel-Air suite to the British press saying, "The BBC refused to react to a bid of nine and three quarter million dollars made by ITV for the two *Jaws* pictures... we do not believe the programme value of this particular package is sufficient to warrant this sort of money." Halliwell was "flabbergasted," saying, "Going to the press like that is a typical example of the kind of antagonism that never used to exist." Not only had Rugheimer broken the golden rule of not revealing what the other side was prepared to pay, but he had discredited the package and called into question ITV's judgement. However, in sacrificing *Jaws* he had paved the way for any future big spending by the other side to be seen as profligacy. With the *Gone with the Wind* auction scheduled for a month later – and with the IBA watching on intently – it might well have been a clever move.

A week before the auction, Alasdair Milne was asked how much they wanted David O. Selznick's Oscar-winner and he replied, "There are some films you can't *not* buy." The 56-film package included *Singin' in the Rain* and *Ben Hur* (1959 version), *Seven Brides for Seven Brothers* and *The Dirty Dozen*, which despite being big titles had all been previously screened in the 1970s. In fact, *Broadcast* went one further and said that only *Gone with the Wind* and one other film in the package had *never* been shown on British television before.

The details of the auction were recounted in a very entertaining article by Peter Lennon for *The Sunday Times*, which included a delightful cartoon of Halliwell and Rugheimer staring intently at one another across a table strewn with cans of film. In reality they did not actually sit face to face. Bill Davis, the agent acting on behalf of MGM, came over to London from his office in Amsterdam to conduct the sale from a suite at the Athenaeum Hotel. Halliwell bid by telephone from his Golden Square office but Rugheimer was there in person. Not wishing to give either side an advantage, Davis isolated him in another room so both would have to place their bids remotely. It is a safe bet that Halliwell had his purchase team listening intently on the other line – and perhaps a glass of *crème de menthe frappé* to hand?

The auction began at an agreed base figure of $8.7million, with $50,000 being the minimum increase. At 10:59 Halliwell opened the bidding and Rugheimer hit back almost immediately. Over the next hour they traded back and forth, with Halliwell raising in aggressive fashion with double bids of $100k, to which the BBC countered with a steady stream of minimum increments, usually after a few minutes' interval. It was Halliwell who broke the $10m barrier but as the clock struck noon Rugheimer was back in front. A delay of fifteen minutes followed, during which one can imagine feverish discussions taking place. At 12:15, and with no response from ITV forthcoming, Davis knocked the lot down to the BBC for $10,550,000. The Corporation had bought *Gone with the Wind* for unlimited showings over fifteen years, plus the other movies totalling some 300 hours' worth of screen time.

The complaints about overspending duly followed, countered by the old argument that it all added up to much less than the cost of making brand new programmes to fill an equivalent amount of time. The package included some films which were tied up for a few years while previous deals ran their course – and some, ironically, were actually holed up in *ITV's* vaults. Sir Paul Fox recalled the auction:

> Alasdair Milne was absolutely determined that the BBC were going to outgun us. And the price went up and up and in the end Leslie said, "Look, this isn't worth it." And we withdrew and they got it. To be fair, *Gone with the Wind* wasn't of great interest to the network, largely because it was 240 minutes long. It wasn't just Gunnar, it was Alasdair Milne who needed it – he wanted it as a trophy.

Halliwell concurred, saying at the time, "We could have pushed them up and up but what was the point?" He asked some MGM reps what they felt the rest of the package had been worth. One and a half million was the response, implying that the BBC had paid nine million dollars for one movie, a suggestion which Rugheimer dismissed as "Rubbish, absolute rubbish."

Still, the BBC had their prize and scheduled the premiere for Christmas 1981, split over two nights due to the film's length. It turned out to be not even the most popular BBC programme for that week, being fifth and seventh in their list. ITV, however, had squeezed in the premiere of *Jaws* in October and topped the ratings for the *whole month*, with an estimated audience of 23.25 million viewers. Halliwell always argued that he had got the better value deal, but he had been prepared to pay over ten million dollars for *Gone with the Wind* himself, so he could not sit too high up on his horse.

Alan Howden, who took over buying for the BBC after Rugheimer left in the early eighties, called *Gone with the Wind* "a nuclear weapon, something that could never actually be used... what do you do for an encore?" The realisation had set in that the number of blockbusting films which could be shown to a family audience, without offending anyone over content or presentation, was approaching zero – something Halliwell had predicted several years before. There would, of course, be other prizes to tussle over in the next few years, such as *Star Wars*, *Raiders of the Lost Ark* and *E.T*, but nothing would ever match the feverish interest – or the price – of *Gone with the Wind*.

We have been surprised by the BBC and their way of going about things ... but all it has done is to sharpen our wits wonderfully ... while they have been making the rules, we have been winning the game.

By the early eighties, Leslie Halliwell had become a major player in the TV industry. He had bought some of the most successful films and shows of the previous decade, with the disappointments being easily offset by the triumphs: the Bond films, *Jaws*, *The Six Million Dollar Man*, *The Incredible Hulk* and *Charlie's Angels*, to name only a few. Along the way he had forged invaluable relationships with US studio executives, both in London and Los Angeles, and his vast knowledge of the industry had made him an indispensable member of the Purchase Group. He had met dozens of famous names and travelled to international destinations he could only have dreamed of when growing up in Bolton.

But he had made enemies, too. Film-makers were annoyed at the way their product was presented on television, and that they and the distributors did not receive enough money for it because of the ITV/BBC duopoly. Reviewers blamed him at least partially for the deluge of American 'trash' which filled the peak-time schedules, and more than one article described him as "stalking" – whether around the corridors of international trade fairs or the film world in general, as if he was some kind of malevolent presence. The stories of him "holding court" at Cannes and giving the IBA a piece of his mind conflict with the amenable and boyishly enthusiastic character who appeared on *Clapperboard*.

His appearance raised a few eyebrows as well. By now the full beard was a permanent fixture and he had taken to walking with a cane after foot surgery. He sported a silver medallion on a lace string in preference to a tie and was once observed exiting the NFT wearing a cloak and a sombrero. David Quinlan met him whilst writing for the *TV Times* and told me, "I found him brisk (some might say brusque!), confident and authoritative; a big man physically and personality-wise." Others found him pompous; stuck in his ways, and he did not suffer fools. One interviewer described him revealingly as "a stocky man with a Brigham Young beard and a way of giving you frequent glances of expansive disdain." Another thought him "unshakeable in his firmly-held opinions" – all of which contributed to his reputation as a bad tempered gruff, a reputation that solidified with the publication of his second major encyclopaedic work of the cinema – arguably an even greater achievement than *The Filmgoer's Companion* – and one which would give him free rein to air his opinions and to vent his frustrations…

1977 saw the release of the first edition of *Halliwell's Film Guide*…

8

Two Untrained Index Fingers

- Halliwell's Film Guide -

The wave of books about the cinema which Halliwell had helped to start with *The Filmgoer's Companion* in 1965, had by the mid-seventies become a deluge of encyclopaedias, histories and biographies. This, combined with the enormous popularity of movies being shown on television, had made him well aware of the demand for a one-volume guidebook specifically for film titles. Having often been asked why he did not produce a complete compendium himself, Halliwell resisted at first, suspecting that "no one volume could hope to be comprehensive ... the attempt would be pointless, for the book would be cluttered up with endless lists of routine second features of long ago, which no one in his right mind would even wish to remember, let alone see again."

The *Companion* had always included some eight hundred entries for specific films of significance, in addition to its primary function of listing personalities, themes and technical terms, but many readers had been annoyed to find that Halliwell's choice of what constituted a significant work conflicted with theirs. Typically eager to please, he set himself the task of producing a film guide which could incorporate brief information about every title "likely or worthy of remembrance by the keen filmgoer or student." With what Philip French would later call "an appalling cultural insularity," Halliwell initially chose to concentrate on English speaking titles only, covering the period from the beginning of the sound era up to the present day. He felt it would not be fair to include just a handful of silent films given the thousands that had been made in the early days, and similarly thought he could not do adequate justice to foreign language films. His selection policy did, however, give him "fifty years of product to play with," and he set himself a target of 8,000 entries.

In terms of research, given the number of movie-related titles jamming the shelves of bookshops – and the enormous library he had by then himself assembled – Halliwell could now stand on the shoulders of other giants. Perhaps the most significant of these was New Yorker Leonard Maltin, who had been a journalist in America for several years and in 1969 published his paperback, *TV Movies*, designed as a guide for the sit-at-home film fan. Maltin similarly chose to cover some 8,000 titles, in neat capsule entries with brief assessments and a star rating from one to four. The book's two column design with no gaps between the entries made the pages look a little busy, and the synopses often sacrificed a little clarity for the sake of brevity – *The Return of Jesse James*: "Compact budget western dealing with rumours that lookalike for outlaws is notorious gunslinger." *Eight Iron Men*: "WW2 actioner focusing on a group of soldiers, strain they undergo during continued enemy attack."

Halliwell further drew on the work of James Robert Parish, who in 1969 published *The American Movies Reference Book: the Sound Era*. Denis Gifford weighed in with *The British Film Catalogue 1895-1970*, and Douglas Eames documented in *The MGM Story* all 1,738 films produced by the famous studio up until 1974. Finally, the *Monthly Film Bulletin*, published by the British Film Institute, had since 1934 provided brief credits and a review of every film released theatrically in Britain. Halliwell referred to the contributors of the *Bulletin* as "unsung anonymous heroes," and all of the above were acknowledged in the 1st edition of *Halliwell's Film Guide*, published in 1977.

The UK version came in a black book jacket, with the title in large yellow and orange block capitals, in the shadow writing font which would characterise his encyclopaedias from then on. The cover featured the single image of a stack of film cans, with one open and spilling its contents. Later editions would follow in the same style: bright coloured covers with large shadow writing and one image of a movie personality, such as Marilyn Monroe, Harold Lloyd or Basil Rathbone.

Halliwell, then forty-eight, included nearly everything which had played as a main feature in Britain or America up until August 1976, as well as second features with "special merit." He omitted "the absolutely routine, and specifically excluded a few hundred westerns on the Audie Murphy and Randolph Scott level or below." One may debate the merits of a film guide which excluded *The Battleship Potemkin*, *Intolerance*, *Les Enfants du Paradis*, *La Règle du Jeu*, and nearly all of Chaplin and Keaton's best work, but Halliwell stated clearly that the restrictions applied only to the 1st edition. Once the *Guide* was off and running, he could then concentrate on filling the gaps, and he claimed at the time to have some three thousand additional titles already "half-researched."

The 1st edition was dedicated "to the memory of my Mother, who first took me to the pictures… and to everyone who has since joined me there…" In a style reminiscent of his dedications in the *Companion*, he proceeded to list several movies which he was glad to see never actually got made, despite publicity announcing their imminence. Included were *The Dancing Nun*, *The Bride of Sherlock Holmes* and *Son of Psycho*. He added a footnote to what was already a rather lengthy dedication, asking why American place names were so popular in film titles: "Why have the British not responded to *Oklahoma!* with *Accrington!*, to *Thunder Bay* with *Wigan Pier*, to *Bad Day at Black Rock* with *Sunday in Scunthorpe*?" I think he answered his own question there.

The actual guide followed the strict alphabetisation style of a reference book, by taking a word at a time rather than the whole title, thus *O Lucky Man* appeared before *Objective Burma*, an approach some found confusing. Each title was rated from no stars to four, followed by the purely factual information such as production studio, year of release and running time. A brief synopsis of each film was supplied, "with brevity and accuracy the keynote," followed by an assessment of the film's merits and its significant cast and crew members. Many entries were further embellished by quotes from the *Monthly Film Bulletin* and *Variety*, as well as critics such as Pauline Kael and Judith Crist. To add a touch of glamour, as he had with the 4th edition of the *Companion*, Halliwell included many stills and posters, usually of fairly obscure titles and not necessarily the most obvious shots from the more famous films. Among the inclusions was a spectacular image from the 1970s disaster movie *Earthquake*, showing the destruction of Los Angeles, to which he added, "The special effects models were great; unfortunately the characters of the story were cardboard." Pithy comments like that would endear him to film fans as much as they would infuriate the critical *intelligentsia*.

Halliwell's brilliant talent for condensing information was evident in the plot synopses. For *Gone with the Wind* he wrote, "An egotistic Southern girl survives the Civil War but finally loses the only man she cares for." Seventeen words to describe a nearly four hour film. Despite such brevity, though, he still managed to give away the ending of many films, as in that very example. *Casablanca*, *The Blue Angel* and *Five Easy Pieces* were similarly afflicted, and Halliwell even quite unforgiveably gave away the final twist of *Don't Look Now*.

Several hundred TV movies were somewhat incongruously included in the 1st edition. Halliwell had delighted in discovering these productions in the late sixties and early seventies, as they were being made under similar conditions to the old Hollywood, eschewing the more controversial aspects of modern cinema releases. The selections included feature length pilots for TV series which the average referrer may have been surprised to find in a film guide, such as *Charlie's Angels* and *The Streets of San Francisco*. After reassessing for the next edition, however, he wisely removed these items to his *Teleguide*.

The reception to this second great encyclopaedic work was predictably mixed. John Russell Taylor wrote in *The Times Educational Supplement*, "Leslie Halliwell returns to the attack with another indispensable work. It is a unique handy guide … in its totality it does something which has not hitherto been done; it brings together a vast amount of information in one convenient volume, and is something no filmgoer or film teacher can afford to be without." The December 1977 issue of *Film Review* was similarly impressed: "One never ceases to marvel at the patience and industry of Leslie Halliwell. Now [he] staggers us again with a gargantuan work of reference … the work involved in such a compilation simply boggles the mind." Philip French knew that it was not quite the pioneering work some had thought it to be, writing, "[Halliwell's] expensive *Film Guide* comes in the wake of various American paperbacks offering capsule comments on thousands of movies at a tenth the price." American magazine *Choice* commented, "The purely factual information is available elsewhere, and of course other respected critics have published their evaluations of many of the films. However, nowhere else has such a wealth of information been condensed into a single volume."

Leonard Maltin was impressed enough to own copies of both the *Companion* and the *Film Guide*. I asked him if he was at all miffed about Halliwell's books bearing a striking resemblance to his own work. "I wasn't miffed," he told me, "because they are two different types of books and there is room out there for all of us. I used them for research. As always, you have to check facts several times because there were errors [in my book]." Anthony Quinton offered insight into the combination of Halliwell's encyclopaedias, writing in *The Times Literary Supplement*, "Used in conjunction with the *Companion* it is magnificent. During dull patches in films one can go from one book to the other, details under the persons and themes enumerated in the older work, sending one to the detail of particular films in the other." He further pointed out an essential difference between the *Companion* and the *Guide*. In the former, "only a minute fraction of the total is Leslie Halliwell's own choice of words ... in the *Film Guide*, however, he is operating under much less ruthless formal constraints." The loosening of those constraints made its presence felt in four major areas of subjectivity. Firstly, and perhaps most controversially of all, in the star ratings…

Four stars, then, indicate a film outstanding in many ways, a milestone in cinema history, remarkable for acting, direction, writing, photography or some other aspect of technique.

Halliwell devoted the largest section of his 'Explanatory Notes' to the rating system he had employed, as he must have known the controversy it would cause. The system itself was borrowed from *Picturegoer*, in which Lionel Collier's film reviews of the 1940s had denoted quality via the presence of asterisks, with four being the highest. "I have tried to give credit for what seemed excellent or innovative at the time," he wrote, almost imploringly, "I have tried to judge each film by its own standards ... and I have re-scrutinised it now to see what historical or artistic interest it retains." The star ratings were designed to indicate the level of *interest* each film was thought to have... in Halliwell's opinion, of course.

So, from the bottom up, a film which gained no stars at all was to be regarded as a "totally routine production or worse." These were "watchable but at least equally missable," and as such encompassed everything from appallingly bad all the way up to *average* – in other words, the overwhelming majority of all the films that had ever been made! Not surprisingly, this was the most populated category – although it was a close run thing – and begged the question: why would anyone go to such enormous lengths to produce a film guide which concluded that the majority of its entries were not worth watching? The answer would be found in an essay at the back of the book.

Next up, one star, which would "draw attention to minor points of merit," such as a good leading performance or a strong piece of writing which, for whatever reason, did not result in a truly memorable film. It could be a "failed giant or a second feature with a few interesting ideas among the dross." In Halliwell's guide, stars were *earned*, not just handed out liberally the way they were in other books. Two stars indicated "a good level of competence and a generally entertaining film." This category represented titles which were clearly above average but still to be recommended with reservations – still not wholly *good*. That came with the addition of the third star, denoting "a very high standard of professional excellence or high historical interest." This category was reserved for everything which was good without any qualifications at all, but which stopped just short of true greatness, of true historical importance.

Four stars would quite predictably prove to be the least populated category. In the 1st edition, which actually encompassed just under 8,000 entries, only 124 films achieved the highest rating. Throughout the seven editions of the *Film Guide* which Halliwell himself compiled, 153 distinct titles would receive four stars. Some did not appear in the earlier editions; some were demoted along the way – with a major cull occurring between the 6th and 7th editions – but only three were ever promoted: *Napoleon*, *The Band Wagon* and *Dumbo*. The final total for the 7th Edition was 130, and the most recent film to get the award was *Bonnie and Clyde*... released in 1967!

To obtain Halliwell's highest rating, a film had to be not only a superb entertainment, but it was additionally required to have something special about its production which set it apart from other good films, such as the montage effects in *The Battleship Potemkin*, or the zither music in *The Third Man*, or the remarkable earthquake sequence in *San Francisco*. If a film was of great historical interest, though, that would be qualification enough, thus *The Jazz Singer* and, in later editions, *The Birth of a Nation*, would receive four stars more for the impact they had on the industry than for any inherent entertainment value they offered. The former is still a reasonable effort but *Birth* is almost unwatchable nowadays due to its unpalatable racial attitudes.

Jim Emerson wrote in the *Chicago Tribune* that as a critic, Halliwell was "something of a grumpy old English fuddy-duddy. [He] saves his stars only for special occasions and rarely has anything good to say about any movie made after 1960." Leslie Kane added in *Reference Services Review*, "One might find cause to argue with Halliwell's 4-star rating system as he is admittedly predisposed to movies of the 1930s and 1940s." The *New Statesman*'s John Coleman wrote in 1979, "The compiler's rating system is as infuriating as ever."

No matter how strenuously Halliwell maintained his stance that the ratings denoted historical interest, the representation of four-star titles across the decades quite clearly demonstrated a prejudice against the later years. In the 7th edition, only 20 films from the fifties and sixties *combined* received top marks, compared with 50 in the forties alone, and another 48 in the thirties. However, the four-star films were not simply a list of his own personal favourites, a fact verified by his 1982 book *Halliwell's Hundred*, in which he selected all his most cherished titles and many of the four-star films from the *Film Guide* do not appear. As the introduction stated, he admired the likes of Eisenstein and Kurosawa without loving them.

But those stars, or the lack of them, would confuse and infuriate many readers. Indeed, so rare was the top mark that Charles Champlin, a long-time admirer of Halliwell's work, wrote in his review for the *Los Angeles Times*, "He rates films from no asterisks to *three*" (emphasis mine).

[Italics] *denote a contribution of a particularly high standard. Arguments are expected and additions welcomed.*

In *The Filmgoer's Companion*, Halliwell had used italics to highlight the most significant films in an actor's career, a policy which had provoked some quizzical responses from readers. In the *Film Guide*, he again employed italics, although this time they were bestowed upon individuals, so directors, writers and actors could all be so honoured if their work was considered worthy enough. This additional aspect of subjectivity was another that came to fascinate and infuriate the referrer. For the classic 1941 John Huston-directed version of *The Maltese Falcon*, every member of the cast and crew listed received italics... except one: Gladys George. She played the widow of Humphrey Bogart's partner and performed capably enough. Any other compiler might have just given everyone italics simply to honour a great movie, but not Halliwell.

Several performances which the Academy considered worthy of an Oscar failed to impress him. Marlon Brando was so honoured for *The Godfather* but went unrecognised by the *Film Guide*'s author, who elsewhere wrote that Brando was "so facially wired that he can scarcely talk." Robert De Niro's performance in *Raging Bull* was similarly commended by the Academy, but he too remained staunchly un-italicised in the *Guide*. John Russell Taylor called Halliwell the "master of the italic" in *The Times Educational Supplement*, going on to say, "We are often left speculating as to why an obscure character player should be signalled in one place and an important director not in another."

Halliwell sometimes strayed out of his remit by italicising the name of the author or playwright on whose work a film was based. Thus, Margaret Mitchell received italics for writing *Gone with the Wind* and Arthur Miller was similarly commended for *Death of a Salesman*. Since he had almost always seen the play a film was based upon, or read the book, it would seem he was just showing off about how cultured he was. Producers were largely overlooked in this area, probably because their performances were more difficult to assess directly from what was on the screen. In the cases where Halliwell did give a producer italics, it was likely due to specialist knowledge about the making of the picture in question, such as Michael Todd's contribution to *Around the World in Eighty Days* and Hal B. Wallis's for *Casablanca*. As a result, the Gene Kelly musical *An American in Paris* was the only film in which every contributor listed, including producer Arthur Freed, was awarded italics.

I think I may claim to have as reasonable a set of hang-ups as anyone now writing about films, except that I tend to hark back towards the old rather than the new, which is not a bad qualification for the job in hand.

Halliwell claimed in the 1st edition that his assessments were "intended as an amalgam of the general view." In a 1987 interview he further insisted that he tried to give as balanced an opinion as possible, making a concerted effort to read all the reviews of more recent releases and to take a consensus of opinions. In some cases he had not actually *seen* the films in question. On a trip to Australia to publicise the 3rd edition, he admitted to a Perth reporter, "I suppose I've seen about two-thirds of the entries in the book." To another Australian newspaper he added, "Perhaps in the next edition I should indicate whether I have seen a work or not."

All the same, the assessments in *Halliwell's Film Guide* would provide movie fans with their best glimpse into the mindset of its creator. He added the comment, "It will be seen that my judgements are fairly harsh, but I hope they are consistent." His hope was fulfilled almost completely: whether the reader agreed with him or not, the consistency of the opinions expressed throughout the *Guide* was one of its most magnificent qualities. Furthermore, they were the ultimate expression of the 'Halliwell touch', that gift for terse appraisal which had begun in his notebooks as a youngster, inspired once again by Lionel Collier, and developed through his experiences at *Varsity* and in *The Filmgoer's Companion.* Some of them are little gems of succinctness, others are pearls of wisdom. Whether it was the totally routine second features, which warranted no more than a three or four word dismissal, or the spectacularly bad which demanded a more rigorous going over, it was these assessments that gave the *Guide* its distinctive charm.

For the most routine of productions one generally finds the briefest reviews. Thus, *The Big City* rated as "Minor star melodrama" and *The Case of the Curious Bride* as "Smoothish mystery." Other appraisals of standard fare – in their entirety – were "Competent remake," "Dullish star vehicle," "Humdrum flagwaver," "Tolerable second feature," "Watchable potboiler" and "Routine escapist hokum." Occasionally, bad movies were also dealt with concisely. Indeed, the shortest review ever appeared in the 1st edition for a TV movie called *All My Darling Daughters' Anniversary*, which was assessed in one word, "Dim." The Sean Connery film *Zardoz* prompted, "Pompous, boring fantasy for the so-called intelligentsia," and *The Fall of the House of Usher* rated, "Dismally inept low-budgeter, a pain to sit through." Trendy 1966 drama *The Idol* prompted, "Stupefyingly boring generation-gap sex drama" and Sam Peckinpah's *Convoy* provoked, "A virtually plotless anthology of wanton destruction. Too noisy to sleep through."

For the truly insulting, however, a more sophisticated put-down was required. Disaster movie sequel *Beyond the Poseidon Adventure* prompted, "Dreary alternative ending ... with cardboard character studies, cut-price action, and tenth-rate technicalities." Cult sixties movie *Girl on a Motorcycle* was "an incredibly plotless and ill-conceived piece of sub-porn claptrap, existing only as a long series of colour supplement photographs." *No Orchids for Miss Blandish* was described as an "hilariously awful gangster movie from a bestselling shocker. Everyone concerned is all at sea, and the result is one of the worst films ever made." Mitchell Leisen's 1955 effort *Bedevilled* was trounced, "Absurd high-flown bosh, unsuitably CinemaScoped in ugly colour, and surprisingly badly handled by old professionals."

Ken Russell was on the end of many a diatribe. *The Music Lovers* was declared an "absurd fantasia ... up to a point hysterically (and unintentionally) funny, then rather sickening." *Crimes of Passion* was "an hysterically overheated stew of sex and murder; one to walk away from," whereas *Lisztomania* was "the most excessive and obscene of all the director's controversial works." Halliwell's most withering criticism of Russell's output, though, was reserved for *The Devils*, which he felt was his "most outrageously sick film to date, campy, idiosyncratic and in howling bad taste from beginning to end ... a pointless pantomime for misogynists."

Waggish humour occasionally crept in, with *Oliver's Story* rating, "Love means never having to watch this trendy rubbish." For the 1979 horror *Damien: Omen II* he wrote simply, "Once was enough," and of the economically viable but artistically bereft *Carry On* series, Halliwell noted that most of them "were written (or recollected) by Talbot Rothwell." Elsewhere, he expounded his philosophy on films he loved to hate, "I believe that a film judged to be among the worst ever made should have a long way to fall. That is, it should have started with a reasonable budget, big stars and the best of intentions." Into this category fell such as *The Story of Mankind*: "Hilarious charade, one of the worst films ever made, but full of surprises, bad performances and a wide range of stock shots." Perhaps the turkey of all time, however, was the 1967 version of the James Bond story *Casino Royale*, which prompted, "Woeful all-star kaleidoscope; a way-out spoof which generates far fewer laughs than the original. One of the most shameless wastes of time and talent in screen history."

The good reviews were in there, though, and the affection Halliwell displayed for the medium at its very best made finding them well worth the effort. In general, his view on the best films was, "I lean to the theory that great films are great not because they are planned that way, but because of a happy combination of circumstances which strikes the public imagination and makes them both unique and beyond criticism." Into this category fell, predictably enough, *Lost Horizon*, which rated, "A supreme example of Hollywood moonshine, with perfect casting, direction and music." *The Grapes of Wrath* "could scarcely be improved upon ... a poem of a film." *Trouble in Paradise* was declared "a masterpiece of light comedy, with sparkling dialogue, innuendo, great performances and masterly cinematic narrative." *Brief Encounter* was described as "an outstanding example of good middle-class cinema turned by sheer professional craft into a masterpiece." *The Lady Vanishes* prompted, "Brilliantly funny, meticulously detailed entertainment," and *The Bride of Frankenstein* was "the screen's sophisticated masterpiece of black comedy ... every scene has its own delights." The assessment for his favourite film of all, *Citizen Kane*, summed up Halliwell's whole outlook on the movies: "Almost every shot and every line is utterly absorbing both as entertainment and as craft."

Anthony Quinton, in *The Times Literary Supplement*, called the *Film Guide*'s assessments "the most intoxicatingly Halliwellian part of the book." Philip French, not surprisingly, was less impressed, writing in the *New Statesman* that Halliwell had "unwisely decided to advance into the area of criticism and revaluation for which his talents are ill-suited." He went on to say, "There is in the book scarcely a single arresting opinion ... one never wants to argue with his views – they're so dull and conventional in both content and expression." Halliwell had ridden roughshod over the slack narration and flat handling of *Jaws*, which had only recently been overtaken as the most successful film ever made, so how could his comments possibly have been conventional? Quite the opposite, his refusal to adapt to the new style of movies brought about by the permissiveness of the sixties and seventies had put him in a distinct minority. French used as an example *Man of the West*, directed in 1958 by Anthony Mann, which he called "one of the best westerns ever made," but which Halliwell dismissed as, "Talkative, set-bound, cliché-ridden star western with minor compensations." French asked how Halliwell's appraisal compared to Andrew Sarris's review of the same film: "Mann's visual style is the American style which most closely resembles that of Antonioni in the liberal progression through landscape from the vegetable to the mineral world..." No comment necessary.

Another reviewer observed that Halliwell's opinions were becoming "increasingly weary and blimpish," to which he responded with the comment, "I feel myself to be neither, but I remain suspicious of the films of the last fifteen years or so, which have followed fashion to the exclusion of permanent value." John Nangle summed it up beautifully in *Films in Review*, writing of the 5th edition:

> [Halliwell's] crusty opinions and testy outspokenness have surely at one time or another enraged the many film buffs who consider his less-than-elegant put-downs of their favourite stars or films the doddering mutterings of an ancient Anglophile. That is until they re-see the so-called classic he is disparaging, or reconsider the alleged superstar they had never really viewed without a tint of Hollywood hype blinding their gaze.
>
> [Halliwell is] a man who truly treasures film, knows it thoroughly and certainly isn't afraid to offend, no matter how outrageous his acerbic, spleenish verbal cannonballs. At times, these abbreviated lines may seem too cursory a disposal of a debatable entry. Yet, my feeling is that Halliwell is so clever a writer and educated so deeply in his field that he teaches us a fuller appreciation of the values of movies by his constant references to earlier films and witty sense of movie excess and pretence.

It was possible to trace Halliwell's disillusionment with the cinema through the *Film Guide*'s assessments, especially with regard to the 1970s. Censorship had been almost completely abandoned, ushering in the era of sex, violence and bad language which would dominate the industry from then on – turning many people away and virtually ending the traditional family trip to the pictures. As previously examined, it additionally caused a great deal of trouble for TV buyers and schedulers. *The Devils*, *Straw Dogs* and *A Clockwork Orange* were examples of this post-permissive excess, and recognised as such by the *Film Guide*'s author, but *The Exorcist* was by far the most successful of the sensationalist movies of the early seventies. Halliwell found it to be a "spectacularly ludicrous mishmash with uncomfortable attention to physical detail and no talent for narrative or verisimilitude." Liliana Cavani's *The Night Porter*, released in the same year, 1973, was declared, "A downright deplorable film, with no cinematic skill or grace to excuse it; the visuals are as loathsome as the sound is indecipherable, and the sheer pointlessness of it is insulting."

For films which were an offence to his intelligence rather than his sensibilities, look for Robert Altman's self indulgent updating of *The Long Goodbye*, which prompted, "Ugly, boring travesty of a well-respected detective novel." Peter Bogdanovich attempted to recreate the style of an Astaire/Rogers musical with *At Long Last Love*, but "unfortunately true professionalism is lacking and the wrong kind of talent is used. The result is awful to contemplate." Bogdanovich was, like so many new directors of the day, steeped in the Golden Age, and made further attempts to capture its style with *What's Up, Doc?* and *Nickelodeon*. Martin Scorsese, another lifelong devotee of the old Hollywood, attempted his own tribute with *New York, New York*, which was "hampered by gross overlength, unattractive characters and a pessimistic plot." Mel Brooks doffed his cap with *Young Frankenstein*, an affectionate pastiche of a genre close to Halliwell's heart, and he commended it for at least being a decent effort, "The gleamingly reminiscent photography is the best of it, the script being far from consistently funny, but there are splendid moments." John Carpenter, one of the finest directors to emerge during the decade, was another who drew on influences from the old days and gained Halliwell's grudging respect for doing so. His 1976 film *Assault on Precinct 13* rated, "Violent but basically efficient and old-fashioned programmer which shows that not all the expertise of the forties in this then-familiar field has been lost."

However, with budgets sky rocketing, the 1970s was a decade

chiefly characterised by wasteful excesses such as the expensively cast *Lucky Lady*: "Whatever can be done wrong with such a story has been done ... none of it holds the interest for a single moment." *The Last Tycoon* depicted a fictional Golden Age mogul based on Irving Thalberg, but the film was an "astonishingly inept and boring big budget all-star melodrama [which] bogs down in interminable dialogue scenes, leaving its famous cast all at sea." The making of *Apocalypse Now* has long since passed into legend and the end result was considered to be a "pretentious war movie made even more hollow-sounding by the incomprehensible performance of Brando as the mad martinet. Some vivid scenes along the way... but these hardly atone for the director's delusion that prodigal expenditure of time and money will result in great art."

Box office successes were few and offered no guarantee of a rave, as the likes of *Superman* attested, for which Halliwell pointed out in a footnote, "Reprehensible records were set by Brando getting three million dollars for a ten-minute performance ... and by the incredible 7½ minute credit roll at the end." The hugely successful Bond movie *The Spy Who Loved Me* was dismissed as a "witless spy extravaganza," but the biggest of them all, *Star Wars*, was praised – although not without qualification – "Some disappointment may be felt with the actual experience of watching it ... but it's certainly good harmless fun, put together with style and imagination."

The best of the 1970s was to be found in the likes of *M*A*S*H*, *The Godfather*, *Cabaret*, *Don't Look Now*, *The French Connection* and *The Towering Inferno*. But possibly Halliwell's most favourable review for any film released during the decade was for the almost forgotten Robert Redford comedy heist thriller, *The Hot Rock*, from the pen of screenwriting legend William Goldman. He found it to be an "enjoyable variation on the caper theme, with relaxed comic performances and highly skilled technical back-up. It's refreshing to come across a film which hits its targets so splendidly." All of these creditable efforts were awarded three stars – four, it would seem, was simply no longer possible.

Where is the good humour in Jaws? *Where is the heart in* The Exorcist? *These are rides on fairground ghost trains: one pays for the thrill, but one comes out more depressed than uplifted.*

If the star ratings, the italics and the assessments had not yet convinced the referrer of Halliwell's cinema philosophy, then the essay tucked away at the back of the book would ram home the message once and for all. 'The Decline and Fall of the Movie' was his lament to the Golden Age, the culmination of his journey from film-obsessed childhood to disillusioned middle age. It was further, by his own admission, "a deliberate hatchet job by a disappointed fan who has turned devil's advocate." The essay was written in 1977 and appeared in all seven editions of the *Film Guide* edited by Halliwell himself, with only a few minor changes made along the way. It was his attempt to "shed light on a confused and unhappy segment of cinema history," i.e. the 1970s, but many of the points raised are still valid today. At the very least it served as an historical account of the journey the American film industry had taken from the studio system of the 1930s and 40s, through the anti-television experiments of the 50s; on to the permissive 60s and finally to the maverick (or megalomaniac) director cult of the 70s.

He began with an introduction to justify his effort, stating, "I have spent more than forty years seeing, talking about and writing about films, so my affection for the medium in its Golden Age can hardly be doubted." He pointed out that even back then the worthwhile movies were few and far between, and that most of what was produced was "ghastly rubbish." He quoted Jonathan Swift, who wrote, "I hate and detest that animal called man, although I heartily love John, Peter, Thomas and so forth." And that, in a nutshell, was the *raison d'être* of *Halliwell's Film Guide*. The book encapsulated its author's 'Johns', 'Peters' and 'Thomases' – the tips of the icebergs, the cream of the crop – those films which justified his spending half a lifetime at the cinema, and the other half writing about it.

The essay proper began with two examples of the arrogance of modern directors, specifically the fact that neither Stanley Kubrick nor Sam Peckinpah had bothered to explain the titles of *A Clockwork Orange* and *Straw Dogs* respectively. Halliwell commented that the new film-makers were "concerned only to over-spend enormous budgets while putting across some garbled self-satisfying message." He blamed "long-haired publications" such as *Sight & Sound* for promoting the idea of the director as *auteur*, and pointed up the lack of humour in the modern generation and their "absurd pretensions."

He then proceeded to trace the seeds of this purported decline as being firmly sown by the post-war uncertainty over television and the film industry's various attempts to fight it. One result was the increase in location photography, which made films more realistic but removed the magic, "for the real Paris was by no means so romantic and mysterious as Paramount's back-lot." Other innovations such as 3-D and CinemaScope – which he had personally experienced at the Rex – were duly scrutinised, as was the breakdown of the studio system. He conceded that censorship had been absurdly tight but complained that the virtual abandonment of it had merely ushered in the era of exploitation, "led by maverick Ken Russells rather than conscientious Irving Thalbergs." The critics did not help, by being so determined to find deeper meanings in everything and to elevate the medium to the level of serious art. "The new cinema journalism simply encouraged the worst motives of the new breed of film-maker," he railed, "who came to know that whatever idiocy he perpetrated would be staunchly defended … and psychoanalysed."

Richard J. Kelly, writing in *American Reference Books Annual*, thought 'The Decline and Fall of the Movie' was "an embarrassingly wrong-headed essay … which decries every development since the 1930s and 1940s, from colour to shooting on location. Although admittedly written with devil's advocate slant, the essay accomplishes nothing except to call the reader's attention to some of the biases and enthusiasms at work in both the *Companion* and the present volume." Charles Champlin in the *Los Angeles Times* called it "an angry epitaph" but admitted that Halliwell's "indictment will be seconded by many who have written off movies totally (as he hasn't) and there is truth in it." Champlin knew that television – or at least Hollywood's reaction to it – had ended the Golden Age, and referred to the old films as "a treasury of artefacts to be fetched out and wondered over, like Tut's accoutrements, and enshrined in the pages of Halliwell's own sad and loving book."

The essay further highlighted the rising costs of cinemagoing and the subsequent fall in attendance. Denis Forman, the man responsible for bringing Halliwell to Granada, wrote in 1982, "The cinema of Hollywood and the Odeon has gone. In 1981 admissions were one-tenth of the 1957 figures, 90 million against 955 million." The fall in attendance following the war had inevitably led to many closures, which – according to John Spraos in his book *The Decline of the*

Cinema – did not make people more likely to seek out entertainment further afield: instead, apathy simply kept them at home. After all, the cinemas themselves were nowhere near as inviting as in the thirties, when they had provided so much comfort and warmth unattainable elsewhere. Many of the surviving picture houses had fallen into disrepair or had suffered that most unfortunate of cinema indignities: division into separate screens. Indeed, the Bolton Odeon was 'tripled' in 1972, with the stalls area becoming two separate screens, and the Lido was re-branded 'Studio 1&2' after converting its café into another screen and incorporating a disco in 1973. Halliwell's point, though, was that the *type* of movies then being made was another contributing factor to the cinema's downfall. "If my thesis were not largely true," he protested, "how would one explain the enormous popularity of old movies on television, or the recent deluge of books about them?" The Christmas period of 1976 had seen over sixty films broadcast but the most "discussed and appreciated" were apparently *White Heat*, *A Night at the Opera* and *Yankee Doodle Dandy*. Peter Biskind, in *Easy Riders, Raging Bulls*, celebrates the seventies as being the great decade for maverick film-makers. In reality, a few talented baby boomers fresh out of film school, each with one or maybe two successes behind him, were given carte blanche to overspend wildly on self indulgent projects, very few of which ever justified their enormous costs, in terms of either profit or artistry.

Philip French typically pulled no punches about Halliwell's essay, though: "He sounds more like a choleric colonel writing to the *Telegraph*. He sets about the corrupters of the cinema in a style that combines the worst of both Whitehouse and Milhous. It is sad to see someone so confused by his anger and so angered by his confusion." I contacted Mr. French and put that last quote to him, asking if his opinions about the 'Decline' essay – or that particular period of the cinema – had changed at all. He responded:

> I stand by everything I said about Halliwell's 'The Decline and Fall of the Movie' in the passage you quote. Like the 1960s for world cinema, the 1970s was a remarkable decade for the revival of American cinema. Many of us have had doubts about the triumphalism that resulted from aspects of the 1970s, e.g. the role of blockbusters, new forms of distribution and the subsequent domination of US commercial cinema – but Halliwell did little to

encourage a taste for movies in foreign languages, or from the new cinema, in his books or through his TV programming.

With regards to Halliwell's concentration being primarily focused on English language films, encyclopaedist David Quinlan explained, "The author was writing for an audience and obviously considered the bulk of his readers would not be interested in less well known foreign films." Shaun Usher, a film critic for the *Daily Mail*, also responded to me on this particular point:

> The criticism of Halliwell's guide misses the point. As a lifelong picturegoer, I'm eccentric enough to use at least half a dozen guides [and] Halliwell's is right for its purpose and market ... if one wants the straight skinny on 'films with writing underneath' then there are specialist publications dealing with that field.
>
> [The opinion] springs from some reviewers' anxiety to demonstrate that they're intellectuals who know better. In all arts fields, anything suiting the majority audience, let alone making the creators money, is A Bad Thing. The consolation is that time continues to be the decisive judge: most of what nose-in-air critics rave about is forgotten within a year or two; good stuff survives on its merits.

Part of the appeal back in the Golden Age had been the lavish, escapist entertainments which took people out of themselves and gave them a sense of wonder. But in the 1970s the studios were no longer interested in whimsical fantasies: everything had to be gritty and realistic, with dishevelled characters and downbeat locations. The cheerful optimism of the likes of Fred Astaire and Cary Grant and Claudette Colbert was long gone – the audience no longer needed to use its imagination, and it was left without heroes to look up to. The bad language and the violence kept many people away but the box office successes of *The French Connection* and *The Godfather* amply demonstrated that people *would* turn out in large numbers if there was something worth watching. However, *Star Wars* – the most successful of them all – proved beyond question that the audience still preferred fantasy to reality.

As if to prove this very point, at the beginning of the 1980s a film was released which would change the movie business forever. United

Artists, impressed by the success of *The Deer Hunter* in 1978, gave director Michael Cimino a free hand to make a lengthy, downbeat western called *Heaven's Gate*, a film so spectacularly mis-timed that it crippled the studio. By then, what American writers called the juvenilisation of the cinema was in full swing, ushered in by the enormous box office successes of *Jaws* and *Star Wars*, and all the imitations they inspired. Halliwell wrote of *Heaven's Gate* that it hopefully marked "the last time a whiz kid with one success behind him is given a blank cheque to indulge in self-abuse."

In later editions of the *Guide*, he added two postscripts to the 'Decline' essay, mostly re-affirming his original sentiments. His final word on the subject was, "Commercially, as a mass-entertainment, the cinema still needs a saviour." With hindsight it could be argued that the saviour had already arrived. Halliwell was yearning for the days when *adults* went to the cinema in droves, to be entertained by sophisticated comedies and intelligent adventures, but the films of Lucas and Spielberg brought in a whole new cinema audience. From the eighties onwards it was teenagers who were making up the largest demographic. Richard Sylbert, once head of production at Paramount, summed it up, "The whole culture became adolescent – and the grosses improved enormously." The studios and the exhibitors quickly cottoned on to the fact that the audience had changed, and subsequently the films and indeed the cinemas themselves needed to change along with them. Audiences of the 1980s would be tempted in by plush new multiplexes, incorporating bars, restaurants and bowling alleys, and films which adhered to Alan Alda's three basic rules of the movies: "Defy authority, destroy property... and take people's clothes off."

With the gritty realism of the previous decade gone, the 1980s would be characterised by slick, adolescent action movies such as *Top Gun*, which Halliwell assessed as "a feast of hardware and noisy music; not much story," and *Rambo: First Blood Part II* – "Absurdly overwrought comic strip action which shamefully caught the mood of America at the time." Slasher movies were another popular variety, such as *Friday the Thirteenth: The Final Chapter* – "The awful mixture as before: would that the title meant what it says" – and *Creepshow 2* – "Cheapjack sequel, of no interest whatsoever." The decade saw the birth of a new genre, the 'teen movie', as represented by *The Breakfast Club*, which Halliwell called an "abysmal apologia for loutish teenage behaviour." Comedies in general were dumbed down to hitherto undreamed-of depths. Far from the inspired lunacy of Laurel & Hardy or the Marx Brothers, eighties audiences had to contend with the likes of *Police Academy* – "Appallingly unfunny" – and *Spies Like Us* – "Inept attempts at humour fall flat throughout this dreary venture" – and *Porky's* – "Ghastly teenage goings-on taking cinema bad taste about as far as it will get."

But, there were once again some notable exceptions: the Chevy Chase vehicle *Fletch* sparked Halliwell's interest, as he commented, "A lightness of touch unusual for the eighties makes this comedy mystery more welcome than most." *An American Werewolf in London* and *Diner* both received praise for being worthy efforts, and there were even a few triumphs like *Gandhi*, *Chariots of Fire*, *The Killing Fields* and *Back to the Future*. Woody Allen's *Hannah and her Sisters* was deemed to be a "brilliantly assembled and thoroughly enjoyable mélange of fine acting and New Yorkish one-liners" – and the Harrison Ford thriller *Witness* prompted, "This is one of those lucky movies which works out well on all counts and shows that there are still craftsmen lurking in Hollywood."

However, Halliwell would never fall in love with the newer movies the way he had with the older ones. He beautifully summed up his stance in the introduction to *Halliwell's Hundred*, a collection of essays on his favourite films:

Of today's crop I have soon had my fill. Most of them are obscurely told; they tell me things I don't wish to know, in language I find offensive; and they concern characters whom I would willingly cross the road to avoid. Cheap colour makes them unattractive to look at, and all the old studio crafts, so laboriously learned over a quarter of a century, appear to have been jettisoned in favour of obscenely large budgets, which allow the film-maker to wander restlessly around the world crashing real aeroplanes and giving a distorted view of real locations, instead of setting his own and the audience's imaginations to work.

Halliwell's Film Guide progressed through many changes over the years, eventually comprising some 16,000 entries in its 7th edition, the last compiled by Halliwell himself. The major silent and foreign language films had indeed found their way in, along with all those routine second features which "no one in his right mind would wish to remember." When asked how he went about updating the book, Halliwell replied, "One keeps up to date with magazines like *Variety* and the *Film Bulletin* and *Screenworld*, and books of that sort which come out every week or year and that information goes in ... but one reads things and makes notes." In a talk at the Edinburgh Book Festival in 1983, he remarked, "The *Film Guide* has been oddly enough more successful than *The Filmgoer's Companion*. That's probably because the *Companion* has had rivals which have grown up over the years – there's a very good one by a man called Ephraim Katz, which is why we're trying to change the aspect of ours next year. Whereas the *Film Guide* hasn't really got any rivals. No doubt one will turn up."

Notable additions to the *Guide* included another essay, 'A Word on Shape', which examined the effects wide screens had on the showing of films at the cinema and on television – by then a favourite whinge. His exasperation at the widescreen conversion of *Gone with the Wind* was a particular delight. Having cut off the top and bottom of the image, the distributors then attempted to sell a pan-and-scan version of the remainder to television. Halliwell called this "the ultimate buffoonery"!

In the 6th edition, published in 1987, he lamented the closing of the Odeon cinema in Bolton, which he had watched rise brick by brick back in the 1930s. That left at the time only one working cinema in the town, the Lido, then called the Cannon. A most welcome inclusion in the 5th edition was the Top Tens page, which showed the results of the British Film Institute's critical polls as well as including Halliwell's own ten favourite films. *Citizen Kane* was number one in his list, with other predictable inclusions being *Lost Horizon*, *The Bride of Frankenstein* and *Trouble in Paradise*.

The 5th edition's flyleaf further displayed a head and shoulders picture of its author, in a shirt and tie, and with large spectacles and a full beard covering that famous chin. This was the classic 1980s image of him which appeared in many articles and books, and the one with which readers became most familiar. The barest hint of a smile gave him the appearance of a wise old uncle seated in his favourite armchair, as if about to lean back and explain to you exactly why it was that all of your favourite films were in fact rubbish.

In an age long before the internet, *Halliwell's Film Guide* and *The Filmgoer's Companion* provided cinema fans and journalists of the time with their only handy sources of information about the movies, and the men and women who made them. The *Film Guide* itself was suffused with the personality – and prejudices – of its creator, and was for seven editions not only a vast mine of information, but also a remarkably consistent collection of opinions, intelligent observations and affection for a bygone age.

Philip French did not see it way, however, saying of Halliwell:

> I thought him crudely opinionated, an intelligent anti-intellectual who concealed his dislike of the world of ideas by talking about 'pseudo-intellectuals' and 'eggheads'. It seemed to me he made his mind up too easily, had banished doubt, didn't engage in self-questioning, and was too much the saloon-bar thinker, committed to conventional opinion on all matters. From the point of view of facts (credits, dates etc.) his books were valuable and useful, but his mind was too closely reined in.

Others were more impressed by the work he had put in, whether they agreed with his opinions or not. David Bartholomew wrote in *Library Journal Book Review*, "The redoubtable Halliwell has compiled an eminently valuable work, an immense undertaking. In form and function there is no other comparable source." Trade magazine *Variety* trumpeted the 6th edition thus, "A host of similar film guides have sprung up in recent years, nearly all with something to offer, but Halliwell's is still the one to beat." Anthony Quinton in *The Times Literary Supplement* observed, "Immersed in the enjoyment of these fine books, one should look up for a moment to admire the quite astonishing combination of industry and authority in one man which has brought them into existence." One should indeed.

> *When I pick it up, with something of an effort, I can scarcely believe that I typed every word with my two over-worked and untrained index fingers. But I did.*

Readers of *Halliwell's Film Guide*, especially those of a younger generation, may have gained the impression that its author was an old curmudgeon, a fuddy-duddy out of step with modern attitudes and developments. The picture on the flyleaf did not help as it gave him the air of an old headmaster pouring scorn on anything new. But that image was in complete contrast to his actual nature: the ebullient, sometimes boisterous individual with seemingly boundless enthusiasm for his favourite subject. Besides, rather than railing against the cinema for how bad it had become, Halliwell wanted much more to celebrate it for how good it *could* be. At the beginning of the eighties, those like him who remembered the Golden Age first hand were all comfortably middle-aged, whether it was the parents sitting at home with the 'zapper' in their hand or the journalists writing about films in newspapers and magazines. It was from them that the enormous popularity of old movies was being driven: people were reliving their childhood memories.

There was a demand and Halliwell wanted to tap into it. He knew that ITV had been sitting on an enormous film archive for fifteen years, as he had played a significant part in its accumulation. He was the only person who not only knew exactly what they had but who also knew its value. At the Rex in Cambridge he had learned how to package films in double-bills to bring in full houses, but his opportunities to compile seasons for ITV were limited as the network desired high ratings: it did not have 'a BBC2' to cater for more specialist interests.

Halliwell longed for the chance to show his 'golden oldies' to an appreciative audience one last time, before those who remembered them so fondly were gone forever and the era confined to the history books…

In 1982 he would get his chance…

9

A Store of Riches

- Channel 4 and the return to Shangri-La, 1981-86 -

In the early 1980s, the American production companies were growing increasingly frustrated with the market situation in the UK. The gentlemen's agreement between the BBC and ITV that neither would attempt to poach each other's shows was in direct contrast to other countries, where the availability of a new season would trigger a bidding war between networks. The studios were "constantly irritated" by having to "sell their wares in a one-price deal to Leslie Halliwell and the purchasing committee," when fifteen separate companies *plus* the BBC could otherwise have been bidding. Kevin O'Sullivan, the president of US production company Lorimar, remarked, "ITV and the BBC don't compete, they collude to keep prices down … Canada, with half the population of the UK pays two times the price per hour." Lorimar produced *Dallas*, one of the biggest shows of the time, and which had been snapped up by the BBC after being turned down by Halliwell and Paul Fox when the pilot was shown to them in 1978. Sir Paul recalled:

> I remember the chap who tried to sell us *Dallas*, English chap called Colin Campbell And, it was at the end of the week of the screenings and we'd bought quite a bit of stuff. I'm not saying we'd exhausted our budget but we'd bought enough. And then Colin showed us *Dallas* and he said, "Gunnar's very keen." That was always the sales pitch – *Gunnar's very keen* – and they'd hope that you'd pay more.

The show was distributed in the UK by Worldvision Enterprises, whose frustration with the lack of competition led them to begin a dispute which would last for the next four years... and cost *three* men their jobs.

For the 1981/82 season of *Dallas*, Worldvision decided to up the asking price from $35,000 to $40,000 per episode, and when the purchasing teams from the UK were in Hollywood for their regular buying trip, the Americans played their hand. Rugheimer and the BBC stoutly refused to pay the new price, citing an agreement they had previously made with Colin Campbell, one of the founders of Worldvision, that the price would remain the same. The Americans then approached Halliwell with the oh-so-hypothetical question, "*Would* you be interested in picking up the show *if* the BBC don't come up with a better offer?" Despite Halliwell's claims that shows like *Dallas* were too difficult for ITV to schedule, he was not about to throw away ten million prime-time viewers a week, and so replied that he would have to think about it. That was good enough for Worldvision, who promptly announced that the show would go to the highest bidder.

Rugheimer was incensed when he heard that the Americans were reneging on their agreement and the BBC immediately filed a lawsuit against them. Halliwell and Paul Fox both stated publicly that they had made no firm offer – although *The Sunday Times* later claimed to be in possession of "confidential documents" indicating that the purchasing committee *had* discussed an attempt to poach the show from the BBC. Halliwell recalled, "We did not try to steal *Dallas* ... Worldvision tried very hard to make us an offer and the BBC was fully aware of the situation." Some welcomed the confrontation. Elkan Allan wrote an article in *The Times* calling for an "eyeball-to-eyeball" battle, asking, "What is the point of having a theoretically competitive television set-up if they don't compete?"

Worldvision stood their ground but after the legal dust had settled the BBC retained the show at the original price... and Colin Campbell was fired. The *Dallas* fuss was cited as a "contributing factor" to his dismissal, even though Worldvision denied the agreement he was supposed to have made had ever existed. The following year they again tried to increase the price, this time prompting Rugheimer to denigrate the show in the press and claim that the BBC was ready to drop it anyway.

Concurrently to all of this, the independent companies Halliwell represented were making noises about being given responsibility for buying shows on their own, rather than having to accept the decisions of the Purchase Group. Kevin Goldstein-Jackson, the hotshot chief executive of new independent company Television South West, was particularly outspoken in his encouragement of the regional separation of buying. Pictured in *Broadcast* magazine with collar-length hair, an open shirt and large spectacles, Goldstein-Jackson opined that the independents should be channels in their own right rather than having to kowtow to the big five. With this in mind he approached Halliwell at MIP, in the Riviera sunshine, and asked him if the regionals could be allowed to make a unilateral bid for *Dallas* now that the BBC were not interested, claiming that five other companies were willing to come in with him (although none of the *big* five). It is almost certain that Halliwell gave him one of those famous 'glances of expansive disdain', before going on to explain that the show had been running for too many seasons and that they did not want to be seen to be picking up the BBC's leftovers. Halliwell was overheard relating this incident to the other members of his team during one of those champagne cocktail-sipping 'court sessions' – to a response of "uncharacteristically uncharitable remarks" from his rapt subjects. Goldstein-Jackson was far from appeased and stated publicly that he thought the real reason behind Halliwell's reluctance to bid was that he did not want to upset the gentlemen's agreement, which was the networks' only way of keeping prices down.

With Worldvision digging their heels in, Lorimar made a move of which J. R. Ewing himself would have been proud. They went behind their own distributors' backs and negotiated a secret deal with the BBC directly. Rugheimer was cock-a-hoop, and announced his victory to the press, prompting Worldvision to sue both the BBC *and* Lorimar. An out of court settlement was reached in which the Corporation once again retained the show at the original price, but with *Lorimar* having to make up the shortfall of $5,000 per episode to Worldvision. So the producers of the show ended up paying their own distributors the price increase!

As if things could not get any more bizarre, in 1985 Brian Cowgill of Thames stepped in. He had ruffled some feathers a few years before with that rogue bid for *The Sound of Music*, and had in addition been present on the 1981 Hollywood trip where the possible 'theft' of *Dallas* had been discussed. He was obviously frustrated by the subsequent failures of ITV to secure the show and – perhaps inspired by Goldstein-Jackson's posturing – he and his programme controller Muir Sutherland made another secret deal for *Dallas*, this time behind both the BBC's *and* ITV's backs. Sir Paul Fox again:

> Brian Cowgill leaves the BBC and goes to Thames Television, and Brian – tough Lancastrian – said, "We're going to need some hits over here," and firstly he bought Morecambe and Wise. Paid a fortune, way over what the BBC were paying. And the second thing Brian said was, "We must get *Dallas*." Now ITV bought American television series as an organisation, as a consortium, rather than each company being allowed to. Brian wasn't having that – he said "I'm going to get it." The chap who was in charge of Worldvision said, "OK, I'll sell it to Thames." Brian thought he had a wonderful coup and thought the network would say 'you are our saviour.'

Cowgill was in line for the job of ITV chairman at the time but his audacious plan backfired spectacularly. When the deal became public the Purchase Group were furious; the IBA stepped in and both Cowgill and Sutherland lost their jobs. The arguments raged on for the rest of the year until ITV was eventually forced to sell the show back to the BBC, in one of the most embarrassing 'episodes' in British TV history. A full analysis of the story and the motives of those involved would make a pretty decent book in itself but unfortunately for *this* author, Leslie Halliwell was only involved peripherally. He had been aware, though, of Cowgill's intentions: he recalled a Worldvision employee saying to him, "Thames had made it plain ... that they alone would buy *Dallas* given the chance." But it was not Halliwell's style to get involved: he was too much in favour of maintaining the status quo. Indeed, I asked Sir Paul, "Didn't you want the show?" and he replied, "That wasn't the issue. We didn't want warfare to break out." As for the American soaps themselves, Halliwell would later scathingly – but quite typically – dismiss the whole genre as…

> *…the depiction of rich American families as collections of scoundrels and perverts who never have much to do beyond dressing in tennis or evening wear, and hanging around*

expensive but under-populated sets from which flatly to deliver lines of naïve bitchery.

Discussions had been going on throughout the seventies about the possibility of a fourth UK television channel. Royal Commissions debated, official papers were written, bills were passed and finally, after the Conservative election victory in 1979, Channel 4 was given the green light. It would be a commercial channel, wholly owned by the IBA and uniquely funded by the other independent companies. Paul Bonner was appointed Channel Controller and Jeremy Isaacs became Chief Executive. The IBA's policy statement expressed its wish that the channel would "have as a particular charge the service of special interests," and the Broadcasting Act of 1981 further stipulated that the programmes should "appeal to tastes and interests not generally catered for by ITV." In addition, the Act included the admonishment that "nothing is included in the programmes which offends against good taste or decency." Most of the channel's problems in its first year would be regarding that last point.

Isaacs said, "No one will expect a new television channel with less than £30,000 an hour to spend on programmes to be anything other than heavily dependent on film made for the cinema." And with that in mind two film buyers were appointed: Derek Hill would handle UK and foreign language movies, and Leslie Halliwell would be responsible for American imports – maintaining the emphasis on specialist interest. Paul Bonner commented, "The endless round of negotiations with film studios and distributors, and the semi-competitive battles with the BBC for UK rights had grown tedious for Halliwell. Channel 4 offered him a new opportunity." Isaacs added, "[He] was a film buff; a walking encyclopaedia. He wanted not just to purchase material for us but to help schedule it, which he had never been able to do satisfactorily for the ITV network."

Broadcast magazine saw the sense in using films as a vital part of the line-up, "First, they're very cheap, and C4 has the added advantage [of] the old movies stashed away in Leslie Halliwell's vaults that would never see the light of day on ITV1 ... if properly dressed up in seasons you can build up a loyal audience." Halliwell had been saying the same thing for years. He would still continue to buy for ITV, though, and remain employed by Granada, working out of his Golden Square office a stone's throw from Channel 4's premises in Charlotte Street. For him 'specialist interest' meant only one thing: old movies. In addition to scouring ITV's vaults, he used his influence with distributors to see what other bargains he could pick up, and they were happy to do deals on account of the channel being new and wanting to establish a relationship. Instead of bartering for specific groups of movies, though, his approach was just to grab all he could and then see what he had at the end of it. Isaacs commented, "Eagerly he got to work on our behalf, chasing rarities [and] diverting goodies from ITV's vast store." How he must have relished this unexpected opportunity to celebrate the Golden Age once more.

The Channel 4 board members, senior staff and commissioning editors met for the first time to discuss programme policy at a conference centre in Lane End, Buckinghamshire, over a weekend in July 1981. For Isaacs this was "the core group that was to create both the spirit and the substance of Channel 4." A group shot featuring thirty-one of the great and the good of the channel appeared in *Broadcast*, all lined up together on the nine hole golf course. Sir Richard Attenborough was among them in his capacity as Deputy Chairman – although his time with the channel was limited due to his directing the epic *Gandhi* at the time. Halliwell stands with his arms behind his back, smiling affably. He wears a long, oriental-style shirt with a cardigan, casual trousers and is sporting the obligatory full beard and glasses – and is that a medallion there just visible? He looks broad shouldered, a little plump and is taller than most of the people in his row. Paul Bonner, however, towers above them all, as befits the channel controller.

On the morning of the last day of the conference, Halliwell spoke to the group about what he intended to bring to the channel. He offered an "archive night," beginning with the films of Samuel Goldwyn and continuing with the works of other great film-makers such as Hitchcock and John Ford – though not their most famous titles by any stretch. He took the same approach with his selections featuring famous stars such as Gary Cooper, Mary Pickford and Ronald Colman. In keeping with the new channel's direction, Halliwell was choosing films which had been previously neglected. They did not necessarily have high reputations but would at least have something about them that would be of *interest*. Isaacs called them "rare birds indeed," but Halliwell additionally threw in a few more recent titles within the channel's price range, just to maintain a balance.

Channel 4 may have been looming on the horizon but Halliwell was still very much a part of the ITV Purchase Group, and in early 1982 he secured the hottest property of the decade – at the time the most successful movie ever made – George Lucas's space adventure, *Star Wars*. And he got it without so much as a scuffle. Indeed, that quote from Paul Bonner which refers to "*semi*-competitive battles" is quite appropriate, as the president of 20th Century Fox, Harris Kattleman, came over to London to meet Halliwell and they fixed the deal over lunch, "between the soup and the fish course." The BBC got *Chariots of Fire* and ITV got *Star Wars*, for three runs over seven years. Simple as that... how Michael Winner would fume! Halliwell did pay four million dollars for it, however, which was the most ITV had ever spent on a single film, but he told an *Express* reporter that the supply of movies for peak time viewing had all but dried up, adding, "*Star Wars* plus *Superman* ... and *Jaws 2* are the last big blockbusters we can expect to see on our ITV screens for some while."

To no-one's surprise, *Star Wars* topped the ratings when it was shown in October 1982, and was the most popular broadcast of the month. Halliwell still grumbled about the estimated figure of 16.8 million viewers, though, saying, "For top money I would expect 20 million." Other observers at the time were actually questioning the statistics themselves, with the argument that the rise in popularity of the video recorder was adding a time-shift factor to viewing habits, absent from the research.

Of the three contentious subjects [the audience] *are bored by sex and repelled by violence but they get hot under the collar about bad language.*

Halliwell was fifty-three when Channel 4 launched on Tuesday 2nd November, 1982. Isaacs wrote, "As a come-on I front loaded the first ten evenings with good movies." Some of these were made by the channel's own production company, Film Four, such as *P'tang Yang Kipperbang* and *Walter*, but the others were bought in and Halliwell was directly credited with having acquired four of them. On the Friday night, *Woodstock*, the three hour film of the famous music festival was shown, and Paddy Chayefsky's Oscar-winning satire on the TV industry, *Network*, went out on the Saturday night (was Halliwell making a jibe at the new channel here?) Two 1930s Howard Hughes films followed: the World War I dogfight movie *Hell's Angels* on the Saturday afternoon, and Paul Muni closed the weekend schedule in the gangster classic *Scarface*.

Unfortunately, none of these selections made the channel's own top ten ratings list, but Halliwell would have a number one hit in the second week with the 1977 American Football movie, *Semi-Tough*, starring Burt Reynolds and Kris Kristofferson, scheduled for the Tuesday premiere slot. Isaacs thought it would dovetail nicely with the channel's coverage of the sport, writing, "It never occurred to me in my innocence that there must be some good reason why neither ITV nor the BBC had snapped it up." He watched the film for the first time when it was broadcast and nearly fell off his chair: "It was wall-to-wall foul-mouthed locker-room badinage, at 9pm with no warning," he cried. Nearly four million other viewers also tuned in, though, making it the most popular Channel 4 broadcast of the week, and despite his initial shock Isaacs remained determined to show films uncut – they would just have to schedule them better. Halliwell said, "We started off by showing theatrical films such as *Semi-Tough* and *Equus* ... but we found ourselves in no end of trouble because of the bad language. C4 don't like to cut films, so you usually find that they can't be shown until 11pm, unless you are going to emasculate them."

The channel came under fire almost immediately for the content of its shows and films, with Mary Whitehouse, founder of the National Viewers' and Listeners' Association, complaining about bad language in a letter to the Attorney-General, in which she specifically mentioned *Woodstock* and *Network*. She further voiced her disapproval of ITV's showing of *Alien*, which Halliwell had bought for the network and scheduled for 10.30pm, after the World Cup Final. Whitehouse declared her association had carried out a survey which found that "*Alien* caused boys to have nightmares ... and affected their behaviours at school." (The only behavioural effects which *I* observed at school, however, were that everyone was talking about what a good film it was). Whitehouse expressed her delight when Halliwell cancelled a proposed showing of the James Caan thriller *The Gambler*. The film had been advertised in the *TV Times* but Halliwell reviewed it and declared, "There was too much bad language to edit out … we apologise to people who wanted to see the film, but bad language causes more upset among viewers than violence."

That old conflict between his personal and professional tastes was apparent again. Halliwell made no secret of his antipathy towards the excesses of the modern age – "Films that rely on four letter words simply show the ignorance and lack of intelligence of the people who made them" – and since those excesses were now causing him scheduling headaches and viewer complaints, he had even more reason to be resentful… but that did not stop him from trying to show them. In the case of Martin Scorsese's boxing drama *Raging Bull*, Channel 4 had been prepared to show the full cinema version but *accidentally* showed the cut version, prompting the usual complaints from purists. Halliwell's viewpoint was made clear in an NFT interview in 1987, where he responded to questions about showing cut versions: "I'm perfectly happy that people see the version they want as long as they don't insist that *I* see it. I have seen *Raging Bull*, obviously, and it's such a heavy going and unpleasant film about unpleasant people that it wouldn't be among my personal favourites. On the other hand … I respect its intentions and I respect the desire of people who think it's a masterpiece to see it in that version."

He positively invited trouble with some of his choices for Channel 4, though, especially with the season called 'What the Censor Saw', among whose titles were originally to have been *Straw Dogs* and *Last Tango in Paris*, two of the most notorious films of the seventies. Not surprisingly, the IBA had kittens when they saw the schedule. "*Straw Dogs* in particular is like a red rag to a bull," Halliwell observed, "The IBA remains convinced it would incur the combined wrath of God and Mary Whitehouse." But he went on to say that although he himself thought it was just a very bad film, it should still have been shown so that people could see what all the fuss was about. The IBA denied instructing him to withdraw the films, claiming instead that it was done as a result of "mutual discussion." The season eventually featured titles which had been controversial in their day but had latterly lost their propensity to offend, such as the Mae West vehicle *I'm No Angel*, and Preston Sturges's *The Miracle of Morgan's Creek*.

Some reporters accused the new channel of being trendy and only appealing to minorities – which was precisely what it had been instructed to be in the first place. But, with the ratings even lower than expected, Isaacs found himself under pressure. He announced that there would be no re-launch but that there would be some concessions to light entertainment. Cecil Korer, a commissioning editor for the channel, had been on a buying trip to Los Angeles with the Purchase Group and later returned there to scout for more programmes on his own. He heard about a comedy set in a Boston bar and snapped it up – prompting a stiff letter from Halliwell, saying, "Dear Cecil, can we please try to keep our channels straight?" He explained that ITV had expressed some interest in the show and added somewhat melodramatically, "That's the way civil wars start." *Cheers* would become one of Channel 4's biggest successes of the decade.

Halliwell had more colleague trouble with Kevin Goldstein-Jackson, the regional executive who had campaigned for the decentralisation of buying. Goldstein-Jackson gave a two page interview for the *Sunday Independent* in which he denounced ITV's festive offerings as "rubbish." He refused to show the planned Christmas Day movie, *The Black Hole*, bought by Halliwell, allegedly for $750,000, saying, "It is going to die, I know it is. It died at the cinema." In its place, by rather bizarre logic, would be the Peter Falk comedy *The In-Laws*. He went on, "As far as I know Leslie Halliwell is given no budget to work to. We're not consulted on whether we want to spend half a million on *Raise the Titanic*; we just get a bill informing us that we have to pay such and such amount by such and such a time." Halliwell responded that *The Black Hole* was the "thinking man's *Star Wars*" and that it did far better at the box office than the Falk movie, which he suggested was inappropriate for Christmas Day on account of its Jewish humour. In the event, neither film made the regional or countrywide top ten, or indeed the top 50 for the whole month.

Halliwell did not contribute a great deal to Channel 4's new drive for light entertainment but he did indirectly supply two of its most popular shows. Firstly, the hospital drama *St. Elsewhere*, which he described as "a bobby dazzler, tremendous quality, a super piece of work." Apparently the BBC had bought the show without seeing it; then balked at the pilot and "wriggled out of the deal." Halliwell saw two hours and bagged it for ITV, but they could not find a suitable slot in the schedules and so it went to Channel 4. *Hill Street Blues* had been shown previously on Thames but had never been properly networked, to Halliwell's annoyance, so he reluctantly handed that over as well. He described both shows as "Slice of life melodramas ... with a large cast of characters all professionally upstaging each other, on their way to possible tragedy at the hands of cynically 'honest' scriptwriters."

St. Elsewhere and *Hill Street Blues* regularly drew audiences of around five million, which was fine for Channel 4 but not in the same league as ITV, who were trouncing all-comers at the time. The ratings for December 1982 show ITV broadcasts occupying the top *eighteen* places, the Bond film *Moonraker* being the highest placed film. The trend continued into the first week of January with *Superman* and *Jaws 2* beating anything shown by the opposition, and over the following year more of Halliwell's purchases would prove to be successful.

Among the shows he managed to keep hold of for ITV, and in keeping with his time honoured approach of buying 'hokum', was *The A-Team*, featuring George Peppard leading a gang of mercenaries on civilian missions. Halliwell bought it on the January 1983 L.A. trip, likening it to *The Dirty Dozen*, and it would prove a ratings smash when it aired that autumn, pulling in over thirteen million viewers in its Friday evening slot. If he never did find that other 'Kojak' he was looking for – the long running series which was popular with critics and public alike – then this was probably the closest he came. *The A-Team* was enormously popular for several seasons but, it has to be said, it did not thrill the critics. *Hollywood Reporter* commented, "No one admits to liking it, but everyone watches it." Other shows Halliwell bought, such as *Knight Rider*, *Hart to Hart* and *Airwolf*, all had mixed success with audiences but again they did not ring any critical bells. He once said, "I might have been wrong a couple of times but nothing serious has ever gone down the pan." One show he let slip was *Miami Vice*, which he found "too rough and sleazy ... no-one ever shaved." To his surprise, Alan Howden, who was then buying shows for the BBC, picked it up and did very well with it – but not as well as *The A-Team*.

The cult of the mini-series which had begun in the seventies reached its apogee in the eighties, with a deluge of productions available to the buyers. Indeed, it was a mini-series that brought Channel 4 its first major audience figures, with the Jenny Seagrove saga *A Woman of Substance* bringing in nearly 14 million viewers for its final episode. Halliwell's major success in this field came with the 18-hour World War II drama *The Winds of War*, starring Robert Mitchum and Ali MacGraw, and which he bought from Paramount at the 1983 Monte Carlo trade fair. The series had cost $40m to make, with a further $25m spent on pre-screening publicity, and when run on consecutive nights in the US it pulled in a bewildering *140 million* viewers. It cost Halliwell less than $500,000 to buy for ITV and drew a steady – but very healthy – audience of 13 million when shown in Britain. He commented, "When you look at a mini-series and the Hollywood people want you to spend 100,000 dollars an hour for it, you've got to see a few armies marching. Those are the criteria: the money has got to show on that small screen."

There was controversy when the BBC ran *The Thorn Birds* against Granada's sedate epic *The Jewel in the Crown*, and promptly cleaned up in the ratings. Critics – and even politicians – cried out at the Corporation's lowering of standards, calling *Birds* "meretricious rubbish" whilst hailing *Jewel* as "marvellous." Halliwell called the scheduling a "cardinal sin" but felt that criticism of the series was harsh. Although he did not like it personally, he said that the whole affair was "giving American television production a worse name than it deserved." He would himself have a hit with some smart scheduling, when the sci-fi invasion series *V* ran against the BBC's coverage of the 1984 Olympic Games, pulling in around 10 million viewers for each of its five episodes. However, the resultant spin-off series which he later bought was a flop.

In a 1984 article for *Primetime* magazine, Halliwell listed sixteen mini-series which had either recently been bought or which were on the market, including *Lace*, *Princess Daisy* and *The Key to Rebecca*. He added, "There probably is not enough scheduling time available for British audiences to witness all the results." He did note, however, that none of them had come from Universal, who had begun the trend back in the seventies. The genre was showing its age. Rising costs reduced their epic sweep to that of *Dallas*-style soap operas, with a resultant drop in quality. Halliwell noted that "invariably the narrative is jumbled, the diction poor, the spectacle mere child's play; while the actors seem to have been introduced only recently to their costumes." He was particularly scathing about *Hollywood Wives* for its cheap sets and bad acting, saying, "We're sorry we ever bought it. I think we'll stay divorced from [the sequel]." Apart from the expense, the studios came to the realisation that there was no second run for mini-series, and within a few years the genre had all but fizzled out.

> *Nostalgia is only a trendy word to describe something which people have at last learned to appreciate because it has been taken away from them.*

In the summer of 1983, BBC2 ran a glorious season of Universal's old monster movies, featuring all the Dracula, Frankenstein, Wolf Man and Mummy films in late Saturday night double-bills. But there was one missing. Halliwell had captured the elusive Invisible Man for Channel 4 and proceeded to run all the films in sequence, on Sunday nights. They might be generally regarded as the weakest of Universal's monster features, but the first, starring Claude Rains and directed by James Whale, is an undisputed classic. It reached second spot in Channel 4's list of top programmes for the week, and the rest pulled in regular audiences of around 2 million. 'Samuel Goldwyn presents…' featured a season of films from the legendary Hollywood producer, including *Wuthering Heights* with Laurence Olivier and Merle Oberon, and *The Westerner* with Gary Cooper and Walter Brennan. Halliwell managed to use his influence to get Goldwyn's son, himself a producer, to introduce each film.

And that was just the beginning. Over the next few years Channel 4 would flood the airwaves with a deluge of films. Those of a certain vintage were selected personally by Halliwell, either from existing stock or sought out using his vast knowledge and buying expertise, and all were presented to an admittedly specialised but undeniably appreciative audience, in season after season after season…

'Milestones of the Movies' featured significant classics such as *Green Pastures* and *Pygmalion*, whilst 'Long Lost Movies' revived, among others, Chaplin's *A Woman of Paris*, unseen in fifty years. 'Weekends with the Stars' was vague enough to feature just about anyone, and there were in addition tribute seasons for James Cagney and Cary Grant soon after their deaths. Jeremy Isaacs wrote that Halliwell was "lovingly combing the libraries for the neglected masterworks of the period he cared for most … he resurrected the B-movie; Mister Moto sleuthed again…" Greta Garbo's birthday was celebrated with an appropriate title or two, similarly Laurence

Olivier's and the anniversary of James Dean's death. The list went on and on, with Halliwell eagerly filling up those precious Saturday afternoon and Sunday night slots with gems from his treasure chest, and remarking, "What a store of riches has been revealed!"

To cater for the slightly more up to date there was 'The Swinging Sixties', which included Richard Burton in *Look Back in Anger* and Albert Finney in *Saturday Night and Sunday Morning*. And for the very up to date there were still the Tuesday night premieres – provided they were of specialist interest – such as Ken Russell's *Altered States*, John Boorman's *Excalibur*, and the violent Australian film *The Chant of Jimmy Blacksmith*.

But it was mostly oldies, if for no other reason than there were just so many of them. Halliwell said, "Films from the past had never been dealt with satisfactorily on television. ITV has never really found a way of using very old films, and Channel 4 felt that this was one minority interest they could satisfy." He even managed to recreate that BBC2 season of Universal monsters, running them in sequence and adding one or two choice rarities such as *The Vampire Bat* and *The Old Dark House*. He would sometimes try to outdo himself: if nineteen titles in a James Cagney season had felt like some sort of a record, then he would better it with a *hundred film* season of comedies, which he called "the biggest cavalcade of laughter in the history of British television." Some of the collections were somewhat spurious, however: a season of films with the word 'song' in the title?

But it was not just a question of pulling out every film made before 1955 and hoping for the best. Halliwell had strict criteria about what was to be shown and refused to compromise on quality, in both senses of the word. He declared that every film of a certain vintage had been "chosen by me, and I stake my reputation on its having a certain amount of interest," whether it was the film which got Carl Laemmle fired from Universal in 1936 (*Sutter's Gold*) or Errol Flynn's first role (*The Case of the Curious Bride* – as a corpse).

In the other sense of the word quality, he was often dealing with films which were half a century old, and felt there was no point in "reviving these elderly entertainments if one had continually to apologise for fuzzy, scratched, jumpy prints which reduced the original value to a fraction." The channel was prepared to pay for brand new 35mm prints to be struck and would make video tape copies of every film they received, in order to maintain their condition. But sometimes a fair degree of detective work was required in order to source a decent print to begin with. In the first instance, Halliwell had to find out who owned a movie. Studio mergers and acquisitions had often left back catalogues in the hands of third parties, and many properties were tied up in complex legal wrangles. Sometimes the rights for the same film would be held by different people, or they would be held by a director or producer for a certain amount of time before reverting to somebody else entirely.

In the cases of both *The Old Dark House* and *The Cat and the Canary*, the studios which made the movies still owned them but had lost the rights to the original plays on which they were based – to a smart lawyer charging 50% of any sale. The Alec Guinness comedy *Father Brown* was repeatedly disclaimed by Columbia until Halliwell remembered that it had been released under the title *The Detective* in the States. The negative was tracked down in New York but was accompanied by a note saying that the rights had been lost but would revert back to the studio in 1986. Halliwell remembered that G. K. Chesterton, who had written the original story on which the film was based, had died in 1936, and knew that author's rights last until fifty years after death. Columbia was holding out so as not to have to pay Chesterton's estate – Halliwell did not want to wait and so paid the appropriate fee.

Another name change occurred with the Dana Andrews thriller *Night of the Demon*, which according to Halliwell was the only film in existence of an M. R. James ghost story. This had to be played under its US title *Curse of the Demon*, but the print which turned up had the added benefit of two extra scenes not present in the UK version. *All That Money Can Buy*, the marvellous William Dieterle variation on *Faust* – which Halliwell had likened to *Citizen Kane* in its use of the "whole cinematic box of tricks" – was finally traced under the title *Daniel and the Devil*. Unfortunately he could only obtain a cut version but said philosophically, "It contains all the best scenes and will have to do." The broadcast of *The Court Jester* occurred two days before Paramount lost the rights back to Danny Kaye, who had in the meantime died, prompting Halliwell to remark, "Heaven knows what is going to happen…"

He received many requests for *Call Me Madam*, *Alexander's Ragtime Band* and *Annie Get Your Gun*, all of which featured the music of Irving Berlin, who at the time was clinging on to life at ninety-six, but still demanding prohibitively large fees for the use of his music. The films of his old favourites Laurel & Hardy were denied to him, however, being tied up in a $3million dollar legal dispute at the time. Halliwell sometimes had to tell the studios themselves exactly what they had. In the case of the 1948 second feature *The Fatal Night* – which he had identified from several viewer requests that described it but could not quite name it – he had to insist to Columbia that they had in fact made the film, and he had a still in his possession proving it. One can imagine him on the phone, "Look, you can wave this still at someone and ask what happened – there must be records!" One can further imagine the helpless expression of the poor individual on the other end of the line.

In some cases, prints had been struck for television companies years before and simply never returned to the distributors. With negatives either degrading or simply being thrown out, these errant copies were occasionally all that remained. It turned out that Granada owned the only surviving prints of several British movies which had been bought in the sixties and left in the vaults. *Night Train to Munich*, a delightful piece of wartime 'hokum' starring Rex Harrison, was one of the few titles still being held back by the Film Industry Defence Organisation, so Halliwell promptly negotiated its release.

Sometimes it was a jigsaw puzzle. He had to piece together the Claude Rains version of *The Phantom of the Opera*, in which a good quality 35mm print turned up in Amsterdam, minus opening and closing titles, which were instead supplied from a battered print found in Ireland. In other cases amateur film enthusiasts owned 16mm copies, and Halliwell had to negotiate with one over the Conrad Veidt thriller *The Passing of the Third Floor Back*, a picture thought completely lost due to an accident with the negative. The collector was worried about being sued but Halliwell struck a deal with Rank, who had previously owned the property. However, just before transmission a Rank representative called asking where to send the brand new 35mm print they had just prepared. Halliwell was aghast, "I was told there hadn't been a print for fifty years!"

Two significant works were treated scandalously by their owners. The 1931 version of *Dr Jekyll and Mr Hyde* had been deliberately destroyed when Metro had remade it, limply, with Spencer Tracy ten years later. A similar fate was to befall the original *Gaslight*, starring Anton Walbrook, also remade in the forties. Fortunately, in both cases someone had the great good sense – and probably risked their job – to hide a copy.

In the case of *Frankenstein*, there were rumours for years about a scene being cut soon after the film was released, where the monster innocently throws a young girl into a lake thinking she will float like a flower, but instead she drowns. In one version the scene ended at the moment the monster was reaching toward her – giving a totally different impression as to what had taken place. Halliwell was actually allowed into the very vaults of Universal to search for the missing footage (*Oh look just let me do it, will you!*) – but to no avail. The missing scene was finally unearthed by the British National Film Archive, who in addition played a major role in the restoration of *Lost Horizon*. Halliwell wrote, "One often thanks heaven for the National Film Archive, which since 1934 has been taking better care of movies than the people who own them."

He positively bubbles with excitement in several articles of the time, commending interviewers to the various seasons and reeling off lists of titles he had exhumed from celluloid graves; following up with a cheery, "What more could you want?" His motives were almost profound, "It would be unthinkable to let the work of Fred Astaire or Charles Laughton moulder in obscure vaults when they can still be enjoyed by an audience numbered in millions … they are the art form of the 20th century: to let them pass from sight would be as barbarous as to burn a Picasso or a Matisse."

Halliwell was additionally put in charge of scheduling, which he could finally do to his complete satisfaction, but he found it to be a tricky business. If the channel had a contract to show a particular film for two runs then he had to make sure they got value for money, and, recognising that not everyone at the time had a 'video', if a film was scheduled late at night for its first run he would find an afternoon slot for it the second time around. He admitted, "Juggling with timing is extremely difficult to accomplish. The nice thing is when you get three hours on a Saturday afternoon and you can invent a double-bill, or when you've got a slot on Sunday evening and you can start at 10.15pm … at the moment I'm going even more hairless than usual trying to fit in the autumn schedule." With 160 slots to fill he had to give priority to the titles whose contracts were expiring, adding, "It isn't easy but it's fun."

And it was not just feature films. Halliwell himself introduced a season of those wartime documentaries which had so impressed him back in the forties, and which he had obtained for Granada thirty years later. The season was called *The British at War* and was similar to another show he had made for Granada two years before, called *Home Front*. For *Home Front* he introduced each film sitting casually in an office chair in a fairly darkened set, with three wartime posters on large boards behind him. Wearing a shirt and tie with a tan jacket and his full beard now greying in the centre, he has a typically authoritative but somewhat playful air about him, and clearly enjoys highlighting small details of each production with a slightly mischievous relish.

Of the riveting nine-minute documentary made for the American market, *London Can Take It*, Halliwell said that it "inspired a lot of people I knew to stop moaning and get on with the job of winning the war." He introduced Humphrey Jennings's masterpiece *Listen to Britain* as "an absolute copper-bottomed classic … much more effective than a hundred weight of history books." For *Shunter Black's Night Off*, in which a railway worker is called back into action when a German bomb hits the station, he declared it "one of those tense little action dramas which the Government did so well," and added that the main character's occupation was "the sort of job I might have enjoyed myself when I was a bit nimbler." *The British at War* followed in late 1984 on Thursday afternoons, running into January 1985 and featured more terrific Ministry of Information productions, including *Western Approaches*, *Desert Victory* and *The True Glory*. Halliwell introduced each episode from the Cabinet War Rooms in Whitehall.

That same year, he was interviewed by Teeside local radio for a programme all about the cinema. He was questioned on many different aspects of the medium, such as producers, silent movies, heart-throbs, gangster films and comedies, and he talked for three or four minutes on each. On the subject of directors he observed, "I have a strange feeling that a lot of critics are wrong when they attribute the merit of a film, the overall merit or demerit, to a director, because a film is in the hands of many people, and although the director is very important you don't start with a director: a film starts with a script. And that's why in my books, in giving credits for films, I always give the writer first because I think without the writer there can be no film." Of those marvellous character actors which had been one of the many attractions in his early days of cinemagoing, he commented, "They used to be under contract to particular studios and you knew if you went to an MGM film Frank Morgan would probably be in it, and in an RKO film you might see Edward Everett Horton and so on. If you went to the pictures once or twice a week as I used to, these people became as familiar as your own family. And they were all actors who probably were very limited, a lot of them. I mean, they only did that one thing but they did that one thing beautifully."

Having often been criticised over the years for not seeming to promote foreign language films very much, Halliwell relates here the stumbling block he found himself up against in his efforts. "The English generally do not like reading subtitles," he said, "If you put a subtitled film on, the audience drops to a tenth. And we *tried*, ITV tried some years ago, putting on a series of French films which we called 'The Continental'. I went to Paris and particularly chose about twelve films which had very strong mystery plots, and we thought as long as people were interested in the plot they won't complain about the dubbing. But they did complain. People don't like dubbing either, so one's stuck."

To say he speaks with authority is an understatement. Throughout the programme a succession of anecdotes and quotations flow liberally from his agile mind, and the names of countless actors and films come immediately to him at the merest prompting. He seems to talk as quickly as he thinks, sometimes forgetting to take a breath, and he never misses an opportunity to mention an upcoming attraction on Channel 4. Which was not surprising, as the response to all his buying, scheduling and introducing had been "overwhelmingly affirmative." He wrote that "an enormous postbag from delighted viewers has made the effort more than worthwhile." The viewing figures confirmed it, with *The Battle of the River Plate* and *Green for Danger* both drawing audiences of nearly four million, and *Night Train to Munich* and *The Roaring Twenties* just over three million. Among his biggest successes were *The Jolson Story*, with Larry Parks impersonating the famous jazz singer, and the Bob Hope comedy *The Ghost Breakers*. Halliwell exclaimed, "When you can show Conrad Veidt in *The Passing of the Third Floor Back* to an audience of five million you really feel that you have achieved something." He further enthused, "There are cries of delight from all around the country when you play Deanna Durbin or Jeanette McDonald." Indeed, there were cries from Durbin herself when she wrote him from her home in France to say that she was buried under a pile of fan mail, on account of one of his seasons.

In one week alone he answered 43 letters of enquiry and received three alone praising him for 'finding' Rita Hayworth in *Angels over Broadway*. Within all this correspondence there was only one complaint, from a lady in Godalming who rang up to say she thought the films were "too old to suit her taste." He replied that the channel had been conceived to appeal to minority interests, and fans of modern movies were adequately catered for elsewhere. He rationalised the audience reaction as being not only simple nostalgia but due in large part to the "abundance of brilliant talent on screen in those days," going on to say in one article that young people of his personal acquaintance were surprised at how good the films were, despite them being in black and white. One other quality he felt the oldies had over modern movies was optimism, and that they came from an age when films appealed to the whole family, which the more modern productions no longer did.

The parallels with the Rex are as clear as day. Thirty years on and Halliwell was again using his vast knowledge to source films of particular interest; dealing with distributors and film archives to get the best possible material, and showing it all to an appreciative audience – which no longer numbered in the hundreds but the millions. He said, "I'm having a marvellous time ... it's fascinating work." One can picture him whistling away at his desk after taking a call from some old lady in Surbiton, thanking him for the trip down memory lane he had just provided her with.

He additionally contributed a regular piece for the channel's own magazine, *See 4*, under the heading 'Leslie Halliwell's film notes'. Just scanning through any entry reminds one instantly of 'Next week's films', as he directs viewers to the latest batch of rarities with unashamed enthusiasm: "There's a six-week Deanna Durbin season including four premieres ... at long last we have a shining Technicolor print of the much requested Chopin biopic *A Song to Remember* ... some splendidly nostalgic pieces will be presented ... the titles are irresistible ... we anticipate that a great many people will retire late on Saturday evenings ... requests from viewers are always welcome ... the barrel is far from empty ... keep watching Channel 4: it's the best movie show in town!"

If that was not enough, he contributed a weekly half page to the *TV Times*, in which he would respond to requests for films or general queries with typical gusto – "Channel 4's recent showing of *The Best Man* entertained but confused PG of Hartlepool ... although he had never seen it before, he remembers an American political film in which a candidate was smeared and yet he's sure it wasn't Cliff Robertson ... Quite right, PG: the other film was *Advise and Consent* (1962)."

Readers tested his memory by supplying what moments they could recall from films and hoping he could provide the title: "I was able to tell SJ of Norwich that the James Mason film in which there are three paths through a bog, only one of which is safe, is *The Night Has Eyes*, made in 1942 ... likely to be shown on Channel 4 in the New Year ... WT of London remembers a film in which a blind man is trapped between the gates of a level crossing ... I'm pretty sure that this is *Faces in the Dark* (1960), starring John Gregson ... I am taken to task by BP of Stockport for saying that Cornel Wilde played Robin Hood in *The Bandit of Sherwood Forest* (1946). In fact it seems he played the *son of* ... it was Russell Hicks who played the aged swashbuckler."

Other commentators also appreciated Halliwell's efforts: *Broadcast* called him "distinctly in vogue through his choice of golden oldies for C4." *The Times* said, "Scarcely a day goes by without Channel 4 offering further proof that it has the best movie policy of any of the four channels." Even Alan Howden of the BBC was forced to admit grudgingly, "Channel 4 has introduced a strong degree of competition in an area where BBC2 had a monopoly." Film historian Jeffrey Richards recalled, "For lovers of the golden age of the cinema like myself, Channel 4 became a source of unalloyed delight as time and again one encountered films one had only ever read about and never expected to see."

If the viewers were pleased, Halliwell's employers were ecstatic. Paul Bonner wrote, "Channel 4 was very fortunate in having available Leslie Halliwell's intimate knowledge," and Jeremy Isaacs said he had made an "unsurpassed contribution" to the channel's success. The British Film Institute agreed: in 1985 they gave Halliwell an award "for the selection and acquisition of films with a view to creative scheduling."

No-one else could have done all this. It required not only huge reserves of knowledge but also the application of industry which could only come from great enthusiasm and fondness for the subject. Had Conway at last found his lost horizon?

> *I know people think I'm old-fashioned. And I only hope I'm wrong about the way in which television today is headed. But the answer lies with the public and what they will finally accept ... they have the on-off switch.*

If Halliwell's passion for Channel 4's golden oldies knew no bounds, it seemed to run in inverse proportion to his feelings about buying new films and shows for ITV – in changing times. A relatively poor audience figure for the network premiere of *Raiders of the Lost Ark* was blamed on the film having been released to buy on video long before the broadcast. Barrie Brown of the BBC was sympathetic, "When a repeat of *Porridge* gets a larger audience than [*Raiders*] you have to start thinking very carefully." Halliwell added, "A film used to go theatrical and then onto TV. Now it goes theatrical, then there's video, cable and then broadcast – yet the suppliers are still trying to get the same money out of us."

The problem he had been complaining about for years was that the prime-time slots could no longer be given over to films. Old movies were for specialist interest only and most of the newer ones were not intended for a family audience – and now the viewing figures were dwindling anyway due to competition from video. This in turn had caused the networks to concentrate solely on TV productions: the mini-series and other entertainments from the US, prompting criticism from the press about quality. With cable and satellite looming in everyone's future, Halliwell was growing tired of being asked the same question at all the trade fairs: "How are you going to fill all the dozens of channels in the future?" for the simple reason that he did not have an answer.

"Twenty years ago I bought a hundred films at a time," he said, "all suitable for family viewing. Now we can't buy a hundred a year between us and the BBC." As for the new shows he commented, "I was in a screening room recently in Los Angeles and I just couldn't believe the garbage I was hearing." Everything was starting to look familiar, causing him to remark, "Most of what I see ... leads me to believe that I've seen all of the permutations of what you can do."

However, the trade press thought perhaps *he* was the problem: an article in *Television Weekly* asked, "Is Leslie Halliwell a man who has watched too many American TV series and films – disliking more and more of them – for too many years? Does he despise what he watches so much that he has gradually come to belittle and misjudge the ... mass popular audience who lap up *Dallas* and *Columbo*?"

In addition to this, the Peacock Report, which emerged from a committee set up by the government to look into television finance, had proposed to end the BBC and ITV's "cosy duopoly," and words like 'deregulation' were being bandied about. Halliwell balked at the idea of television following the cinema's lead and showing all the sex, violence and bad language he so despised. "My fear," he said, "is that in the next few years there will be a tendency to extend the boundaries of what is permissible ... the doors are open to all sorts of excess."

And so, in November 1986, at the age of fifty-seven, Halliwell announced his decision to retire, saying to *Screen International*, "It's all got a lot more complicated over the past few years and it is perhaps time for me to leave." To *Broadcast* he added, "I have been doing this job for 20 years [and] with the new media arriving it is time someone should come in who can look forward to that." *The Sunday Telegraph* added, "When you can't see the high ground any more, in other words, it is time to go."

Halliwell would, however, continue in an advisory role for Channel 4 on a two year contract, to deal with all the old movies he had now acquired for them and which nobody else knew what to do with. He declared somewhat portentously, "I am the only one who knows all the details of what I have bought for Channel 4. It would take an awful long time for anyone else to get to know the weight and value of each title in my book of purchases."

So how would Halliwell spend his retirement years? He would write about the movies, of course...

10

A Matter of Life and Death

- The final years, 1987-89 -

To mark his retirement in 1987, the National Film Theatre invited Leslie Halliwell to select a number of his favourite films, to be shown in a short season at their famous South Bank repertory cinema. Not surprisingly, his choices were all from the Golden Age, and in his programme notes he explained that they were all movies which had meant a great deal to him over the years; they all benefited from being watched by an audience and most of them contained the "gift of elegant understatement." The season ran throughout July under the title 'Halliwell's Handful'.

Among the treasures on offer, he was delighted to present a brand new print of *Lost Horizon*, after its ten year restoration by the UCLA Film and Television Archive. The version he had obtained was 14 minutes longer than any shown since 1942, and he said of it, "It's amazing how the texture of the film has improved." Other titles included *The 39 Steps*, which his programme notes described as "classic early Hitchcock, disregarding logic and reality for the sake of thrills." For *Destry Rides Again* he wrote, "Precision is the watchword here, making old elements seem like new." *A Matter of Life and Death* was referred to as a "giddy masterwork," and for *Sullivan's Travels* he confessed to having fallen "madly in love" with Veronica Lake at the time. His introduction concluded with the words, "I count them indeed amongst my best friends: Destry, and Conway, and Sullivan, and Hannay, and of course Stan and Ollie."

One evening of the season was devoted to an onstage interview conducted by Brian Baxter of the BBC, in which Halliwell discussed his famous encyclopaedias and his career as a film buyer. The event's programme asked, "Was this job the paid holiday it seems to outsiders, and how did he square it with his more famous role as Public Film Buff Number One?" A recording of the interview survives at the British Film Institute Library.

Baxter introduces him by briefly describing his various roles at Granada and saying, "He never had an official title, he tells me." The interview was preceded by a clip of the creation sequence from *The Bride of Frankenstein*, after which Halliwell comes bounding onto the stage to warm applause. He is in a jovial mood and proceeds to recount with boyish enthusiasm – in that clear and commanding voice – his first experience of *Bride* at the Bolton Rialto in 1944. He especially remembered how he had begun to appreciate for the first time how much work went into the production of a motion picture, with set designers, photographers, and especially editors all making a vital contribution.

"It may not have been the only clip which turned me into a film buff," he recalls, "but it was certainly prime among them." He goes on to say that whenever people ask him for his favourite he replies *Citizen Kane*, as it is "such a compendium of movie art," but that *Bride*, though more specialised, is probably his number two. Baxter then proceeds to question him on his selections for the NFT season, making special mention of there being no films made after 1946; no colour films and no foreign language films. Halliwell counters that he considers *A Matter of Life and Death* to be a colour film and that a rights issue had prevented him from obtaining René Clair's *Le Million*.

"Also 1930s..."

"Yes of course," he responds, and continues beneath the audience's laughter, "I could have done all kinds of seasons [but I] chose films which had delighted me not just once but a number of times over the years ... films which come up fresh each time with wit [and] cinematic expertise."

Baxter presses him further, saying that out of the thousands of films and TV shows he watched in his capacity as a buyer, he must have seen one or two in the last thirty years which had provided him with some enjoyment.

"Yes but not of this *kind*. There are perhaps films of the last twenty years that I *admire* but they haven't meant so much to me in my life." He then digresses to the cinematic technique of Lubitsch's *Trouble in Paradise*, but Baxter refuses to let him off –

"Sorry to labour the point, but…"

"That's all right, labour away."

Baxter proceeds rather clumsily to make the same argument again, adding the old question about how he equates his personal and professional tastes. Halliwell gives his by-then standard response: he had a responsibility to buy films and shows which *other people* would want to see, and that ITV never previously had the benefit of 'a BBC2' for specialist interests.

"For the first time, when Channel 4 came along, I was really programming for myself. All the years at ITV I was doing the best job I could for other people. Now it doesn't mean to say I *despised* what I bought. I thought *The Beverly Hillbillies*, *The Naked City* and *The Munsters* were all terrific but they just weren't *me*." He wraps up his answer rather poetically, "In our heart of hearts we go back to the time when something meant something to us and we kept on enjoying it … I am somewhere lost back there in the Rialto Bolton in 1944."

Baxter then turns to Halliwell's encyclopaedias and questions him on the rather throwaway nature of some of the entries. He asks why, instead of dismissing Bresson as a "French film director of mainly austere films" and Ozu as a "Japanese director since 1927," it might be better to point the enquirer to a more detailed reference book. Halliwell replies that his books are for the mainstream filmgoers who were only likely to have seen what was shown at the local Odeon, and that he tended to avoid including foreign language films shown only at film festivals… but he promises to improve the entry on Ozu.

The discussion then moves on to his work for Channel 4 and he describes enthusiastically his scheduling for the channel. He responds to the charge that television often treats films with a degree of contempt by pointing out that people would be surprised at how often a film is broadcast in a longer version than was ever released in UK cinemas. In many cases films were cut by exhibitors for the purposes of timing, or to squeeze them into double-bills, whereas Channel 4 always shows the most complete version available.

The conversation is then opened up to the audience and one

question emerges which I myself would dearly love to have asked him: "Why do you often give away the ending of films in your synopses?" He seems taken aback and fumbles for an answer, "Well I try not to… unless it's one that everyone knows the ending of." And whilst the audience giggles, Baxter for once fails to press him and instead proceeds with another question about the type of comments people write in with. Halliwell says that he often gets letters from readers pointing out mistakes and omissions, but that sometimes even the most irate are not always correct when he double checks. An audience member then asks, "What do you think the fashionable critics think of you, like Derek Malcolm?"

"Well, they probably despise me. Derek Malcolm might use my books but would write a different book himself. There are a lot of people who want my type of book but it's not the only type there is." He then describes some other similar works and takes pride in pointing out that the *Oxford Companion* was quickly remaindered whereas his never has been. "If you're interested enough in films you'll get several books and get several different opinions," he concludes. Someone then comments on the lack of silent films on British television and Halliwell counters, "What about *The Wind* and Kevin Brownlow's presentations?"

"I meant British films."

"Ah well, if you saw one or two *British* silents you wouldn't want to see any more. You watch *The Squire of Long Hadley* or *The Lure of Crooning Water* … or *A Debt of Honour* with Clive Brook being eaten by a boa-constrictor which clearly came from Woolworth's." More audience laughter follows as Halliwell rounds off by saying that he tried to put some German silents into a season, such as *The Cabinet of Dr Caligari*, but was told he would not get the same audience figures – "My ratings are not great but they are consistent!" It was the same situation with foreign language movies: because many of his time slots were late at night, the channel felt that audiences would not want to read subtitles at that time.

He then announces that he has brought with him a crib sheet, so that if anyone wants to know whether particular films are under contract to Channel 4, he could tell them without relying on memory. Baxter comments, "That'll take us through the rest of the evening." A few titles are indeed shouted out and Halliwell quickly responds with the relevant information. To the question of how often films elude him, he answers that his film guides are selective anyway, "I mean there's no guarantee that everything goes in there. I can't give you an example off-hand…"

"I can." says the questioner, to the audience's amusement.

"…but I do have a note in the front of my current edition of five films which I discovered to my horror weren't in there and should have been." One audience member points to an obscure Jeff Bridges film called *Success* which had been shown recently by the BBC. "I'd never heard of it," Halliwell declares, "When it came on I literally did not know what it was." He then turns to Baxter, "I mean, had you heard of it?"

"Well, we were showing it…" which gets the biggest laugh of the evening over which Halliwell has to shout, "*Had you heard of it when it was offered to you?*"

"No, I must confess no."

"As far as I know it was never reviewed in *Variety*."

He is then asked why he thinks there is so much interest in the cinema of old. "It was a bit like Shangri-La," he explains, "They created some kind of a magical world … a lot of very brilliant writing went into those films [and] there was a tremendous zest which has been lost … they caused you to look up at the stars, whereas these days too often you're being asked to look down at the gutter."

The first female voice of the evening is then heard, asking, "Where do you think the film is going?"

"The cinemas themselves are deteriorating. The cinema was far more comfortable than your home back then and now it's the other way around … I grew up in the days when it was a family entertainment. That's not possible now because the films are aimed at one particular age group. It's a shame because the cinema was so popular and so fashionable."

Baxter wraps things up by asking what Halliwell thinks when he looks back over his life and career. "I think I've had a very enjoyable fifty years out of it," he observes, and of his golden oldies specifically he says, "These films survive pretty well even when they're interrupted by commercials. You don't deride other forms of art; you don't deride music and painting because it's fifty years old … so it has pleased me to be able to maintain these films in the public eye."

Throughout the discussion, Halliwell is a thoroughly engaging subject, and the criticisms thrown at him flow like water off a duck's back. His knowledge and passion shine through and, with a voice that dominates the room, one would think he could easily have gone on to a career in public speaking during retirement.

> *Less and less do I go to the movies. But perhaps once I've resigned I'll start going more – maybe somebody will ask me to be a film critic.*

Leslie Halliwell's published works span five decades. In terms of articles, it all began in 1946 with that piece for *Picturegoer* about plots in musicals. He went on to contribute dozens more to his school magazine *The Boltonian*, and later to *Varsity* and the other student publications at Cambridge, before spending those few unhappy months actually writing for *Picturegoer* for a living in 1952. The following year, *The Spectator* printed the previously mentioned 'Continuous Performance', regarding his management of the Rex Cinema in Cambridge, and two further Rex-related articles subsequently turned up in *Sight & Sound*. Another about the influx of foreign language films in British cinemas was published in lifestyle magazine *Everybody's* in 1956.

The commitments of family life and his job at Granada may have taken up all his time in the early sixties, as no other articles seem to turn up until after *The Filmgoer's Companion* was published. In 1966, however, he began contributing some very lengthy pieces to *Films and Filming* magazine, most of which ran to several pages and were often split across separate issues. In the very edition in which *Who's Afraid of Virginia Woolf?* was reviewed, he supplied an essay on film title changes, spread over six three-column pages. Almost inevitably, there was a response in the following issue's letters page: "In Leslie Halliwell's fascinating article on Title Changes he lists the second remake of *To Have and Have Not* as *The Gun Runners*. He is, however, confusing two different films here…" etc. This was the article which he eventually incorporated into *The Filmgoer's Companion*. *Films and Filming* was a London-based highbrow monthly, with issues occasionally running to over a hundred pages. They featured foreign language films as much as English speaking ones and were not averse to printing the occasional nude still – all in the name of art, of course. Halliwell found in the publication an outlet for his vast knowledge of the medium, and he embarked upon a history of talking pictures up to the beginning of the Second World War – under the umbrella title 'Merely Stupendous' – using periodicals such as *Bioscope* and *Film Weekly* as his sources. Beginning with a study of the last days of the silent era, he then moved on to the emergence of sound, writing, "Let us take a detailed look at the talkies of that first year…" before proceeding to examine them film by film over the next four pages. The 'article' itself eventually ran to seven parts, stretched over the next *fifteen* issues of the magazine. Its final instalment brought in Bolton and all the picture houses he frequented in his younger days, and most of *this* would form the basis of Halliwell's own memoir, *Seats in all Parts*, published nearly twenty years later. One chapter of *Seats* was taken from another *Films and Filming* article called 'The Baron, the Count and their Ghoul Friends', which appeared in the summer of 1969 and concerned his special affection for horror films.

In 1970, Halliwell supplied a series of three short pieces to the *Bolton Evening News* which told of life in the town during his father's day. In the first he related his disappointment at returning to his home town to find that things had changed for the worse, writing, "It is bad enough for me, a former resident, to come back to Bolton in my middle age and find it bereft of most of the things that made it a place of busy wonderment in the thirties and forties." He went on to say that his father had died recently at the age of eighty-seven, after living his last few years with his family in the South. Before he passed away, though, Halliwell had managed to get Jim to set down some recollections of his hometown, and these form the basis of the subsequent articles.

From November 1973 to August 1975, Halliwell contributed a regular full page article to the film monthly *Photoplay*, entitled 'Telemovies', and which began as a round-up of the latest made-for-TV films. The articles offered typically exhaustive lists of upcoming titles, which it was clearly in Halliwell's best interests to promote on account of having bought so many for ITV. He praised producers for their "old fashioned expertise" and for using their talent rather than overspending, but the inevitable rise in costs paved the way for what he called the "rebirth of the one-hour series." The article then became a hybrid, with shows like *Kojak* and *The Six Million Dollar Man* putting in appearances, and provided its author with a forum to bemoan the actions of American networks, such as the cancellation of

Planet of the Apes half-way through its run, leaving no time to resolve its plotlines satisfactorily.

In the late seventies, Halliwell wrote several book reviews for *The Times Literary Supplement*, predictably giving short shrift to authors who dared to find any deeper meaning in films where he felt none was intended. He judged Alain Silver and Elizabeth Ward's *Film Noir* to be "a determination to wring from modish mass entertainment a psychological preoccupation with the world's discord and man's malaise, and to turn political statement fit for expression into an expensive and unnecessary book." Richard Koszarski's *Hollywood Directors 1914-1940* consisted of "mainly dull little essays which may not be very long but make dreary reading for any but the most committed researcher." Of a book about Bob Hope he declared that it contained "vapid journalism which any hack could have accomplished."

In the 1980s there were the previously mentioned articles in *TV Times* and *See 4*, and a host of interviews and submissions to various trade papers. But, his final contributions to a national newspaper came in 1987, when from March to October he was given a whole page of the *Daily Mail*'s Saturday TV section. 'Halliwell's Screen Choice' featured previews of the weekend and following week's major programmes, set out day by day. "His supreme judgement will help you to comprehensively plan your week's viewing," the paper proudly announced (split infinitive theirs). The article consisted of typically terse assessments of the week's fare and included a section on films called 'Pick of the Flicks', as well as his nomination for item of the week, 'Halliwell's Highlight'.

In general, he was more accommodating than one might expect, without ever compromising his opinions. He managed typically on occasion to hark back to the good old days, writing on March 28th, "The fact that I retire this week after two decades as ITV's film buyer has set me thinking about the days when I first encountered TV 30 years ago." He goes on to claim that television was more persuasive then, and that the medium was at its best when featuring "eminent talking heads." He mentions A. J. P. Taylor and Mortimer Wheeler, who "fixed us with an ancient mariner eye and delighted us for half-an-hour or more without the benefit of electronic effects." What a pity that such an insightful observation should be buried in the TV section of the *Daily Mail*.

He often promoted the offerings of BBC2 and Channel 4, the latter of which he was still helping out with the scheduling of films: "So much that is genuinely entertaining and informative now appears on those two stations." It was almost a re-run of the situation in Cambridge where he was at the same time movie critic for *Varsity* and adviser to George Webb. Halliwell brought some of his inside knowledge to bear, describing the difficulties faced by the Purchase Group in trying to predict audience taste. Among the shows recently bought by his ex-colleagues which were not expected to be hits were *Murder, She Wrote* – considered too old-fashioned; *The Golden Girls* – thought to be too crude and *The Equalizer*, which was felt unlikely to run for more than half a season. All of them went on to much better success than predicted, leading Halliwell to comment, "Pity, then, the programme buyers all desperately trying to anticipate what you'll like!" He asked of the Richard Briers comedy *All in Good Faith*, "Why isn't this mildly amusing vicar show doing better in the ratings?" and said of arts programme *Saturday Review*, "I hope to discover from the profile of film director David Lynch what other people see in him." Of *The Clothes Show*, hosted by Selina Scott, he announced, "I suppose there may be viewers filled with enthusiasm for this youth-oriented bundle of fashion news ... with its punkish pretensions and staccato visuals, but I find it literally impossible to watch without upsetting my blood pressure."

Sometimes his introductions were a little on the gloomy side. "Apart from old reliables *QED* and *Panorama* ... the afternoon movies are the best part of an otherwise dull week." But he mostly remained up-beat: "Even during a poorish run-down to Easter, I have no difficulty in selecting at least a dozen items which should sharpen my thinking processes, as well as keeping me entertained." His tastes varied from documentaries such as *Horizon* to the more entertainment based shows such as *Crazy like a Fox* ("I'm hooked on this amiable comedy mystery series") and more serious drama like *Have His Carcase* ("a must on my calendar ... I've even watched the Saturday repeats.") He also revealed his new found interest in snooker – the only time in literally thousands of pages of print that he ever expressed any fondness for a sport.

The final instalment of 'Halliwell's Screen Choice' appeared on October 10th, 1987, and was introduced with the words, "After seven months of musing on programmes to come, I leave you with no earth-

A MATTER OF LIFE AND DEATH

shattering conclusions of my own." He goes on to give a pretty good one at least, in response to readers' letters complaining about British television being too earnest, with its excessive number of documentaries about the Third World and pollution etc…

> *We still have the best television in the world, or the least worst ... but virtue can be dull without a little spice, and a touch of star quality accompanied by wit and human understanding does no harm at all.*

In terms of books, Halliwell's film encyclopaedias were only a small part of a much larger body of work – none of which is currently in print, nor has been for many years. His experience as a researcher and occasional contributor to the Granada programme *Clapperboard* resulted in a 1975 collaborative effort with Graham Murray, another researcher for the programme, entitled *The Clapperboard Book of the Cinema*. Aimed squarely at the younger market, but disappointingly bereft of colour, its 125 pages were nevertheless packed full of articles and pictures of interest to the curious reader even now. One featured a detailed description of Hollywood, with a helpful map of exactly where in Los Angeles all the major studios were situated. Others concerned 'How the Movies Began' and 'How Films Found Their Voice'. Halliwell's touch is evident in the pieces on monster movies and *Citizen Kane*, and in 'Our Dear old Friends: The Gentle Art of Mr Laurel and Mr Hardy'.

The young film fan of the time might well have wondered why no more recent productions were mentioned, but the book freely admits to being rooted in the past, adding the generalisation, "Much of this book has been about the early days of film, or its golden age, which most people agree was the thirties and forties." The chapter called 'Don't Always Believe What you Read in the Papers' reproduced some excellent movie posters, which made highly exaggerated claims about the content of the productions they advertised. "Since the beginning of movies," the text ran, "it has been the fashion to advertise them in superlatives, as though each one that came along was the greatest thing that ever happened." The posters include *The Animal Kingdom*, for which the authors question the veracity of the claim that it was "2 billion years in the making!" *International Lady* promised "A thousand thrills" prompting the enquiry, "Did anyone count them?" *Woman in White* announced that "its every scene is on the screen," provoking the response, "A flagrant lie! Wilkie Collins's Victorian mystery is enormously long and complex..." The chapter concludes rather patronisingly with the admonishment, "We don't say that all cinema advertising is misleading ... we suggest that you should use your common sense when reading it."

A more detailed examination of publicity material features in Halliwell's 1976 book, *Mountain of Dreams: The Golden Years of Paramount*. In the introduction he states that it should not be taken as a definitive history of the studio – although the brief chronicle he provides in the opening chapter would satisfy any casual researcher. But he hoped that it would "enable the student, the fan and the nostalgia buff to examine from an unusual angle the output of one important studio in those exciting Hollywood years."

Each film sold to exhibitors in the old days was accompanied by a press book featuring various advertisements which could be reproduced for magazines and newspapers. Most of them were not preserved but Paramount had kept many of theirs, hence the choice of studio for this collection. It featured publicity for some eight hundred films, grouped under subject headings and accompanied by brief notes of introduction, as well as the expected pithy comments. For the chapter called 'The Suaves' Halliwell made the somewhat bizarre observation, "In these days of film heroes sporting long dirty hair, appearing to have only recently encountered the English language and going to bed in their clothes, it must be difficult for young audiences to imagine a time when the leading idols were sophisticated, mature men who had experienced most of the attractions the world could offer."

Paramount was the home of light entertainment, producing the early Marx Brothers films, Maurice Chevalier's musicals and the Hope/Crosby 'Road' films. "It tended to eschew realism," Halliwell comments, "and is usually remembered by historians for its sardonic high-life romances resulting from the employment of mainly European talents." Talents such as Ernst Lubitsch and Marlene Dietrich, who have their own dedicated sections in the book. As does Preston Sturges, whose finest film *Sullivan's Travels* "got its worst advertising: the campaign was planned entirely around the sultry charms of Veronica Lake (who was dressed as a boy almost throughout the movie) and the serious elements were not even hinted at." Indeed, for a studio so at home with its image the reader might be surprised at how many of their films were mis-sold, with the publicists seemingly "ill at ease with the studio's more ambitious, serious or sophisticated productions. They knew how to sell Crosby, Hope and Lamour but whenever a soupçon of taste was required … they fumbled it."

Halliwell does not fumble this book, presenting for posterity some fascinating glimpses into the mindset of the movie publicists. The only criticism is that it is all once again in black and white, whereas the originals would have been awash with colour. Perhaps such an undertaking was prohibitively expensive to publish in the mid-seventies, but it would have been a glorious sight.

His third encyclopaedic work was another collaborative effort. *Halliwell's Television Companion*, which began life as the *Teleguide* in 1979, ran for three editions only and was modelled after both *The Filmgoer's Companion* and the *Film Guide*, typically focusing on British and American output. Philip Purser, the TV critic for the *Sunday Telegraph*, was the co-author, and he remembered Halliwell to me in a letter:

> I had first met him in the 1960s-70s when I chaired a weird little committee set up by the National Film Archive to select television programmes for preservation, and he was one of the panel. [We sat] around a table to debate the respective claims of Earl Mountbatten or Eric Morecambe to have their latest works preserved. I think I probably liked him for his bluff, no-nonsense attitude.

Purser described the original *Teleguide* as "poor: the American entries passable, British television covered quite inadequately." Halliwell was himself aware of its deficiencies and would occasionally enquire as to whether Purser had kept his old reviews, but he confessed only to having "wodges of smelly old cuttings stuffed into boxes and drawers." He felt disinclined to guide Halliwell through all this material and was equally reluctant simply to hand over all his hard work. Instead, Purser's agent struck a deal for a collaboration, but the job of sifting through the morass of clippings led him to write, "Contract in haste, repent at the grindstone. God it was a chore!" The two worked separately, with Purser focusing on

British productions and Halliwell, with all his transatlantic experience, handling the American side. The resulting *Television Companion* featured separate entries for personalities and productions, as well as genres such as mini-series and television movies. Many of the shows were embellished with quotes from *Variety* and the *TV Guide*, and the combination of information and judgement was once again present, with one dust cover proudly proclaiming that "in this book opinions are never disguised as fact."

In the introduction Halliwell wrote, "Which of us is Dr Jekyll and which Mr Hyde must be left for the reader to decide." With him carping about the lack of television shows that "speak with wit, clarity and discretion to the large audience," and Purser complaining in his postscript that recent developments in television production have "handed over to the director a writer's medium," the reader might have been forgiven for concluding that they were both Mr Hyde.

Halliwell continued, "I hope that this book will have some value for the student of the year 2000 and later ... primarily it is intended for the thoughtful viewer of the eighties, in search of useful information or instant nostalgia." A star rating system was once again employed, denoting the extent of a show's "social/historical/artistic interest," and a casual glance through the pages predictably reveals that stars were scarce. In addition, rosettes were bestowed upon significant personalities admitting them to 'Halliwell's Hall of Fame'. Ed Sullivan, Jack Benny and Lucille Ball were among the American stars so honoured, and Eric Morecambe, Alan Whicker and John Cleese likewise for the British.

"Both Philip and I feel free to disagree in print with each other's opinions," Halliwell declared, and these disputes do give the book an extra dimension, as the reader can only benefit when two intelligent men oppose one another's views. Purser awarded *Yes Minister* three stars and described it as "quite funny," prompting Halliwell to chip in, "I'd give it four stars at least." Halliwell wrote of *Mastermind* that it was "relentlessly highbrow," but Purser countered with, "Not really highbrow at all. Like all quizzes, mainly a test of recall." *Nice Time*, an irreverent Granada show with Kenny Everett and Germaine Greer, was awarded four stars by Purser who considered it "the funniest, most inventive, least consequential entertainment of all time." Halliwell hit back, "It had its occasional moments, but I can't see how it could justify more than two stars." Purser was equally unimpressed with his opposite number awarding full marks to the 1975 series *Edward the Seventh*, commenting that it gave him "the fidgets."

Halliwell's choice of four-star programmes reflected his belief that the best shows – as with films – were those which could be both artful and popular: quality shows which appealed to the majority, rather than "a minority of would-be highbrows." Thus, *Dragnet* was awarded the maximum and described as "simple but revolutionary," and *The Twilight Zone* was likewise commended for being "the kind of pacy imaginative entertainment which TV has since forgotten how to do." Other American shows rated highest included *The Muppet Show*, *You'll Never Get Rich*, *I Love Lucy* and *M*A*S*H*. Among the British efforts achieving top marks were the intellectual epics *Jesus of Nazareth* and *Brideshead Revisited*, as well as the more accessible *Steptoe & Son* and *Till Death Us Do Part*.

Unlike the author's other encyclopaedic works, however, the *Television Companion* failed to make any critical friends. The American magazine *Reference Services Review* said of the 1st edition, "As usual, Halliwell is arbitrary in his selections and the subjectivity of his criticisms is annoying as is the lack of detail." *British Book News* commented, "It is obviously intended to appeal to both the British and the American reader and, consequently, will probably satisfy neither." Typically, Halliwell invited comments and criticism: "bouquets and brickbats" to be sent to his Golden Square office. He received the latter from Barry Took, the "endearing British humorist," as the *Companion* described him. He was less than endearing in his review of the 2nd edition for *The Stage & Television Today*, which appeared under the headline, 'Should be pulped but will probably sell very well'! Took described the book as "amazingly inaccurate"; he found Halliwell to be patronising, and felt that both authors' comments were "frequently dismissive and often downright bitchy." Among his specific grumbles were that the book mis-credited *Bootsie and Snudge*, a comedy he had created with Marty Feldman at Granada in the sixties. Took remembered Halliwell working for the company at the time, claiming he wore "a white storeman's coat and busied himself about the building in Golden Square in a perfectly orderly if puzzling way. I never met anyone who knew what he did."

Halliwell responded in a letter the following week, writing, "Since Barry has misremembered my function at Granada twenty years ago – I never wore a white coat in my entire life – I think I can be pardoned for misremembering his contribution to *Bootsie and Snudge*." He pointed out that neither he nor Purser were infallible and added that Took's "points of view" were welcome, further promising to try harder next time. In the 3rd edition of the *Television Companion*, published in 1986, the entry for *Bootsie and Snudge* had indeed been improved.

Mr Purser sent me a clipping of an even more unfavourable review from a magazine called *City Limits*, in which John Lyttle referred to the *Television Companion*'s authors as having "twin haughty, harridan sensibilities." He further accused them of pandering to "genteel populism" with public school-type attitudes; complained that the book contained "not a single fresh thought or observation," and summed it up as "toffee-nosed tosh"! Astonishing that something as apparently innocuous as an encyclopaedia should provoke such hostile reactions. Purser called it a "lunatic and despicable review," and recalled Halliwell being just as furious about it as he was.

> *I hope I have been able to convey the delight with which I am filled at each repeated viewing of this elegant bric-a-brac from a less grittily realistic age.*

Halliwell's publishers began to encourage him to write not just encyclopaedias but about the films he particularly enjoyed, and this led to the publication of two collections of essays on individual movies, beginning in 1982 with *Halliwell's Hundred*. Anyone in search of a convenient digest of his philosophy on films should look no further than the introduction to this book, for it is two and a half pages of Halliwell gold dust. He briefly describes the hardships of 1930s Bolton and the escape that the cinema offered, where "the otherwise deprived might for three hours enjoy blissful comfort in a perfumed atmosphere, watching on a giant lustrous screen the activities of characters more fortunate than themselves." He continues to take a brilliantly succinct sideswipe at modern movies, quoted at the end of Chapter 8, before explaining his choices for inclusion in the book. "I do not nominate these films as the greatest ever made," he wrote, "Few of them indeed are serious works of art, fewer still milestones of film history," thus explaining the absence of *The Battleship Potemkin*, *The Birth of a Nation*, *Alexander Nevsky*, *Seven Samurai* etc. As he stated, he admired the likes of Eisenstein and

Kurosawa without loving them. Instead, the inclusions are films which were all made "with great craft and competence under the old studio system which was so abused and is now so much missed."

Each chapter featured an examination – or "revaluation" – of usually one major film, with a few related titles additionally covered so that the actual total far exceeded a hundred. For example, *Singin' in the Rain* and *The Band Wagon* appeared as main features, with the other splendid Arthur Freed musicals, *On the Town* and *An American in Paris*, providing solid support. In some cases related titles were coupled, such as *The Wizard of Oz* with *The Blue Bird*, and *Sunset Boulevard* with *Ace in the Hole* – like literary versions of those double-bills he was so fond of putting together at the Rex and on Channel 4.

Halliwell had managed to re-watch all of the key titles included in the book for the purpose of gaining a fresh perspective, and he was not above poking a bit of mischievous fun at his choices. For the chapter on *The Adventures of Robin Hood*, which focused on the marvellous Errol Flynn version of the story, he additionally describes Douglas Fairbanks's 1922 silent production, commenting that *his* merry men "hop, skip and jump all over the place when they might have saved their valuable strength on occasion by walking."

For *Dr Jekyll and Mr Hyde*, he wrote, "This fifty-year-old film has excitement and ingenuity in every frame: there is no way at all in which it could be improved by the techniques of the eighties." For *The Jolson Story* he bemoaned the lack of comparable entertainments, "What is there for the middle-aged fans of 1980 to recall with such affection? What film has enough bouncing optimism to do so many people so much good as *The Jolson Story*? The chapter on *The Palm Beach Story* contains the most brilliant distillation of the style of Preston Sturges, and for *Destry Rides Again* he wrote, "This highly polished family entertainment is a gleaming example of how every talent in a Hollywood studio used to be bendable to a common aim, which was to give the audience a thoroughly good time in the most professional way possible."

Halliwell included some films which he loved to hate, such as the Bela Lugosi film *Night Monster*, which he assessed, "This gem of incompetence was written by one Clarence Upson Young, whom I strongly suspect to have been a pimply schoolboy, whose derivative and pusillanimous farrago was accepted by Universal on a desperate afternoon when they had several actors sitting around waiting for a script. Any script."

This is Halliwell's finest non-encyclopaedic work. It is affectionate without being pandering; informative but never patronising, a book into which its author has poured his love and respect for the mass medium which at its very best reached for – and sometimes touched – the giddy heights of both entertainment and art. What a tonic it is after 'The Decline and Fall of the Movie', and all the criticism provoked by his throwaway opinions and dismissive stance in the *Film Guide*.

Roger Manvell in *British Book News* called it "a warm-hearted book, the product of a man who knows more than most and enjoys all he knows." Peter Craig, by contrast, completely missed the point in *American Film*, writing, "The personal approach makes for mixed results: the *Blue Angel* chapter is little more than a self-congratulatory account of how Halliwell convinced a revival theatre owner to book the film." The chapter in question highlights brilliantly the effect a great movie can have on an assembled audience, which was surely the intention of the whole book. Most of the best films ever made are to be found within the pages of *Halliwell's Hundred*, all recounted by the greatest cinema aficionado of them all, on top form – what more could you ask for?

A follow-up duly appeared in 1986 under the title *Halliwell's Harvest*, which unfortunately suffers from a touch of 'after the Lord Mayor's show' (or should that be Mayer's?) It follows the same format but with fewer titles and the addition of three lengthy essays at the end. The choices this time were heavily influenced by the films being re-discovered on television, and in particular those which the author had recently brought to Channel 4.

"It may be objected that in some cases I have more bad than good to say of my choices," Halliwell wrote, "this is because I am judging by the highest standards I can summon … In other words I am following the precept of Polonius, being cruel only to be kind." Unfortunately that kindness is lost on the reader. Since all the best titles are in the first book anyway, for him to be so critical of his own selections here makes for a difficult read. Having once again caught up with each film recently, he all too often expresses his disappointment with them, and since his other publications feature plenty of his dislikes – and indeed this book itself contains a whole essay on bad films – the reader might be left wondering why he made the effort at all. For the *noir* classic *Laura* Halliwell wrote, "What once was thought to be Preminger's best film by miles ... can now be seen as not far ahead of his others, ponderously shot and lacking rhythm in the editing." Even a film which appeared to get wholehearted approval, such as the James Cagney gangster thriller *G-Men*, the author could not resist taking a swipe at its poor dialogue. Steven Spielberg's *E.T.* was bizarrely shoehorned in – no doubt as a token gesture to modernity – but it just looks completely out of place and Halliwell does not say a single positive thing about it.

Strangely, the critics seem to have been more impressed with this collection than its predecessor, with Paul Stuewe writing in *Quill & Quire* that the book is "a veritable cornucopia of fine writing about great viewing, a rewarding read for anyone with even the slightest interest in films," and adding, "How pleasant, among many felicities, to find the 'dream ending' to *The Woman in the Window* firmly defended." The essays at the end of the book may feel like heavy-going to some but Ivan Butler in *Film Review Annual* called them "highly entertaining and stimulating," and John Nangle in *Films in Review* assessed the book as "a delightfully sprawling, always entertaining detour through his exhaustive memory bank of celluloid pleasures."

Hundred and *Harvest* both served to illustrate how well travelled Halliwell was, and indeed how much culture he had absorbed in his lifetime. For *Dracula* he describes reading the novel as an undergraduate on the train returning from a West End show. The Bette Davis tearjerker, *The Great Lie*, was encountered in a Norwegian coastal town, and *Yankee Doodle Dandy* brightened up a stay at the Kahala Hilton in Hawaii, on a stopover coming back from Australia. A depressing visit to Harlem underpins the chapter on *Stormy Weather*, while *Roxie Hart* was overshadowed by Bob Fosse's excellent 1970s stage musical *Chicago*: "I can't listen now to Roxie's testimony about both grabbing for the gun without hearing the superlative precision of the chorus which belted it out on the Broadway stage." *The Jolson Story* sparked further theatrical memories of seeing Ruby Keeler on stage in a 1970 revival of *No No Nanette*. And tales of San Francisco mark the entry for the Clark Gable film named after the famous city, as well as the frantic farce *Hellzapoppin*.

Halliwell's Hundred and *Halliwell's Harvest are dedicated to the proposition that art should not be despised because it is popular.*

In 1985, Halliwell published his memoir, *Seats in all Parts*, which carried the all too prescient subtitle *Half a Lifetime at the Movies*. The details of his early cinemagoing with his mother and his school days were recounted, and the story continued through his army service and Cambridge, and ended with him leaving the Rex. Its dedication ran, "I think my mother would have liked to read this book." It is a fascinating account and provides rich rewards for the social or cinema historian (as well as the budding biographer!) but it does feature Halliwell's worst writing trait: the tendency towards *lists*. Because he so often felt compelled to be exhaustive in his descriptions, full inventories of mostly forgotten stars in mostly forgotten films appear all too regularly. Richard Caplan in the *New York Times* noted, "The effect of many one-line reviews is a tedium that mars this otherwise entertaining book."

Seats in all Parts is Halliwell's very own trip down memory lane, recounting with rose tinted affection the harsh times he lived through and how he came to escape from them, both figuratively and actually. John Nangle in *Films in Review* found its author's tales "too whimsical for words, with a preciousness that is so fey and British that it reads like an Ealing comedy." *The Sunday Times* pointed out that "the prose style is waggish [and the] picture captions are arch." Philip French was surprisingly more favourable, recognising the book's potential as a piece of social history by calling it "a richly detailed record of the great age of the picture palaces, a belated Mass-Observation report." David Elliot of *Booklist* wrote that it was a "fond, breezy memoir ... a nostalgic bouquet laid upon the grave [of the movie theatre]," and film historian Jeffrey Richards called it "a vivid, heartwarming recollection of a film-obsessed childhood ... he indelibly recaptured that now half-forgotten world of uniformed commissioners and queues, the A picture, the B picture and full supporting programme."

In 1986, the first in what was intended to be a series of books about particular genres of film appeared: *The Dead That Walk*, which tackled horror. In the mid-eighties, though, when the term implied splatter movies and video nasties, Halliwell's eye was as ever fixed firmly on the past, with the major focus being on those Universal monster movies of the thirties and forties, where dark shadows and gargoyle-like faces could send tingles down the spines of a shivering audience at the local Odeon. Focusing on three main protagonists: Dracula, the Frankenstein Monster and the Mummy, Halliwell began with their literary sources and touched on any relevant German expressionist treatments. He proceeded to examine the Universal features in detail before going on to cover Hammer's revivification of them in the fifties, and finally mopping up any related film or TV versions. In an interview for *Films and Filming* he remarked, "I took horror because it's a genre I've always enjoyed – within limits – and there's a lot to say and quote." American critic Roger Lewis was unimpressed: "There is a book of befitting brio to be written about horror films. Leslie Halliwell's *The Dead That Walk* is not that book. Very thin stuff, from a writer who has already spread himself a bit thin." Sean French (son of Philip) began his review for "long-haired publication" *Sight & Sound* thus:

> There is a creature ... which has been stalking the film world for many years. A semi-legendary creature, which rarely ventures out of the darkness. It is seemingly immortal and has even made a successful transition to television where it wields fearsome powers. It has evoked strong, hostile emotions in filmgoers, though in some it has inspired an odd affection and awe. Its name is Leslie Halliwell.

He goes on to describe the author's style as "jaunty plot summaries linked in a most leaden fashion"; further complains about his lack of enthusiasm and points out, "Halliwell is a film buff rather than a critic." A chip off the old block indeed! Once again the implication is that only critics can write about the movies because it is only they who truly understand the medium. John Nangle was more complimentary for *Films in Review*, pointing out the author's "seldom-middling opinions" – and he had no problem detecting enthusiasm, writing, "You can see he truly loves the genre."

The Dead That Walk is typically comprehensive and generally an entertaining read, but the long extracts from original novels and stories are an unnecessary distraction. It is much more successful when dealing with the films of Lugosi and Karloff, and in particular the script excerpts of scenes absent from released versions. The

Hammer films were dealt with respectfully but Halliwell was quite prepared to poke a little fun: "Black Park, near Pinewood ... rapidly became hilariously recognisable whenever Dracula's funereal carriage was driven back and forth along the foreshore, which was roughly twice per film." Also enjoyable is his increasing bemusement with the strains placed upon the audience's credulity by the creators of the Mummy series. "*The Mummy's Curse* has too great a lapse of the logic required even from a low-budget horror series on its last legs," he wrote. The main problem was that the monster was discovered in a Louisiana swamp, having fallen in at the end of the previous episode – "Ah yes, the swamp, murmurs the audience to itself; but wasn't that in New England?" Other similar lapses of sense led him to conclude, "This is Universal, where many apparent truths flourish for the duration of the movie, but whither as soon as the lights go up."

Double-Take and Fade Away, the next book in the series, examined comedy from its earliest historical sources, through American vaudeville and British music hall, and on into films and television. The subject is vast, and typically the author feels compelled to be all-encompassing, so the tendency towards lists is again apparent. The section on British film comedy of the thirties is covered title by title, and that on American sitcoms of the sixties and seventies *year by year* – "1967 was pretty much all lemons..." The book is its best when dealing with the routines of old music hall stars such as Frank Randle and Max Miller, of whom Halliwell had personal experience at the Grand Theatre in Bolton: his descriptions place the reader right there in the sixth row. Especially enjoyable are the transcripts of some of Abbott & Costello's sketches, and Danny Kaye's classic "the pellet with the poison's in the vessel with the pestle" routine from *The Court Jester*. It is in this book that one of Halliwell's best witticisms appears, writing that Blake Edwards was "a man of many talents, all minor." His sensibilities are tested towards the end of the book, as he is forced reluctantly to examine the wave of irreverent comedy which was sweeping British television in the eighties. The book concluded with a plea to return to more innocent humour – although he had himself recounted some pretty racy stuff from the music hall days along the way.

He intended to write additional books in the series, including *Transformation Scene*, to be subtitled "Movie characters who are seldom themselves." This would examine how the likes of Lawrence

Talbot of *The Wolf Man*, and Dr Jekyll had fared on the silver screen. After that would come *Somewhere over the Rainbow*, dealing with utopias such as Oz and, of course, Shangri-La. "It might be westerns after that," he told an interviewer, but unfortunately no further volumes in the series were ever published. Other unfinished or unpublished works included a novel about the cut-throat world of the TV industry. Having encountered all sorts of unsavoury characters in his thirty years in the business, Halliwell had ample material to draw on. He wrote of the executives he had met, "Some of them would by their own admission sell their grandmothers for sixpence; others are counted among my best friends; a third group expects to pull one dirty trick after another and not to be taken to task for such misconduct ... let them wait: I know on which of them I shall base the villains of my forthcoming novel."

Another proposed project, which he mentioned in that NFT interview, was his desire to write a book about moviegoing in 1939, the year in which ten (entirely worthy) films were nominated for the Best Picture Academy Award. The idea was for the book to come out in time for the fiftieth anniversary, but circumstances conspired against him. Despite his retirement, Halliwell was still involved in various occupations, including being a member of two National Film Archive committees, one for films and one for television programmes. They met every month or so at the BFI and were primarily concerned with selecting titles for inclusion in the archives. In late 1987, he was further employed to act as a consultant to the American production company Weintraub Screen Entertainment.

That same year, he attended the Richmond Film Society's 25th anniversary open evening, where he was observed "talking with enthusiastic nostalgia of youthful cinemagoing in his native Bolton, and screening a selection of clips from favourite films." Peter Sheil, currently chairman of the Society, recalled the occasion to me in an email, saying, "I remember him being a large bearded gent full of enthusiasm, and as a regular purchaser of his tome (any film fan's bible pre-internet) I was very much in awe of the man."

For the sea was pure and the darkness so soft and comforting, like the black folds of the dress of the lady who had now emerged fully formed from his imagination and was standing to his left...

In 1984, Halliwell had finally published his first collection of ghost stories, inspired by M. R. James. He had kept in touch with his old vicar, Stanley Leatherbarrow, and retained an interest in the genre all his life. He often remarked upon how few films had been made concerning spirits, with *Night of the Demon* and *The Uninvited* being two notable exceptions. *The Ghost of Sherlock Holmes* was the first of his efforts, and of his inspiration he wrote, "It was, I suppose, my admiration of James which prompted me to stand in the shadow of his chilling phrases: but I have always found in fantasy an elegant and amusing form of escape from the often tiresome reality of the world in which we live." In the preface he states that the 'I' in his tales is almost never him, but the unfathomable mysteries of the creative mind nevertheless conjured up a story set at Loews Hotel in Monte Carlo during a six-day TV market, and another about schoolchildren at an agricultural camp in Kirkham. One concerns a soldier doing his National Service in the Education Corps at Winterbourne Dauntsey, and a further tale is about a middle aged married couple living in a semi-detached in Kew.

A Demon Close Behind and *A Demon on the Stair* completed the set, in 1986 and 1988 respectively, and both of these conclude with ghostly poems. All three compilations contain stories set in locations Halliwell had visited during his life, from the sulphur springs and lava flows of Iceland to the arid desert of Death Valley, California, with the odd quaint English village thrown in. One story entitled 'The Past of Mrs Pickering' features an old lady from Bolton revisiting the places of her youth, and recalling her first trip to the cinema... at the Queen's Theatre. The name Haslam turns up more than once, which was Halliwell's mother's maiden name, and another sobriquet, Nicholas Kentish, is slightly adapted from a pseudonym he had used when writing for *Varsity*. Kentish is described as "a movie buff as well as a movie buyer," who, on a business trip to California, takes a trip to Death Valley where he has a strange encounter with some moving rocks.

Another Nicholas who visits Death Valley was the main character in Halliwell's only published novel, *Return to Shangri-La*, which appeared in paperback in 1987. It was a sequel to *Lost Horizon*, with the imaginative premise that the author of the original book, James Hilton, had actually met the real Conway and had simply related his true-life tale as fiction. In Halliwell's story, Nicholas

Brent, a TV producer in the 1980s has an experience in Death Valley which leads him and his explorer companion to undertake an expedition to the Himalayas. When they reach Shangri-La they meet Conway still living his contented existence, by then of considerable age but kept alive by the pure air – and some choice herbs – of the Valley of the Blue Moon. When asked about the book, Halliwell said, "*Lost Horizon* was one of the films which meant a great deal to me … I first saw it when I was about nine years old," adding, "The concept of Shangri-La always lingered in the mind. I tinkered for a few years with the idea of doing a sequel to it."

The novel itself is intriguing and always readable, like an updated Biggles adventure. It uses the same narrative style of *Dracula* and *Dr Jekyll and Mr Hyde*, with the story unfolding through written reports and journal accounts. Some references to films are typically shoehorned in – Shangri-La by then even has a makeshift cinema, and during a showing of John Ford's *The Grapes of Wrath* Brent comments, "I kept imagining myself back in a high street cinema in some English provincial city in the forties, about to catch the last bus home from the stop on the corner." The story only really picks up pace, though, in the final chapter, when a rival team try to muscle their way into the fabled paradise in order to steal its gold. Before that it spends a little too much time in Death Valley: Halliwell was keen to show off his intimate knowledge of the area. He had grown fond of barren landscapes at an early age when wandering across the Lancashire moors, as his old friend James Beattie recalled, "He loved remote places. He adored Death Valley – oh, he went on and on about it… the quietness and remoteness…"

One plot thread not fully realised in the book concerns the main character visiting his doctor, who "hummed and harrumphed at the result of my X-rays and barium meal and … put me down for 'a few other tests' … he did say there was no *immediate* danger." Much of Halliwell's writing was based on experience, but it seems unlikely that he could have known at this time the reality of his own condition. Michael Wright remembered meeting him in early 1988 for a drink and lunch at the Royal Oak in Guildford. Halliwell presented him with a copy of *A Demon on the Stair* as a present for his forthcoming wedding. The next contact Wright had was when his old friend telephoned to say he had been diagnosed with cancer of the oesophagus, and that the outlook was bleak. Halliwell's stepdaughter

Denise recalled that the family were especially surprised at the news, as he had only recently been given a clean bill of health in a medical for Granada. James Beattie told me, "He had complained – well, he didn't *complain*… but he kept saying for a while [patting his neck], 'Got this cold – can't seem to get rid of it.'" Beattie was appearing in a play about aboriginals which his old pal was due to attend, but the performance involved a real fire on the stage, and Halliwell knew the smoke would upset his throat and so had to drop out. Michael Winner remembered him announcing the news over lunch at a restaurant in Marble Arch: "He told me he was dying of cancer and that he wanted to finish his latest film guide…"

In December, Halliwell was honoured by the London Film Critics' Circle with a Special Achievement award, in recognition of the work he had done for the cinema. In their view he had "raised film consciousness" through his encyclopaedias. He was reported to have been "terribly pleased" but mentioned to a friend that the whole idea "sounds much too posh to be me. I just saw a hole in the market that I wanted to plug with the movies I loved, and which nobody else seemed to want to put into a book." He recorded a thank-you message as he was by then too ill to attend the ceremony.

Ruth Halliwell recalled a moment at home when her husband touched his books and said, "I am leaving these behind, anyway…" He was taken to the Princess Alice Hospice in Esher, where he was still trying to finish the 7th edition of the *Film Guide* from his bed. Denise said that her mother seemed to have a firmer grasp of the reality of the situation than he did, and that Ruth had to prevent him from dictating the second part of his memoirs as his condition worsened…

On Saturday 21st January 1989, a month short of his sixtieth birthday, Robert James Leslie Halliwell died.

11

A Tough Act to Follow

- Legacy -

In September 1988, a job advertisement appeared in *The Guardian* newspaper for the position of Production Editor at a new video magazine called *Movie*, a "glossy, perfectly bound, top quality monthly." The successful candidate would require experience and attention to detail, as well as an interest in the cinema… but, the advert stressed, "you don't have to be the son of Leslie Halliwell."

At the time of his death, Halliwell's reputation as 'Public Film Buff Number One' was cemented. With his guides selling thousands of copies and being ubiquitous in library reference sections up and down the country, his work was justly famous and widely regarded as the first port of call for film research. But even if movie fans did not personally own copies of his books, the reviews they read in newspapers and magazines were often aided by his work, as journalists frequently turned to their 'Halliwells' for fact-checking and inspiration. The millions who tuned into Channel 4 to catch an afternoon film were most likely watching one of his personal selections, and those settling down in front of a blockbuster premiere on ITV were benefiting from his buying expertise, whether they were aware of it or not.

As news spread of Halliwell's death, tributes began to pour in. Most of the major newspapers carried obituaries, with *The Times* calling him the "master guide for film and TV audiences," as well as "an unashamed apologist for the golden age of the cinema." His books were described as "not just catalogues of facts but spiced with his own, often idiosyncratic comments." In *The Guardian*, Tim Pulleine asserted that Halliwell had "done much, perhaps most, to popularise film history." He too commented on those famous opinions: "Quaint and bluff though some of his verdicts might have been, they were shot through with a passion for the cinema." The *Los Angeles Times* observed that his books were "as necessary as popcorn [and] sprinkled with writings as heated as those of a Revolutionary War pamphleteer."

Author Jeffrey Richards paid a warm tribute in the *Telegraph* with the headline, 'The irreplaceable filmgoer's companion'. He began, "For a legion of film fans, the death of Leslie Halliwell on Saturday will come as a personal blow, for he had become an indispensable part of their lives." Richards proceeded to highlight how useful the guides had been – as well as how much fun – and felt that Halliwell's work for Channel 4 had brought about "what in effect became a National Film Theatre in the home." Richards was himself a lifelong fan of the Golden Age, and appreciated in particular the more obscure titles which Halliwell "sedulously sought out." He further praised him for "recreating for all of us the joys of that childhood in Bolton long ago, when the silver screen had given him golden dreams. He was its chronicler, its champion and its celebrant. He will be irreplaceable."

TV World echoed the sentiment by suggesting that Halliwell's actual replacement at Granada was not quite in the same league:

> When Leslie Halliwell left the ITV film purchase group, the decision to appoint Don Gale as the new chief buyer for the ITV network caused a few raised eyebrows. Halliwell would be a tough act for anyone to follow – an intellectual with a passion for film, he was one of those impressive larger-than-life characters, every bit the public broadcaster and a breed apart from his successor.

In Halliwell's old school magazine, *The Boltonian*, a Dr. Alastair Finch attributed his own interest in films – leading to appearances on *Film Buff of the Year* and *Mastermind* – to his discovery of Halliwell's books when he was a librarian at the school. Finch attested, "His enormous and undisguised affection for the golden era of the cinema and its stars shines generously in all his work ... though

I never met him I feel a deep sense of loss which I'm sure is shared by his followers."

The funeral was held at the Barn Church in Kew, followed by cremation at Mortlake. Michael Wright was present at the service and three months later he attended a tribute arranged by ITV at the National Film Theatre. Clips were shown from *Lost Horizon, Citizen Kane* and *The Bride of Frankenstein*, and Paul Fox and Jeremy Isaacs were among the speakers. Ruth was there, as were many of Halliwell's ex-colleagues, and the numbers were further swollen by executives from the major American film and television studios. Wright remembered one of them calling Halliwell "a tough negotiator." Channel 4 paid their own tribute with a special screening of *Lost Horizon* in May.

Only a publisher's note served as the introduction to the 7th edition of the *Film Guide*, claiming that the author died shortly after completing work on it. However, he was reported to be still at work on revisions the day before he died, and Alan Frank, a colleague at Granada, told me *he* was corralled into finishing off some of the entries after Halliwell's death. Consequently, the 6th edition of the *Film Guide* was the last compiled wholly by its creator.

Although he desired that both the *Guide* and the *Companion* should continue, by the summer of 1989 Halliwell's publishers were struggling to find a successor. An article appeared in *The Sunday Times* with the headline, 'Halliwell proves a tough act to follow', in which a Grafton editor explained, "The problem is finding someone who combines Leslie's prodigious knowledge of films, but who also matches his personality. We have been approached by seven or eight people and we have some ideas of our own, but it is going to be a difficult job finding a replacement."

Alan Frank was mentioned as a possible candidate but the honour eventually fell to journalist John Walker. However, not only did he supply entries for the newer movies, but Walker proceeded to revise many of Halliwell's previous assessments and star ratings, quite significantly in some cases. The Australian production *The Chant of Jimmy Blacksmith* was originally awarded no stars and received this assessment: "Hard to take moral tale for philosophers with strong stomachs." However, once Mr. Walker got hold of it the movie jumped the full gamut to *four stars* and was given a rave: "One of the great achievements of Australian cinema." Walter Hill's *Southern*

Comfort, concerning National Guardsmen lost in the Louisiana swamps, made a similar ratings leap, with the assessment changing from, "Brutish retread of *Deliverance* with a few nods to Vietnam," to, "Brilliant, compelling, tightly-constructed thriller that manages also to be an allegory of American involvement in Vietnam." Inevitably, the 'Decline' essay was removed from subsequent editions, and despite the *Guide* continuing to be published under the name 'Halliwell', it would have decreasing relevance to its creator's sentiments and opinions.

In 1990, Halliwell was celebrated by the British Film Academy, with a special BAFTA bestowed for his masterful encyclopaedias. Ruth collected the award on his behalf and told a reporter, "Leslie had an inkling he was to get [it] but by then he was very ill. Even so he was pretty pleased. He loved films and everything about them." Five years later, Ruth was involved in a plagiarism case brought against Derek Winnert's *Radio Times Film & Video Guide*, after parts of it were found to be too similar to her late husband's work – even retaining some of Halliwell's own errors. John Walker complained, "It is most unfair that competing film guides should benefit from all his painstaking and time-consuming work." They were successful in the High Court and a "substantial sum" was paid, with the remaining stocks of Winnert's guide having to be pulped.

The Observer was indignant at the outcome and encouraged its readers to get hold of the *Radio Times* book before all the copies went "to the shredder." They reiterated Philip French's comment about Halliwell knowing the credits of everything but the value of nothing; further called his *Film Guide* "turgid" and alleged that it was "regarded by many leading critics as inferior to Winnert's in judgment, wit and style." Two years later the same newspaper reviewed the *Time Out Film Guide* and asserted that, "Unlike Halliwell, the *Time Out* people are critics with ideas, not buffs with glib opinions, and they range far beyond the mainstream cinema."

As time passed on, Halliwell's reputation seemed to diminish even further. *League of Gentlemen* star Mark Gatiss supplied a wretched comment to *The Guardian* in which he imagined that the "dishevelled tramp with the terrible BO who always sits next to you at the pictures is Halliwell's vengeful spirit, seeking to spoil cinemagoers' enjoyment in death just as he did in life." Far from spoiling anything, Halliwell had received awards for his promotion of the cinema and had spent his working life encouraging a greater appreciation of its history. But small minded observers resented him simply because he did not care for the same kind of films that they did.

The emergence of the World Wide Web, and in particular the Internet Movie Database, all but relegated film guidebooks to obsolescence but Halliwell's other achievements were also forgotten. Dorothy Hobson wrote a whole book about the early years of Channel 4 and did not even give him a single mention; the Bolton Little Theatre's website fails to list him among their notable alumni and none of his non-encyclopaedic works is currently in print. Critic Alexander Walker was invited by the editors of *The Dictionary of National Biography* to contribute some words about Halliwell but he "declined on the grounds that he thought him unworthy of inclusion."

Others were more appreciative. Tom Hutchinson of *The Guardian* marked the twentieth anniversary of *Halliwell's Film Guide* with an article celebrating its author for single-handedly inventing the film reference book. He admitted that in the late nineties, guidebooks in general had become a "damaged goods industry," but praised Halliwell for being a pioneer in his field. He referred to him as a "hulkingly amiable man [with] belligerent enthusiasm," and further stated, "Similar books sprang from that original enterprise but they still pale by comparison." Hutchinson concluded, "All film-writers of repute are addicts, rationalising their addiction by passing it on to others. Leslie Halliwell happened to have a bigger fix of faith than most ... he was the only begetter of what has become part of our lives. That's why the dynasty lives on – and still reigns over us."

Even Philip French was respectful of his memory, in an email to me:

> I didn't greatly care for his writing or for the influence he exerted on public opinion by way of his reference works or his TV programming. There was/is nothing personal about this. He was clearly intelligent, knowledgeable and professionally well organised. We met occasionally in the 1980s when we served on the advisory committee of the National Film Archive, that met for lunch at the BFI every month or so. We never became friends, but we were on amicable enough terms.

In 1996, comedian Peter Kay helped to unveil a plaque dedicated to Halliwell at the ABC cinema in Bolton, formerly known as the Lido. The plaque, in the shape of a film frame, was one of 200 similar honours bestowed upon movie notables across the country, to mark the centenary of the cinema. Kay spoke of Halliwell's influence and said, "Like everyone else in the town, every screen, every seat and every film holds many memories." The dedication ran:

> LESLIE HALLIWELL
> Born in Bolton 1929.
> Eminent Film Historian and Author
> A regular visitor to this cinema, then 'The Lido'.

The ABC was described as "Bolton's last stand cinema": it was at the time the only remaining picture house from the Golden Age still functioning as a cinema in the town. The Theatre Royal survived only until the early sixties, and the Queen's switched to Asian films in the seventies before closing in 1980. The Lido/ABC lasted only two more years, however, eventually shutting down upon the opening of the Tonge Moor multiplex, now part of the Cineworld chain. The building was demolished in 2006 and a block of flats now stands in its place. The Odeon reopened as a bingo hall but was itself pulled down in 2007, seventy years after its construction. At the time of writing, the site is still not completely clear, and parts of that old "palatial hall" still remain. When I was there, the shiny black tiles of its rounded corners were visible at the front, and broken brickwork could be seen around the sides – as if the Golden Age refuses to die in Bolton.

With the picture houses and theatres now gone, Churchgate and Deansgate are almost the sole preserve of shops, and with very few pubs or restaurants the place is eerily quiet in the evenings. What a contrast to those heady days of the thirties, when this part of town thrived with activity. Further out, some of the mill factory buildings still stand, now converted either to warehouses or office blocks.

The Cambridge Rex closed in 1972 and was demolished seven years later. The Wessex Place Care Unit now occupies the site, helping people with mental health needs. George Webb died in 1983 after being ill for some time following a serious heart attack. He had given up the cinema business in the late sixties and returned to the motor industry. The *Cambridge Evening News* carried the headline, 'City loses a flamboyant personality', and described him as a household name in the town. They recounted George's acquisition of the cinema and his appointment of Halliwell, whereupon "the place really came alive ... students felt their periods at Cambridge were incomplete without the weekly visit to the Rex."

Clive Halliwell had gone to live at Ravenswood special home many years before his father's death. Leslie saw to it that the copyright for his encyclopaedias reverted to the institution, so that the royalties would ensure his son's continued care. Ruth remained at their Kew residence for a while before moving to an apartment nearby. She passed away in 2002. Stewart Porter, her son by her previous marriage, died two years later at the Suffolk house bought for Leslie's retirement, which was to feature a dedicated annexe for his film library. Ruth once said of her husband, "He was a gentle man who disliked films of violence. And he retained a great pride in his home town."

Sir Paul Fox told me, "I cannot praise Leslie enough in terms of his ethics, for his negotiating skills, and for his knowledge of the industry. The studios appreciated him as a fellow professional and had great, great respect for him at all levels."

My favourite of all the tributes I received, however, was from Michael Wright, Halliwell's friend for forty years. He wrote, "Leslie's personality could at times be overwhelming, but it came so naturally to him that he nearly always managed to get his way without causing offence, and there was not a trace of malice in him."

In 25 years' time the negatives of all my golden oldies may have dwindled into dust.

If Halliwell's influence is now all but forgotten, at least it is still possible to enjoy the films he so cherished. Every title I have mentioned in this book can be obtained from one source or another, and many of them turn up on television from time to time – and not just on specialist channels like TCM. In addition, the National Film Theatre runs many seasons featuring films from the Golden Age, with talks and presentations to accompany them.

Fortunately, the studios themselves seem to have taken great care of their legacy, thanks largely to the efforts of conscientious film-makers such as Martin Scorsese. Warners in particular have kept their old negatives in such fine condition that recent blu-ray releases of *Casablanca*, *An American in Paris* and *The Adventures of Robin Hood* have been of breathtaking quality. But there are many other treasures from the old days to be discovered by inquisitive fans, and who knows what influence they might yet have? Perhaps a new generation of film-makers could be inspired to emulate the techniques of the Golden Age greats? Maybe a small studio somewhere will begin to make slick, sophisticated entertainments to stimulate the mind as well as to pass an evening, and a new audience might emerge to appreciate them. There could be a move away from the tiresome comic book adaptations, the moronic action flicks and the infantile comedies which so beset the industry's current output. And instead of the clash and bang of modern film-making, with its shaky camerawork, frantic cutting and vapid performances, perhaps the creators will adopt a more impressionistic approach. They might inject a lightness of touch into their work and once again strain reality – as their predecessors did – "through the mesh of Hollywood's magic machinery."

Maybe one day Hollywood itself will find a way back to its own lost horizon, a place where gifted screenwriters created characters the audience could look up to, and conjured witty lines to be delivered by talented performers capable of mesmerising an audience. A place where directors were content to move the story along briskly, while stimulating people's imagination via subtle camera movements.

Or, more likely, I will just continue to enjoy the riches the older generation left behind, and once in a while thank Leslie Halliwell for introducing them to me, and for increasing immeasurably my knowledge and appreciation of the cinema.

I can watch the films, but I can never know what it was like to experience them sitting in the plush warmth of a brand new 1930s dream palace, with the grime of a soot-covered mill town banished for a few precious hours. To gaze upon a gleaming new print, freshly struck from a pristine negative, thrown up through light onto a giant four-by-three screen, and appreciated with hushed reverence by a packed house…

Halliwell's Shangri-La, was both a place *and* a time.

References

Abbreviations for newspapers and periodicals:

AB = *Antiquarian Bookman*
ABC = *American Book Collector*
AF = *American Film*
AG = *The Age*
ARB = *American Reference Books Annual*
AW = *Airwaves*
BB = *Books & Bookmen*
BBN = *British Book News*
BC = *Broadcast*, formerly *Television Mail*.
BEN = *Bolton Evening News*
BEP = *Bristol Evening Post*
BJG = *Bolton Journal & Guardian*
BL = *Booklist*
BT = *The Boltonian*
CC = *Choice*
CDN = *Cambridge Daily News*
CEN = *Cambridge Evening News*
CH = *Chicago Tribune*
CT = *Cambridge Today* (formerly *Varsity Supplement*)
DE = *Daily Express*
DM = *Daily Mail*
DT = *Daily Telegraph*
EN = *Evening News*
EQ = *Esquire*
EV = *Everybody's*
FIR = *Films in Review*
FR = *Film Review*
FRA = *Film Review Annual*
GD = *The Guardian*
HP = *Harper's*
IB = *Independent Broadcasting*
ID = *The Independent*
LAT = *Los Angeles Times*

LJB = *Library Journal Book Review*
LS = *The Listener*
MM = *Movie Maker*
NR = *The New Republic*
NYR = *New York Review*
NYT = *New York Times*
OS = *The Observer*
PG = *Picturegoer*
PP = *Photoplay*
PT = *Primetime*
QQ = *Quill & Quire*
RSR = *Reference Services Review*
RTT = *Richmond & Twickenham Times*
S4 = *See 4*
SI = *Screen International*
SK = *Skoop*
SL = *Stills*
SM = *Sunday Mirror*
SO = *Slough Observer*
SP = *The Spectator*
SS = *Sight & Sound*
ST = *The Sunday Times*
STM = *The Sunday Times Magazine*
STT = *The Stage & Television Today*
TES = *The Times Educational Supplement*
TM = *Television Mail*, became *Broadcast* in 1973.
TT = *The Times*
TVT = *TV Times*
TVW = *TV World*
TW = *Television Weekly*
VT = *Variety*
VV = *Video Viewer*
VY = *Varsity*
WA = *The West Australian*

REFERENCES

LH's books (see also bibliography):

CBC = *The Clapperboard Book of the Cinema.*
DTFA = *Double Take and Fade Away*
DTW = *The Dead That Walk*
FC[1-9] = *The Filmgoer's Companion*, with edition number
FG[1-7] = *Halliwell's Film Guide*
GSH = *The Ghost of Sherlock Holmes*
HH = *Halliwell's Hundred*
HV = *Halliwell's Harvest*
MOD = *Mountain of Dreams*
RTSL = *Return to Shangri-La*
SIAP = *Seats in all Parts*
TVC[1-3] = *Halliwell's Television Companion* (or *Teleguide*).

Introduction

Information comes from Fred Hill's *Churchgate* and Gordon Readyhough's *Bolton Town Centre*, as well as *Bolton Memories*, *Bolton's Last Tram* and my own observations at the scene. LH saw *Lost Horizon* at the Theatre Royal according to SIAP, and the BEN puts this occasion in the week beginning 31st January, 1938. It is inconceivable to me that he would not have attended the first night's showing after school, but I don't know it for certain. The Theatre itself was described by Brian Hornsey in *Ninety Years of Cinema in Bolton*, and by LH in FF 04/1968. The weather is from the forecast in the BEN, so that could also be wrong – but it *was* winter in the north of England…

Chapter 1 – Like a Duck to Water

Bolton

Information about the town comes from *When All the World Was Young*, as well as LH's memoir, *Seats in all Parts* (SIAP) – which I have certainly leaned on for the first four chapters. Most of the insights into LH's early life and especially into his own mindset come from here. However, it should be noted that many of the incidents regarding his early cinemagoing with his mother were recounted previously in 'Merely Stupendous', a mammoth seven-part series of articles he contributed to *Films & Filming* in 1967/8. In fact, some of them turned up word for word in SIAP almost twenty years later. In application development, we call that "code reuse"...

Figures for cinema attendance – and the reason for it – are from Jeffrey Richards's wonderful book, *The Age of the Dream Palace*, as well as other works in the 'Cinema and Society' series: *An Everyday Magic, Film-making in 1930s Britain* and *The Unknown 1930s*.

The two 'first' trips

Recounted in both FF 03/1968 and SIAP, as well as a talk LH gave at the Edinburgh Book Festival in 1983 – British Library Sound Archive, ref. C143/17. The Queen's was described as "the coolest cinema in town" in BEN 24/07/1933, where *Madame Butterfly* was advertised on the front page, along with all the other cinemas' fare for the week. "The screen was astonishing" is from SIAP.

Family Life

Jim Halliwell's early life was recollected by his son in BEN 06/10/1970, 07/10/1970 and 08/10/1970, and *From Affetside to Yarrow: Bolton Place Names and their History* provided the derivation of his surname. That Lily's maiden name was Haslam shows up on LH's birth certificate, Apr/May/Jun 1929, Bolton, Vol 8c, Page 480, which records his full name and their address. Other family-related information is from SIAP.

The Golden Age

"For me the greatest days..." is from AW spring 1986, and the coming of sound is described in Barry Norman's excellent *Talking Pictures*, from where "ponderously and portentously" is taken. The Production Code is printed in *Winchester's*.

Ezra Goodman was certainly one observer who felt that the silent era was preferable, in his book *The Fifty Year Decline and Fall of Hollywood*. "To this fluency with words..." is from FF 01/1968. "Filmland was entering its golden age" is from FF 04/1967, and that witty observation about MGM is from FF 03/1968 – all parts of 'Merely Stupendous.'

Garbo is described in *Brewer's Cinema* and *MGM: When the Lion Roars*, and LH's "indestructible" quote is from SIAP.

REFERENCES

"Agreeable light entertainment" comes from MOD.

"Christians killed in a novel and diverting manner" is from FF 02/1968, and "did not seem to have the right kind of dust" is from SIAP. "All cheap sets and shadows" is from the assessment of *Angels with Dirty Faces* in FG5, and *Top Hat* is recounted in SIAP, from where the "image of Fred" quote is taken.

Cinemagoing with Lily

"Like a duck to water" and "it was with my mother" are from SIAP, as is the information about LH's home life. The cinema experience, with its queues and full supporting programmes, is recounted in *The Age of the Dream Palace*. Laurel and Hardy's background is described in *Brewer's Cinema*, and LH's wonderful distillation of their style is in both HH and SIAP. "Our dear old friends" is from FF 04/1968.

Moving house

"I was always grateful" is from BEN 08/10/1970, and the rest of this section is from SIAP.

British films

"...class ridden or downright foolish" is from 'Over the Brink', LH's two-part study of the film industry during wartime, FF 09/1968 – although the observation was made with regards to the thirties. That Boltonians preferred American to British films is borne out by *Mass-Observation at the Movies* and John Sedgwick's *Popular Filmgoing in 1930's Britain*.

Gracie Fields and George Formby get whole chapters devoted to them in *The Age of the Dream Palace* – so does Jessie Matthews, but I couldn't find room for her. "Lancastrians preferred to laugh at hardship" is from HH and the Timbuctoo quote is from SIAP. *Popular Filmgoing* provides the comparison between *Sing as we Go* and *Queen Christina*, and "anything starring the lad from Wigan" is from SIAP. The incident where Formby appeared on stage is in both SIAP and FF 04/1968.

Regarding Mr Hitchcock, "The electrically vivid first flowering" (a beautiful quote), and "It is still among the most entertaining ways" are from HH.

The Isle of Man trip and *Things to Come* are from SIAP and HH.

The BBC's first television broadcast can be attributed to an article called 'From There to Here in Forty Years' from BC 01/11/1976, as well as Denis Forman's piece, 'My Life and TV Times', SS autumn 1982. "We warn the industry" is from 'Merely Stupendous', FF 01/1968.

Lido and Odeon

SIAP again for the décor quote, with the rest a combination of that and 'Merely Stupendous'. *Dr Jekyll* is related in FF 06/1969 and HH, from where "a masterpiece of cinematic flow" is pulled. "Precisely the same type" is from a copy of the Odeon programme for that opening night, preserved at the Bolton History Centre, and which provides details of the night's entertainment.

Lost Horizon

SIAP for the "half-employed" quote and for LH's first time for seeing it. The tie-in ads are from BEN 28/01/1938 and the "record crowds" quote from BEN 01/02/1938. The making of the film is described in *A Catastrophe of Success*.

Going on his own

SIAP, as well as BEN 04/10/1978 for banned from the Tivoli, and AW spring 1986 for "richer than colour." The *King Kong* incident is once again in both SIAP and HH. FF 01/1968 is where the lack of popularity of colour and "the hues had all the richness" are taken.

Estimates on the number of cinemas in the area vary. LH mentions 27 in both BEN 06/10/1970 and BEN 04/10/1978 – as well as that talk at the Edinburgh Book Festival in 1983 – British Library Sound Archive, ref. C143/17. He seemed finally to settle on 28 in SIAP. I could only make it 26 from my research.

Chapter 2 – No Concessions to Low-brows

Wartime

See *Mass-Observation at the Movies* for all information related to the studies, the interview with the Embassy manager, much of the material about Humphrey Jennings and the cinema closures. LH's recollections of the outbreak of war are from a TV series he hosted called *Home Front*, specifically the episode dealing with *The First Days*. Ronald Lowe related his memories to me in a phone call, 14/04/2010. The changing face of cinemas, "semi-disabled" and "I already sensed" are all from a two-part article LH wrote about moviegoing in wartime, entitled 'Over the Brink', to be found in FF 09/1968 and 10/1968. The second tale about LH in Great Lever Park is from *Home Front* and the trip to Surrey is recounted in SIAP.

School

The description of Bolton School is from my own observations, and LH's first day and subsequent loneliness are from SIAP. "At seven o'clock…" is from SK 01/03/1979. I interviewed Ron Edge on 12/04/2009, and James Beattie on 31/07/2010. Malcolm Worrall wrote to me through FriendsReunited.com.

American Films

Kings Row is from HH and SIAP. The *Citizen Kane* excitement is from 'Over the Brink'.

Picturegoer

Their readers' top ten list was reported on by LH in FF 10/1968. Examples of Collier's style are from PG 28/12/1940 and the notebooks were written of in SIAP.

Horror Films

LH wrote another two-part article called 'The Baron, the Count and their Ghoul Friends', which related his tales of watching horror films with his friends. This appeared in FF 06/1969 and 07/1969, and turned up almost word for word in SIAP many years later. "Mental incompetents" is from the latter, however. *The Mummy's Hand* and *Bride of Frankenstein* were additionally featured in HH.

Documentaries

Mass-Observation at the Movies provides a history of the Crown Film Unit. SIAP also used here, and 'Over the Brink' for "the new spirit." LH presented *Home Front* on ITV in 1982, from where "marvellously chilling," "quite different" and "favourite film sequences" are taken. Also, see the documentary *Humphrey Jennings: the Man who Listened to Britain*, included on a DVD of his best work.

British Films

Henry the Fifth is in HH and LH's review of it appears in BT 12/1945 along with the "no concessions" quote. *A Matter of Life and Death* is recalled in HH, as well as SIAP, whence came "British films had reached maturity."

Rejuvenation

"Initially despised me" and "unforgivably bossy" are from SIAP. Many of the articles in *The Boltonian* are referenced in the text, but "no facilities for plays" is from BT 12/1945. The Film Society is recalled in SIAP, HH and HV, and the reports feature in any issue of BT from the period. In SIAP, LH claimed to have written letters to the BEN, but I'll have to take his word for it because I tried in vain to find any. The Literary and Debating Society was reported on regularly but "noteworthy support" is from BT 12/1945. The Empire experiment into foreign language movies is from SIAP, as is the "delirious week" at Stanford Hall. 'Pastoral' is from BT 03/1947. I spoke to Irving Wardle on 02/05/2009.

Theatre

The influx of live performance in Bolton is from SIAP as is LH venturing to Manchester. He was seen in *As You Like It* in BT 07/1947. James Wood's recollection of *Hamlet* was given to me in an email on 27/02/2009, and Irving Wardle's in person. The pictures and review of the production were included in BT 07/1947. "My mother loved it" is from BEN 04/10/1978.

National Service

Predictably related in SIAP but much of this is taken from letters LH wrote to his old school, printed in BT 12/1947, 03/1948 and 03/1949.

Return to Bolton

SIAP for LH's return and Barry Norman's *Talking Pictures* for the changing face of the movie business.

REFERENCES

Chapter 3 – The Scarcest Commodity

College life

Information about college life and entrance figures come from *Portrait of Cambridge 1952* and *An Introduction to Cambridge* (see bibliography). LH's own experience is related in detail in SIAP, from which his quotes are taken. ABC's dominating presence in the city at the time is easily verifiable from adverts and articles in VY and CDN, as well as *Kelly's Directory of Cambridge*.

"Making a furtive egress" is from BT 12/1949. Allen Freer offered his memories of LH to me in an email, 14/09/2009. Michael Wright sent his in a letter, 17/09/2009, as did Eric Cross on 08/10/2009. Jim Norris saw the film posters on LH's walls, and told me so in a phone call on 27/09/2009.

Films

LH's experiences watching *The Philadelphia Story*, *The Third Man*, *Duck Soup*, *Trouble in Paradise* and *The Lady Eve* are from SIAP, HH and HV. The quote about *Morgan's Creek* is from FG5. The Marx Brothers being "the patron saints of Cambridge" comes from Michael Birkett's article in VY 17/11/1949. Peter Darby reminisced to me about the German Society in a telephone conversation, 17/09/2009, and "Ah, to be young again" is from HV.

Varsity

LH's visit to his old school appears in BT 12/1949, and the reviews are in VY 25/02/1950 and CT 03/1950. Incidentally, the latter was the first time in print that he was referred to as 'Leslie Halliwell'. His impressions of *Varsity* are from SIAP, and the issue in which he is almost omnipresent is 04/11/1950. His promotion to Features Editor is from BT 12/1950, as well as his Tripos results which can be further confirmed by the *Cambridge Historical Register*. LH's appearances at the Cambridge Old Boltonians' Dinner and *Alice in Wonderland* are from BT 03/1950. The trip to Italy is related in HV.

'Exit the Monsters' appears in CT 11/1950, and 'Music without Charms' a month later. "It sparkles in my memory" is from HH. LH's appointment to Literary Editor was announced in VY 13/01/1951, where 'A Filmgoer's Guide' also appears. Tom Pevsner's response duly appeared on 20/01/1951.

'Next Week's Films" quotes are from VY 19/01/1952, and the letter of complaint and LH's response appear the week after. "I tried to be fair" is from SIAP.

The Rex

"Luxury had never entered…" is from SIAP. The hypnotist and George Webb's purchase were reported in VY 24/02/1951. LH suggests he won it in a raffle in HH, but said a poker game in a later interview. *Cairo Road*, *Tarzan and the Slave Girl* and *State Secret* were all shown in January according to CDN, so it would seem that George was already in place at the Rex before the sale had fully completed. LH's first impressions are from SIAP, as is his conversation with George – related as a phone call which "ran along these lines." I took that as a licence to alter it slightly and make it a face-to-face.

Acting

"Time is the scarcest commodity" is from LH's editorial in VY 19/04/1952. *1066 and All That* is mentioned in VY 10/02/1952 and BT 07/1952, along with *Coriolanus* and LH's second Tripos exam. "He can be seen in disguise…" (I love that quote) is from BT 07/1951. Other information was obtained from programmes of performances, sent to me by various Cambridge alumni.

Our Town is related in SIAP, BT 04/1952 and BEN 01/01/1952, where Thornton Wilder's letter was reported. The review is from BEN 04/01/1952.

Conflict of interest

"The powers that be…" and "Bookings so far suggest" are from an article called "Films for this term" in VY 19/01/1952, also the source for "a brilliant programme" in 'Next Week's Films'. "Go early" is from VY 09/02/1952, and *Forbidden Jungle* and *Love Happy* both appear the following week.

Editor

"We live in a dream world" is from VY 19/04/1952, and LH's appointment, and George Webb's fine, are reported in VY 08/03/1952. The editorials and their responses duly follow over the next eight issues.

REFERENCES

The Blue Angel

"As a frequent non-paying patron" is from SIAP. *The Blue Angel* was shown in the week of 17/05/1952, according to VY and CDN, and the episode is related in both SIAP and HH, as well as LH's talk at the Edinburgh Book Festival in 1983 – British Library Sound Archive, ref. C143/17.

Summary

"It is neither easy nor desirable…" is from LH's final editorial, VY 07/06/1952. "*Avant-garde* films…" appears in CT 01/1951.

Chapter 4 – A Dream Come True

Film Industry

Talking Pictures once again for industry changes and the end of Clark Gable's contract. When Chaplin, Griffith, Fairbanks and Pickford formed United Artists in 1919, film producer Richard A. Rowland remarked, "The lunatics have taken over the asylum."

Picturegoer

SIAP and James Beattie in person for the flat-share; 'Macbeth' is referred to in the *All About Eve* section of HV. *The Thing* article is in PG 06/09/1952, and other quotes are from PG 16/08/1952 and 23/08/1952, the latter being the source for 'Box Office Ginger'.

A *Picturegoer*-related anomaly persists. LH on more than one occasion recounted an incident where he was dispatched to view Don Siegel's *Invasion of the Body Snatchers*, and was so impressed that he recommended it for the magazine's prestigious Seal of Merit. Given the film's B-movie title, the other staff thought him mad and sent another reviewer for a second opinion, which of course concurred with LH's. A nice story, but he worked there during the summer of 1952… and *Body Snatchers* was not made until 1956! Did he do a second stint there? It seems unlikely as he was on the Rank trainee course at that time, and at least one newspaper report puts him at the Slough Ambassador in November, soon after the *Picturegoer* review of the film was printed. I tried in vain to contact several people who might have helped and so it remains a mystery.

Chesterton Road

"Having never met anybody like George…" is from SIAP, as is "read and sleep and have breakfast." Observations were made by myself at the scene, and the fact that number six was owned by Mrs W. Lavis is confirmed by *Kelly's Directory of Cambridge 1955*. The location of the Rex is clear from a 1953 County Planning Department map, held at the Cambridge Archives.

Early Days

LH's early experiences as a manager, including his attempts at improvements are all from SIAP. The "commission-hungry travelling salesmen" turn up in the articles 'Running the Rex', VY 08/11/1952, and 'Continuous Performance', SP 13/03/1953. 'Strictly for Eggheads', SS 04/1954, is the source for "partial success came our way…" and "we are persevering…"

The King Kong pictures are in VY 01/11/1952 and CDN 01/11/1952. "I believe my performance…" is from HH. The programme booklets are for February, April, May and July of 1953.

Citizen Kane

SIAP and HH, as well as *Brewer's Cinema* for a little history.

Innovations

All are related in SIAP, but the Synchro Screen is reported on in VY 17/01/1953, and 3-D turns up in CDN 24/07/1953 and 07/08/1953. "CinemaScopus Horribilis" is from EV 11/02/1956. The other widescreen quotes are from FC9 and *The Fifty Year Decline and Fall of Hollywood*. "Good enough for *Gone with the Wind*" is from SIAP. George Perry's criticism appears in VY 08/10/1955, with LH's riposte coming the week after and Perry's final word in VY 05/11/1955.

X-Certificate films

These are mentioned in 'Strictly for Eggheads' SS 04/1954. "…suckers for the pornographic" is from VY 08/05/1954, written by Sir Peter Hall, who gave me his recollections by phone of the showing of *Extase*, 18/10/2009. The programme booklet for 02/1953 contains the other quotes and the controversy turns up in VY 07/03/1953.

REFERENCES

Criticism
"Personally I'd love to show…" is from VY 05/03/1955, and "The Rex continues digging…" is from VY 17/01/1953. "…a dream come true" is from SIAP.

The Golden Years
Most of this is from SIAP, including "in my second and third years," "a square peg in a square hole" and "my days were filled with excitement." Michael Wright reminisced of the Norway trip in a letter to me. 'Dracula claims victims' is in VY 26/11/1955. *The Titfield Thunderbolt* premiere is related in DTFA and the Marx Brothers book review is from VY 06/11/1954.

Public Speaking
The 'toast of the school' was proposed in BT 04/1954. 'The Perverted Art' is reported in VY 31/10/1953 and 'The Box Office is debasing the Film' is in BT 12/1955 and VY 22/10/1955.

Film Society
The move to the Rex is reported in VY 16/01/1954 and "mentally lazy" and "desperate appeals" are from VY 01/05/1954. "Pre-LH days" is from VY 08/05/1954.

Journalism
'Strangers in the Train' is from BJG 05/02/1954. The Lina Lopez "perambulating" is from VY 05/02/1955, as is the first instance of Michael Winner writing 'Next Week's Films'. I spoke to him on the phone on 24/04/2009, and the story about George Webb is from VY 04/06/1955.

The Wild One
Obviously SIAP, but also SS summer 1955, DE 22/03/1955, PG 07/05/1955 and CDN 12/04/1955. Michael Winner remembered curry conversations in ST 23/11/2008 and ST 26/12/1993. George Webb's overstatement is from VY 30/04/1955.

Leaving the Rex
SIAP and VY 28/01/1956. Lily's death certificate index is Apr 1956, 10b, 530, Bolton.

Chapter 5 – Just Like Ealing Broadway

Domestic Life

Information gleaned from BMD: Ruth/Edward m11/03/1944, Nottingham; Ruth/Leslie m18/07/1959, Surrey North; Clive b11/04/1961, Kingston Hill, Surrey. In addition, the reminiscences of Halliwell's stepdaughter Denise, Joanna Harrison, Sir Peter Hall, Michael Wright and Alan Frank were all of enormous help.

RTT 27/01/1989 had the information about Leslie's bookstall. The record turnout at the Old Boltonians' dinner is in BT 03/1961. Ruth's quote about looking after him is from BEN 04/04/1992, and LH's about Laurel & Hardy is from SIAP. Stanley Leatherbarrow moving to Malvern is in BEN 04/10/1978.

At the Odeons

BT 12/1956 states that LH had been at Ipswich, *Bolton* and Slough. A journalist in BEN 21/09/1999 further claims that LH actually worked at the Bolton Odeon for six weeks but I could not verify this. Since it was quite possibly his favourite ever picture house, the fact that he never once mentioned in print having actually worked there makes it difficult for me to believe. More likely it was nearby Radcliffe, which he speaks of in both HH and HV.

His tenure at the Slough Ambassador is in the *Twelve Angry Men* section of HH and is further confirmed by SO 30/11/1956. The Hammer revivification is dealt with in DTW and *The Story of Mankind* is from HV.

Playwright

BEN 09/04/1957 has the interview with LH regarding *Make Your Own Bed*, and BEN 22/04/1957 has the "continuous uproar" advert – but unfortunately they do not seem to have reviewed the actual play. *A Night on the Island* turns up in BT 03/1959; is previewed in BEP 31/01/1959 and reviewed in BEP 03/02/1959.

Early career

The History of Broadcasting in the United Kingdom has information about the Rank consortium. LH refers to publicising John Mills and Norman Wisdom in DM 23/5/1987, and his position is mentioned in BT 07/1957. His stint at Southern Television is referred to in BT 03/1959.

Granada

The history of ITV and Granada is from *Granada Television: the First Generation*. LH starting work there is in BT 03/1959, but the fact that he worked there from around this time is confirmed by countless book jackets and other sources. Denis Forman, in his autobiography *Persona Granada*, states that it was Cecil who was looking for an assistant, but LH remembered it being Sidney in SIAP. Sir Denis gave me his recollections in a letter, 28/04/2010.

The *Flashback* anecdote is related in FF 01/1987. LH refers to the Zoo Unit in DM 28/3/1987 and it also crops up in OS 22/03/1987. Details are from *Seven Years with Film & TV Cameras at the London Zoo*. The *Psycho* meeting was related in HV and his secondment by Cecil Bernstein is in OS 22/03/1987.

"Head of the Film Department" is in BT 12/1963. He boasts about buying *The Beverly Hillbillies* in DM 12/09/1987.

FIDO

SS autumn 1982 features an article concerning Sir Denis Forman's experiences and SS summer 1980 includes one about the cinema versus television. FIDO turns up in both, as it does in *The History of Broadcasting in the United Kingdom* and CBC, from where "many second feature producers..." is taken. "57 covenants" is reported in TM 16/10/1959. The buying of films by triumvirate at Granada is from STT 17/01/1985, and LH being in charge of the film department is in BT 12/1963. Lew Grade's antics are mentioned in TM 21/08/1964 and also in an NFT interview with LH which took place on 22/07/1987.

Cinema

The *University Challenge* quote is from DM 11/07/1987. Bamber Gascoigne and Sir Michael Parkinson gave their recollections to me in emails, on 30/09/2009 and 22/07/2009 respectively. *Cinema* itself is previewed in TM 14/08/1964 and its commencement is verified by TVT 07/1964. LH's credit is mentioned every week and see TVT 24/04/1966 for the wide screen edition. Actual episodes and interview subjects are obtainable from the BFI Library's website database. DM 28/03/1987 has LH helping to organise the BAFTAs. David

Shipman's quote is from ID 23/01/1989 and the popularity of films on TV, as well as *Cinema* is in TM 04/12/1964. The week the show hit the number one spot was 16/06/1968, verified by TM a couple of weeks after the event. This publication is also the source for the show's popularity in general and its spin-off, *Clapperboard*.

The Charlie Chaplin anecdote is in HH and is of course anomalous: *The Chaplin Revue* came out in 1959, probably to celebrate his seventieth birthday but *Cinema* was not running then. So, unless the film was re-released for his seventy-fifth..? But Chaplin was born in April and the show did not begin until July so that still doesn't work! It's a good story and I'm sure LH related the events faithfully, but may have just got some of the details wrong.

First US trip

This is a distillation of a two-part article called "America: the Celluloid Myth," which LH contributed to FF 11/1967 and FF 12/1967, as well as TVT 06/05/1967. "The backlots were more or less intact" and "just like Ealing Broadway" are from PT issue 8 1984. The *All About Eve* viewing is from HV and Mae West's 'come-on' is in OS 22/03/1987. King Kong was mentioned in a Granada Memo from 21/02/1969, held at the BFI Library and accompanied by the photograph. It was referred to in BT 07/1962 and Nancy Banks-Smith's observation is from GD 18/12/1976. LH's comment about *Virginia Woolf* is from FF 01/1987.

Chapter 6 – For People Who Like the Movies

The chapter title comes from the introduction to FC1, but for some reason in later editions the definite article was removed, and so the line read, "This book is for people who like movies." No idea why the change was made but I have stuck with the original version.

1st Edition

Hitchcock's quotes all come from the foreword he provided for FC1. The cocktail party is mentioned in the introduction to FC9, OS 22/03/1987, ID 23/01/1989 and LAT 25/01/1980. Reginald Davis-Poynter's obituary is in TT 06/07/2004.

"It started because I felt the need" is from BEN 10/07/1972. The first review is from TLS 16/12/1965, and the "Andy Warhol" remark is from EQ 06/1966. "Overly adjectival" is from AB 14/03/1966. Sales figures are from ST 30/07/1989.

Updates

LAT 25/01/1980 is the source for "everything on casters," "I have a terribly good memory" and "copious notes." "I start off with the best will in the world" is from an NFT interview, 22/07/1987 (see notes for chapter 10). "There aren't many more names missing" is from SK 01/03/1979.

Halliwell's stepdaughter Denise gave me her recollections when I met her at a friend's house, 24/05/2010.

Reviews

Anthony Quinton's "...nobly self-denying," as well as the later "It is hard to imagine life" are from TLS 25/11/1977. Charles Champlin's 2nd ed review is in LAT 29/11/1967 and his 3rd ed in LAT 30/10/1970, which includes the "potato chip" comment. His "iron will" is in LAT 04/05/1979. Jack Conroy's thoughts are in ABC 04/1968; Clifford Terry's in CH 14/01/1968 and Richard Schickel's in HP 11/1970. "You can't actually film-go" and "appalling posters" are from OS 08/12/1974. Ernest Callenbach writes of the quiz book in FQ summer 1979. Benny Green's "Wretchedly provincial" and "the perusal of one entry" are from SP 11/1977.

Criticism

"Joan Crawford blistered me" is from LAT 25/01/1980. The George C. Scott quote was found in CH 18/03/1979. Philip French's comments are all from SP 24/02/1978. I took a bit of dramatic licence here by spreading out his remarks over the two film book chapters. This may have given the impression that he wrote several articles disparaging LH's work, which was not the case.

Competition

Mark Crispin Miller writes in NYR 16/09/1976, Stanley Kauffman in NR 29/12/1978 and George Perry in ST 30/07/1989. Fred Zentner's quote is from ID 23/01/1989 and the other books are listed in the bibliography. Champlin's comparison and "I need you both" quote are from LAT 21/08/1982.

The author himself

LH's "two or three rooms" quote is from WA 26/06/1982. His comments on film careers and italics are from that NFT interview, 22/07/1987. A "pocket cassette of *The Maltese Falcon*" and "my tired eyes are led gently" are from the introductions to FC4 and FC9 respectively, with FC9 also being the source for the rosette quotes and "my first love."

End of FIDO

"…the majority remained undiscovered" is from AW spring 1986. As mentioned in the notes for the previous chapter, the history of FIDO and films on television comes from SS summer 1980 and SS autumn 1982.

TM has the audience figures from 18/08/1968, when four films were in the top 20. LH making his pitch to the controllers and his first purchase are from OS 22/03/1987 and SL 03/1987.

His appointment to the Board of Granada Overseas is in BT 03/1966. A "poky second floor office" is from DM 08/11/1978 and the Chinese prints were observed by Peter Lennon in ST 08/02/1981.

Chapter 7 – Things became Fraught

All audience figures come from *Broadcast* magazine, usually to be found a couple of weeks after the relevant film or show has aired. To find out airdates go to http://infotrac.galegroup.com/default and search the *Times* database. You'll need to enter your library card number. What… you don't have a library card? *You should be ashamed of yourself!*

Purchase Group

Described by LH in STT 17/01/1985, AW 11/1986 and IB 05/1975. See FF 01/1987 for the year of LH's promotion, and almost all the obituaries. I interviewed Sir Paul Fox in his conservatory on 11/04/2010.

End of studio era

Barry Norman's *Talking Pictures* describes the decline of the studios, as do *MGM: When the Lion Roars* and LH in PT issue 8 1984. Debbie Reynolds's remark is from an interview for a BBC documentary called *Musicals, Glorious Musicals*. Have fun tracking *that* down…

Bond Films

LH in OS 22/03/1987 puts the purchase year of the Bond films as 1968, and so does Paul Fox in LS 05/02/1987, but in DM 17/01/1987 LH contradicts himself with, "in the *seventies* I paid less than £1 million for six Bond films." The amount paid is given as £828,000, which I converted to dollars using this website, http://fx.sauder.ubc.ca/etc/USDpages.pdf.

The films are again referred to in BC 31/01/1977, where the Alasdair Milne quote comes from, and Rugheimer gives a slightly higher price in ST 08/02/1981 – as well as another different year, so you tell me! The "tropospheric scatter" is described in BC 03/11/1975.

Rugheimer

Obituaries: DT 30/03/2003 and TT 22/04/2003. Other descriptions appear in ST 08/02/1981, the source for "things became fraught…," and *Independent Television in Britain* (see bibliography). The Michael Winner quote is from a telephone interview I conducted with him on 24/04/2009. Unfortunately I don't have a recording but apparently *he* does.

TV shows

Beretta: SM 20/08/1978.

Charlie's Angels: "a tremendous battle" is from STM 01/10/1978. See also TT 20/11/1981, TW 18/02/1983 and TVW 07/1979.

The Incredible Hulk: "a nice sense of humour" is from STM 01/10/1978. See also TT 20/11/1981.

Kojak and *Starsky*: DM 08/11/1978, OS 22/03/1987 and TVW 07/1979.

The Six Million Dollar Man and *The Streets of San Francisco*: PP 04/1974, IB 05/1975, BC 08/03/1976 and STM 01/10/1978.

Vega$: STM 01/10/1978, EN 27/04/1979.

Films

Ben Hur – "Can Rugheimer top that?" is from BC 08/08/1977.

Gone with the Wind – BC 08/12/1980 reported the FT story with LH's reaction, and "There are some films you can't *not* buy" is from Elkan Allan's article in TT 09/01/1982 (which I have used quite a lot of). The auction and other quotes (*crème de menthe frappé!*) are from the excellent Peter Lennon article in ST 08/02/1981. See BC 09/02/1981 for a full report including "ITV's vaults." Other mentions in TT 03/02/1981 and OS 07/12/1980, and "a nuclear weapon" is from GD 19/08/1985.

Jaws – story reported in BC 02/02/1981. "Thumbs up" is from OS 13/03/1988, and "flabbergasted" is from TT 09/01/1982 – an article which appears to contradict the timing of events. LH's comments here imply that the *Jaws* sale happened *after GWTW*, but too many dateable sources have it the other way round, so that famous memory must have failed him on this occasion.

Network – from the *Edinburgh International Television Festival 1977 – Official Programme*, reproduced for BC 19/12/1977.

Oliver! – BC 20/12/1976 for the rumoured amount, converted using this website, http://fx.sauder.ubc.ca/etc/USDpages.pdf, and 21/02/1977 for Isaacs's quote.

The Sound of Music – "Gunnar dealt a stunning blow" and "Typical Leslie" are again from Peter Lennon in ST 08/02/1981. Reports and reaction are mostly from BC 24/07/1978.

Movies running out

In many articles LH speaks of the well running dry, such as BC 08/03/1976 and 24/08/1984, SI 20/03/1976 and VT 18/04/1979.

Complaints

Prices paid: the Association of Independent Producers' report comes from BC 01/08/1977. "People who own casinos and hotels in California" comes from Tony Smith of the BFI, at the Edinburgh TV Festival, printed in BC 07/09/1981 – which is admittedly a few years on from the section I've used it in but it's a good quote and I felt it was appropriate to the subject matter. Michael Winner's quote is from a telephone interview conducted on 24/04/2009, and "If we clash over one film" comes from DE 23/10/1982.

Quality: the Elkan Allan book launch is reported in GD 16/10/1973, and "How would feature films ever be preserved?"

comes from SI 20/03/1976, which mentions the 14% quota, also to be found in BC 28/11/1977 and 11/05/1984.

Content: *Virginia Woolf* is mentioned by LH in IB 05/1975, along with the TV versions and the "artistically mangled" line. *The Wild Bunch* is from STM 01/10/1978 and *The Killing of Sister George* from BC 08/03/1976. *Dog Day Afternoon* is mentioned in SI 20/03/1976, which is where the "What everyone's scraping around for" quote is taken. LH meeting Coppola is in IB 05/1975.

Timing: "with restraint and with skill" is from the ITA Annual Report and Accounts, 1966-67. "If you turned over five pages of *Wuthering Heights*..." makes me smile every time I read it – Peter Fiddick wrote it for GD 16/10/1973.

Cinemas: see Alasdair Milne's article in BC 31/01/1977, as well as a four-page piece on 'Cinema vs. Television' in SS summer 1980 and Sir Denis Forman's article 'My life and TV times' in SS autumn 1982.

Shape: mostly from LH's essay 'A word on shape', to be found in FG5. "Losing a third" comes from BC 18/05/1981.

TV movies
See TVC3 and IB 05/1975, as well as any issue of *Photoplay* between 11/1973 and 08/1975. "Medical dictionaries" is from VT 18/04/1979. "Laughably low" and "welcome new discipline" are from PP 07/1974.

Trade Fairs
There were MIP reviews every year in BC, usually in early May. LH describes it in AW 11/1986, as well as the other festivals in PT issue 8 1984. The anecdote about the meal is in ID 23/01/1989 and VV 01/05/1983, and the morning dip story is from ST 08/02/1981. The "tirade of monumental proportions" is from BC 09/05/1977.

LH was spotted "stalking the corridors" of Monte Carlo by BC 22/02/1982, which is where both the Colin Davis quote and the industry joke are taken.

TV appearances

"There is little love here," and "Don't you know everything is in colour now?" are both from an article for a Dutch magazine called *Skoop* 01/03/1979, which I used some internet translators to decipher. In addition, see SI 20/03/1976. The bit about *On the Town* is from HV. The TV appearances I have used are from *Looks Familiar* (Thames, 02/01/1974), *Clapperboard North West* (Granada, 17/08/1978) and *Look Here* (LWT, 04/03/1980), and all were viewed at the truly wonderful BFI Library (on frightfully old fashioned videotape!) The other interview is from BEN 04/10/1978.

Buying hokum

See STM 01/10/1978 and EN 27/04/1979 for "early evening action." LH writing off feature films is in SI 20/03/1976. "Purist devotion" is from TT 20/11/1981. "I'm buying for an audience of millions" is from TVW 07/1979, and "I don't have to like everything I buy" is from VV 01/05/1983. "I have been known to conclude deals" is from PT issue 8 1984. The incongruity of LH's personal and professional tastes is mentioned in TW 18/02/1983.

See VT 18/04/1979 for talk of Roman orgies, and "there was no relationship really" is from BC 24/08/1984. "Why you have to put up with this TV trash" is in DM 21/06/1979.

Mini-series

"I'd rather cram them all in one week" is from TVW 07/1979. The birth of the mini-series is recounted in BC 12/03/1979. *The Dain Curse* is from STM 01/10/1978, as is "a firm option" and "marvellous entertainment." *Holocaust* is described in BC 21/08/1978 and *Washington: Behind Closed Doors* in DM 21/06/1979.

L.A. Trips

Looking for a 'Kojak' is from ST 13/02/1983 and Paul Fox was seeing medallions in LS 05/02/1987. LH describes a general trip to L.A. in PT issue 8 1984, and so I have applied this back a few years and combined it with the *Supertrain* article from GD 24/02/1979. "Laughed off the screen" comes from TT 09/01/1982, and "casting a set as its hero" is from VT 18/04/1979. The "55-page report" is in BC 24/08/1984. Once again, my interview with Sir Paul Fox was on 11/04/2010. The complimentary champagne is mentioned in RTSL and LH's meeting with Gracie Fields is recounted in both HH and DTFA. Alan Frank reminisced to me in a phone call, 10/03/2010; June Dromgoole likewise on 12/05/2010.

Summary

"We have been surprised" is from TT 26/11/1981; "looks of expansive disdain" is again from Peter Lennon in ST 08/02/1981, and "unshakeable" is from PP 10/1985. David Quinlan sent me an email on 21/03/2010.

Chapter 8 – Two Untrained Index Fingers

1st Edition

The genesis of the *Film Guide* is mostly gleaned from the introduction to FG1, along with "no one volume could hope to be comprehensive." Philip French's "appalling cultural insularity" comment is from SP 24/02/1978. "Unsung anonymous heroes" is from the introduction.

Response

John Russell Taylor's quotes are from TES 02/06/1978; Philip French's is again in SP 24/02/1978. *Choice* magazine had anonymous heroes, too, and one of them wrote about a "wealth of information" in CH 07/1978. Anthony Quinton offered his insight in TLS 25/11/1977.

Leonard Maltin gave me his comments in an email, 02/12/2009.

Stars

All LH's observations regarding the star system can be found in FG 1-7. The totals were arrived at by the simple but time-consuming process of counting. "…a grumpy old English fuddy-duddy" is from Jim Emerson in CH 02/03/1990. Leslie Kane was "admittedly predisposed" in RSR 01/1979 and John Coleman was "infuriated" in NS 21/12/1979. Charles Champlin was asterisk-ally challenged in LAT 04/05/1979.

Italics

"…so facially wired" is from an essay on bad movies in HV.

John Russell Taylor spoke of the "master of the italic" in TES 02/06/1978.

Assessments

LH's "reasonable set of hang-ups" is from FG1, and the interview is from the NFT 22/07/1987. His confession that he had not seen all the films was in WA 26/06/1982 and AG 13/07/1982... and *only* there – two Australian publications. Did he think he was safe, making the admission so far from home? I for one had always assumed he had seen every film in the guide, and it begs the question "which ones had he not?" Impossible to say with any assurance, but I would guess it was many of the more obscure ones from the early days, and some from the later years when going to the cinema was a pain for him.

All but one of the assessments can be found in FG7, with the "dim" TV movie being in FG1. LH's philosophy on bad films is from TVT 11/04/1987, and that on good films is in the *Adventures of Robin Hood* section of HH. "...increasingly weary and blimpish": unfortunately I failed to track down the source of this quote. LH himself uses it in the introduction to FG5. John Nangle's summation is from FIR 10/1986.

The 'Decline' Essay

Richard J. Kelly wrote in ARB vol 9 1978, and Charles Champlin in LAT 04/05/1979. Philip French's comments are from an email to me on 10/01/2010, and Sean Usher's from a letter, 20/03/2009. Denis Forman's article was in SS autumn 1982. The juvenilisation of the cinema and *Heaven's Gate* are covered in *Talking Pictures*. Alan Alda's movie rules are from the film *Sweet Liberty*.

Summary

The NFT interview is further used here, from 22/07/1987. "...an immense undertaking" is by David Bartholomew in LJB 1979. "...still the one to beat" is from VT 23/12/1987 and Anthony Quinton's comment is from TLS 25/11/1977.

REFERENCES

Chapter 9 – A Store of Riches
Again, audience figures are from *Broadcast* magazine.

Dallas saga

"Constantly irritated" comes from an article called 'US Soap Dealer Lathers BBC', in BC 07/06/1982. Kevin O'Sullivan's quotes are from VT 29/07/1981, as is the reason for Colin Campbell's departure. LH and Paul Fox saw the pilot of *Dallas* according to *Independent Television in Britain, Vol 5*, which is the source for LH saying "we did not try to steal *Dallas*" and "Thames had made it plain…," both of which are quoted from written reports by him submitted to ITV – and are very probably the "confidential documents" spoken of in ST 14/07/1985.

The "hypothetical question" is from Elkan Allan's article in TT 09/01/1982, as is his calling for an "eyeball-to-eyeball battle" and LH saying *Dallas* was too difficult to schedule. Kevin Goldstein-Jackson was interviewed in BC 24/07/1985 and the anecdote about him approaching LH at MIP appeared the week before. For further accounts see BC 28/06/1982, 30/08/1982, 06/09/1982, 11/10/1982; TT 17/01/1985, 19/01/1985, 04/07/1985, 12/07/1985, 24/07/1985, 24/08/1985, 02/10/1985, 14/11/1985, 31/12/1985, 31/05/1986, ST 27/10/1985 and VT 23/01/1985!

"The depiction of rich American families…" is from the introduction to TVC3, and Philip Purser complains about the affair in the postscript to that book.

Formation of Channel 4

Channel 4: the Early Years was used for the brief history of the channel and BC 12/01/1981 has the report about the IBA's programme policy. "No one will expect" is from a Jeremy Isaacs's article in SS autumn 1981, which outlines LH's intentions, and "the endless rounds" is from *ITV in Britain, Vol 6*. LH grabbed all he could in STT 17/01/1985 and the Lane End meeting was reported in BC 03/08/1981.

Star Wars

The sale was reported in DE 23/10/1982, and "for top money I would expect 20 million" is from SL March 1987. Reports of statistical inaccuracies are from an article called 'Is it really a switch off?' in BC 29/11/1982 and 'BARB's C4 underscore' in BC 01/08/1983.

Channel 4 goes on air
"Of the three contentious subjects" and the *Raging Bull* quote are from that NFT 22/07/1987 interview (see notes for Chapter 10). "As a come-on" is from Isaacs's book *Storm over 4*, as is his reaction to *Semi-Tough* and the showing of *Raging Bull*. BC 01/11/1982 has the full first-week schedule with buying credits. LH saying, "We started off by showing" is in STT 17/01/1985, and Mary Whitehouse's complaints come from *Channel 4: the Early Years*, BC 26/07/1982 and GD 11/09/1981 respectively. "Films that rely on four letter words" is from BC 24/08/1984, and the 'What the Censor Saw' season is talked about in BC 31/08/1985.

Light entertainment
"It doesn't much matter..." is from BC 24/08/1984. Isaacs's announcement is from *Channel 4: The Early Years*, and the Korer story is from Maggie Brown's book *A Licence to be Different*. "A bobby dazzler" is from VV May 1983, and *Hill Street* is reported in STT 17/01/1985 and BC 24/08/1984, and the quote is from PT issue 8 1984. *The A-Team* turns up in ST 13/02/1983, and "No one admits to liking it" is from TVC3. The show is further mentioned in STT 17/01/1985, which is where the *Miami Vice* quote comes from, a series Alan Howden is reported to have bought in DE 26/11/1986.

Mini-series
"You've got to see a few armies marching" is from DM 17/01/1987. *A Woman of Substance* was broadcast in January 1985. *The Winds of War* is mentioned in BC 21/02/1983, VV 05/1983 and ST 13/02/1983, and it was shown in September. "Meretricious rubbish" is from one of two articles about *The Thorn Birds* in TT 27/01/1984, with the show turning up again in TT 30/01/1984. LH's quote is from PT issue 8 1984, in which he lists the sixteen new mini-series. *V* going up against the Olympics is from BC 24/08/1984. "Invariably the narrative is jumbled" is from the *Gone with the Wind* part of HH. *Hollywood Wives* is mentioned in TVC3 and DM 17/01/1987 (with the typically restrained headline, 'The pornography fouling our screens'!)

REFERENCES

Golden Oldies

"Nostalgia is only a trendy word" is from 'The Decline and Fall of the Movie', LH's essay in the *Film Guide*, and "a store of riches" itself is from the preface to FC9, also the source for "an enormous postbag." LH's various seasons and all the anecdotes about sourcing and scheduling come from VV 05/1983, STT 17/01/1985, PT 10/1985, AW spring 1986, HH, HV and MM 12/1984 – the latter being where "Look, you can wave this still" is taken – which may have seemed like it was made up. LH really was allowed into the Universal vaults but the line there *was* made up – it's called artistic licence, you know.

"At the moment I'm going even more hairless" is from a sound recording of LH at the NFT 21/07/1987, held at the BFI Library, along with video tapes of *Home Front*. A recording of the Teeside radio interview is available at the British Library Sound Archive, reference number C1000/091/85/1. Quotes from TVT come from 10/11/1984, 17/11/1984, 24/11/1984, 18/10/1986, 08/11/1986, 18/11/1986 and 03/01/1987. Those from S4 come from any issue you like between 1984 and 1988.

"Scarcely a day goes by" is from TT 28/04/1983 and Alan Howden's quote is from BC 11/05/1984. Jeremy Isaacs' is from his book *Storm Over 4*, and Bonner's from PT issue 8 1984. The BFI award is mentioned in BC 28/06/1985.

Retirement

"I know people think I'm old-fashioned" is from DM 17/01/1987 (*The Mail* also being responsible for "all sorts of excess" and "garbage.") Barrie Brown's quote is from BC 25/01/1985, and "a film used to go theatrical" is in BC 24/08/1984. "A man who has watched too many American TV series" is in TW 18/02/1983. The Peacock Report is mentioned in ST 15/02/1987, and LH's retirement was announced in SI 15/06/1986 and BC 11/07/1986. "I am the only one who knows…" is from STT 17/01/1985.

Chapter 10 – A Matter of Life and Death

'Halliwell's Handful'

The season is outlined in the NFT programme for July 1987, and the sound recording is entitled '*The Guardian* Interview: Leslie Halliwell', 22/07/1987, available at the BFI Library under the subject 'Feature film screening policy'.

Articles

"Less and less do I go to the movies" is from FF 01/1987. Most of the other articles have been referenced for previous chapters, but the essay on title changes is in FF 09/1966. BEN 06/10/1970, 07/10/1970 and 08/10/1970 have the pieces about the changing face of Bolton. TLS 08/08/1980, 04/1977 and 11/1977 have the book reviews. See PP 11/1973 – 08/1975 for *Photoplay* articles.

Incidentally, LH's obituary in the *Richmond & Twickenham Times* speaks of a film column he contributed to them in the early sixties. I was intrigued, as I could find no other articles from the period, and being as it was his local newspaper it seemed entirely plausible. However, though I trawled the back issues I could not find a single article with his by-line, or any which were definitely in his style.

'LH's Screen Choice' began in DM 14/03/1987; "Fixed us with an ancient mariner eye" is from DM 10/10/1987. 'The Clothes Show' is mentioned in DM 21/03/1987 and the snooker comment is in DM 28/03/1987. "The afternoon movies…" is in DM 04/04/1987 and "sharpen my thinking processes" are from DM 11/04/1987. "So much that is genuinely entertaining…" is from DM 25/04/1987 and "pity the buyers" is from DM 01/08/1987.

Books

All the books are listed in the bibliography. The *Teleguide* was reviewed in RSR 07/1981 and "probably satisfy neither" is from BBN 01/1980. Barry Took's comments are in STT 21/10/1982, and LH's riposte is in STT 28/10/1982. Philip Purser gave me his recollections in a letter, 19/05/2010. I don't know what issue the *City Limits* review was from, but his response was dated 12/09/1987.

"…elegant bric-a-brac" is from the introduction to HH and "dedicated to the proposition" likewise from HV. Roger Manvell's review was from BBN 11/1982 and Peter Craig's in AF 04/1983. Paul Stuewe assessed HV in QQ 09/1986, Ivan Butler in FRA 1986 and John Nangle in FIR 10/1986.

REFERENCES

For SIAP, ST 14/04/1985 has the "waggish" comment and NYT 23/02/1986 has the "tedium" comment. David Elliot was seeing bouquets in BL 03/1986, and John Nangle's review was from FIR 08/1986. Philip French wrote favourably in OS 28/07/1985 and Jeffrey Richards even more so in DT 23/01/1989. LH was questioned on DTW in FF 01/1987 and Roger Lewis reviewed it in BB 12/1986. Sean French's review is in SS winter 1986 and John Nangle wrote his for FIR 01/1989. Unfinished works are all spoken of in FF 01/1987, the NFT interview 22/07/1987 and VT 18/04/1979 – from where the "grandmothers" quote is taken. "For the sea was pure…" comes from GSH, and the RTSL comments are again from the NFT interview.

Illness

"I am leaving these behind" is from BEN 04/04/1992. "…terribly pleased," "much too posh" and "raised film consciousness" are from GD 30/05/1997. The Critics' Circle award was also mentioned in GD 06/12/1988. RTT 27/01/1989 puts his illness as being from March 1988, as well as the report of him finishing the 7th edition from his hospital room – which both Alan Frank and Halliwell's stepdaughter Denise confirmed.

Chapter 11 – A Tough Act to Follow

Tributes and obituaries

The job advertisement is in GD 26/09/1988. *The Times* obituary is from TT 23/01/1989 and Tim Pulleine's comments are from GD 25/01/1989. "…necessary as popcorn" is from LAT 29/01/1989 and Jeffrey Richards's words are in DT 23/01/1989. "…a breed apart" is from TVW 11/1989, and Dr Alastair Finch wrote in BT 07/1989.

Aftermath

Funeral details are from RTT 03/02/1989. The memorial at the NFT was recalled by Michael Wright and Alan Frank, and is mentioned in BEN 17/04/1989 and ID 20/04/1989. The programme is also available at the BFI library. Channel 4's tribute is from the TV listings in GD 12/05/1989 and 'A tough act to follow' is in ST 30/07/1989.

Recognition

The BAFTA is mentioned in BEN 26/03/1990. The court case is from GD 30/03/1995 and TT 30/03/1995. The reaction is from OS 02/04/1995 and "…glib opinions" is in OS 26/10/1997. Mark Gatiss's article is from GD 25/11/1995. Dorothy Hobson's book was *Channel 4: the Early Years and the Jeremy Isaacs Legacy*. Alexander Walker's decline was reported in OS 09/04/1995. Tom Hutchinson wrote his tribute in GD 30/05/1997, and BEN 22/10/1996 has the plaque story.

Final words

The website http://cinematreasures.org has details on closures and demolitions. George Webb's obituary is in CEN 31/01/1983. Clive's move to Ravenswood is from RTT 27/01/1989, and Joanna Harrison, a friend of the Halliwells, told me about the copyright. BMD once again for other details: Ruth Halliwell d10/08/2002, North Surrey; Stewart Porter d05/08/2004, Gipping and Hartismere.

Michael Wright's tribute was in a letter to me, in which he mentioned the house with the annexe. "He was a gentle man" is from BEN 04/04/1992. "…dwindled to dust" is from BC 24/08/1984 and "Hollywood's magic machinery" is from the *Rebecca* section of HH.

Bibliography

The Age of the Dream Palace – Jeffrey Richards, Routledge & Kegan Paul, 1984.

Bolton Memories – True North Books, 2001.

Bolton Town Centre: A Modern History – Gordon Readyhough, Manchester/Neil Richardson Publishing, 1982.

Brewer's Cinema – Cassell, 1995.

Britain Can Take It: British Cinema in the Second World War – Anthony Aldgate and Jeffrey Richards, I. B. Tauris, 2007.

Cambridge Historical Register, Cambridge, 1949-1952.

Channel 4: the Early Years and the Jeremy Isaacs Legacy – Dorothy Hobson, I. B. Tauris & Co Ltd., 2008.

Churchgate: a Biography of Life in the Early 1930s – Fred Hill, Bolton Museum and Art Gallery, 1982.

The Clapperboard Book of the Cinema – Leslie Halliwell and Graham Murray, Hart-Davis, 1975.

The Dead That Walk – Leslie Halliwell, Grafton, 1986.

A Demon Close Behind – Leslie Halliwell, Hale, 1987.

A Demon on the Stair – Leslie Halliwell, Hale, 1988.

Done Viewing – Philip Purser, Quartet, 1992.

Double Take and Fade Away – Leslie Halliwell, Grafton, 1987.

Easy Riders, Raging Bulls: How the Sex, Drugs and Rock n' Roll Generation Changed Hollywood – Peter Biskind, Bloomsbury, 1998.

An Everyday Magic: Cinema and Cultural Memory – Annette Kuhn, I. B. Tauris, 2002.

The Fifty Year Decline and Fall of Hollywood – Ezra Goodman, McFadden, 1962.

The Filmgoer's Companion – Leslie Halliwell, Granada, 1965.

Film-making in 1930's Britain – Rachel Low, Allen & Unwin, 1985.

Frank Capra: a Catastrophe of Success – Joseph McBride, Simon & Schuster, 1992.

Frank Capra, the Man and his Films – Richard Glatzer and John Raeburn, University of Michigan, 1975.

From Affetside to Yarrow: Bolton Place Names and their History – W. D. Billingham, Ross Anderson Publishing, 1982.

The Ghost of Sherlock Holmes: Seventeen Supernatural Stories – Leslie Halliwell, Panther, 1985.

The Glamorous Years: The Stars & Films of the 1930s – Alfred Brockman, Hamlyn, 1987.

Granada Television: The First Generation – John Finch, Michael Cox, Marjorie Giles, Manchester University Press, 2003.

Halliwell's Filmgoer's Book of Quotes – Leslie Halliwell, Granada, 1973.

Halliwell's Film Guide – Leslie Halliwell, Granada, 1977.

Halliwell's Harvest – Leslie Halliwell, Grafton, 1986.

Halliwell's Hundred – Leslie Halliwell, Paladin, 1982.

Halliwell's Movie Quiz – Leslie Halliwell, Granada, 1977.

Halliwell's Teleguide – Leslie Halliwell and Philip Purser, Granada, 1979.

The History of Broadcasting in the United Kingdom: Competition 1955-1974 – Asa Briggs, Oxford University Press, 1995.

Independent Television Authority Annual Report and Accounts – ITA, 1968-69.

Independent Television in Britain: Volume 2 – Bernard Sendall, MacMillan, 1983.

Independent Television in Britain: Volume 5 – Paul Bonner and Lesley Aston, MacMillan, 1998.

Independent Television in Britain: Volume 6 – Paul Bonner and Lesley Aston, MacMillan, 2003.

In Search of Shangri-La – Michael McRae, Penguin, 2002.

International Encyclopaedia of Film – Dr Roger Manvell and Professor Lewis Jacobs, Rainbird Reference Books Limited, 1972.

The International Film Encyclopaedia – Ephraim Katz, Macmillan, 1979.

An Introduction to Cambridge – S. C. Roberts, Cambridge University Press, 1953.

A Licence to be Different: The Story of Channel 4 – Maggie Brown, BFI, 2007.

Kelly's Directory of Cambridge 1955.

Kent's Directory of Slough 1957.

Lost Horizon – James Hilton, MacMillan, 1933.

Mass-Observation at the Movies – Jeffrey Richards and Dorothy Sheridan, Routledge and Kegan Paul, 1987.

MGM: When the Lion Roars – Peter Hay, Turner Publishing, Inc., 1991.

Mountain of Dreams: The Golden Years of Paramount – Leslie Halliwell, Granada, 1976.

Ninety Years of Cinema in Bolton: An Essay in Celebration of the Cinemas – Brian Hornsey, Fuchsiaprint Stamford, 1995.

Persona Granada: Memories of Sidney Bernstein and the Early Years of Independent Television – Denis Forman, Andre Deutsch Ltd, 1997.

Photographs of Old Bolton – Chris Driver, Hendon Publishing, 1980.

Popular Filmgoing in 1930s Britain: A Choice of Pleasures – John Sedgwick, University of Exeter Press, 2000.

Portrait of Cambridge 1952 – Edited by Graham Dukes, Varsity Newspaper Cambridge, 1952.

Return to Shangri-La – Leslie Halliwell, Grafton, 1987.

Seven Years with Film & TV Cameras at the London Zoo – Sir Solly Zuckerman, Granada, 1965.

Seats in all Parts: Half a Lifetime at the Movies – Leslie Halliwell, Scribner, 1985

Storm Over 4: A Personal Account – Jeremy Isaacs, Weidenfeld & Nicolson Ltd, 1989.

Talking Pictures – Barry Norman, BBC Books, 1987.

TV Movies – Leonard Maltin, Signet books, 1969.

The Unknown 1930s – Jeffrey Richards, I. B. Tauris, 1998.

When all the World Was Young: A Bolton Childhood in the Thirties – Edna MacCuish, Jade Publishing Limited, 1993.

Winner Takes All: A Life of Sorts – Michael Winner, Robson Books, 2004.

The World Film Encyclopaedia: A Universal Screen Guide – Clarence Winchester, London Amalgamated Press, 1933/48.

Index

A

ABC cinemas....49, 56, 57, 67, 71, 83, 91, 92, 99, 100, 250
Academy Award...22, 27, 38, 51, 113, 122, 136, 138, 143, 150, 170, 181, 203, 241
Academy Awards ceremony............123
Adventures of Robin Hood, The...235, 252
Alda, Alan...192
Alien..204
All About Eve....................................117
All That Money Can Buy............32, 211
Allan, Elkan.......................151, 155, 198
Ambassador Cinema, Slough......103, 105, 106
American in Paris, An... 63, 181, 235, 252
Army Education Corps 49, 242
Arts Cinema, Cambridge .56, 63, 71, 74
Astaire & Rogers 62, 112, 122, 186
Astaire, Fred.........12, 13, 141, 191, 213
A-Team, The......................................207
auteur theory 140, 188, 214

B

Band Wagon, The..............................235
BBC2...113, 156, 196, 208, 210, 217, 222, 228
Beattie, James 37, 46, 79, 243, 244
Bel-Air Hotel ...120, 147, 162, 165, 170
Ben Hur......................................150, 170
Berkeley, Busby...........................12, 62
Bernstein, Cecil........110, 111, 112, 113
Bernstein, Sidney...110, 111, 113, 124, 127
Beverly Hillbillies, The 112, 222
Beverly Wilshire Hotel 162, 163, 165
Bioscope...................................125, 226
Birds, The................................114, 169
Birth of a Nation, The 43, 180, 234
Biskind, Peter...................................190
black and white...4, 25, 26, 63, 92, 129, 215, 231

Black Hole, The................................206
block-booking.................10, 52, 78, 143
Blue Angel, The............75, 85, 177, 236
Bogart, Humphrey 12, 119, 126, 181
Bolton Evening News....6, 8, 9, 23, 27, 33, 45, 64, 70, 158, 226
Bolton Little Theatre....45, 61, 69, 70, 249
Bolton School 27, 30, 31, 41, 61
  Film Society......................42, 48, 61
  Literary and Debating Society 37, 46
  Philatelic Society 42
  Poetry Society...............................42
  school plays 47
Boltonian, The...41, 43, 47, 48, 69, 225, 246
Bonner, Paul.....150, 201, 202, 203, 217
Bonnie and Clyde 179
Bootsie and Snudge..........................234
Bradford Road..................................16
Brando, Marlon....97, 98, 138, 181, 187
Bresson, Robert.......................128, 222
Bride of Frankenstein, The... 38, 184, 194, 221, 247
Bristol Little Theatre.......................108
British Academy (BAFTA)..7, 115, 248
British at War, The...................213, 214
British Film Industry.................21, 150
  maturation.....................................45
  resurgence....................................41
  silent films 110, 223
  wartime documentaries................40
British Film Institute (BFI)...7, 87, 93, 110, 111, 125, 175, 194, 221, 241, 249
Broadcast... 113, 115, 150, 155, 156, 170, 199, 201, 202, 217, 218

C

Cagney, James ...12, 119, 209, 210, 237
Cambridge Daily News...61, 63, 84, 86, 91
Cambridge Evening News................250
Cambridge Film Society.....57, 58, 59, 63, 77, 95
Cambridge University Mummers................................60, 69

287

Proctors..............................54, 67, 68
Tripos............................53, 61, 69, 75
Union 54, 73, 94
Camelot..119, 135
Campbell, Colin 197, 198
Cannes................................154, 155, 173
Capitol Cinema, Bolton........6, 9, 14, 15, 19, 33, 158
Capra, Frank............................4, 24, 129
Carpenter, John 186
Casablanca 32, 177, 181, 252
Central Cinema, Cambridge ..57, 64, 95
Champlin, Charles........131, 132, 137, 140, 180, 189
Channel 4 ...222, 223, 228, 235, 236, 245, 246, 247, 249
    controversy 205
    emergence................................201–2
    golden oldies...........................208–17
    launch 203
Chant of Jimmy Blacksmith, The...210, 247
Chaplin, Charlie...9, 15, 115, 116, 126, 176, 209
Charlie's Angels 172, 177
Cheers 206
Chesterton, G. K. 56, 211
Chevalier, Maurice.....................11, 230
Chicago Tribune 137, 180
chicken biryani........................54, 76, 97
Churchgate 1, 2, 14, 19, 158, 250
Cinema (Granada TV programme)...116, 119, 121
cinemagoing
    continuous performance 14, 85
    decline in attendance...52, 107, 123, 189
    organs 14, 22, 23
    queuing...1, 2, 11, 12, 13, 14, 22, 26, 32, 82, 93
    supporting programme...........14, 238
Cinemas Exhibitors' Association (CEA) 112
CinemaScope 99, 100, 101, 107, 189
Citizen Kane...32, 33, 41, 87, 100, 101, 120, 127, 139, 184, 194, 211, 221, 229, 247
Clair, René 89, 126, 141, 221
Clapperboard............115, 158, 173, 229
Clapperboard Book of the Cinema, The 229

Clapperboard North West................158
Colbert, Claudette 11, 126, 191
Collier, Lionel..33, 34, 79, 99, 178, 182
Colman, Ronald...4, 8, 24, 25, 107, 113, 129, 141, 202
Columbia Pictures.........3, 10, 24, 91, 93, 97, 118, 145, 162, 163, 211
Columbo....................................153, 218
Continuous Performance (article)...88, 225
Cooper, Gary.....................................209
Coppola, Francis 87, 152
Coronation Street.....................115, 143
Court Jester, The......................211, 240
Cowgill, Brian..................167, 199, 200
Crawford, Joan..................................138
Cross, Eric.............................55, 59, 69
Crown Film Unit..........................39, 43
Cukor, George.....................32, 56, 120
Curse of Frankenstein, The..............106
Cushing, Peter 106, 107
Cutts, John 124, 125, 131

D

Daily Express............................97, 203
Daily Mail 167, 191, 227, 228
Daily Telegraph 190, 246
Dallas..............................167, 208, 218
    controversy 200
Darby, Peter 58
Davis, Bette......................117, 135, 237
Davis-Poynter, Reginald..........124, 125
de Havilland, Olivia...........................52
Dead That Walk, The 240
Deansgate..250
Death Valley 161, 242, 243
Decline and Fall of the Movie, The (article) 191
DeMille, Cecil B........................11, 143
Demon Close Behind, A 242
Demon on the Stair, A 242, 243
Destry Rides Again 23, 59
Deutsch, Oscar...........................22, 105
Dieterle, William 32, 211
Dietrich, Marlene ...75, 76, 88, 141, 230
Double Indemnity............................118
double-bills........49, 84, 106, 196, 209, 222, 235
Double-Take and Fade Away 240

288

Dr Jekyll and Mr Hyde 22, 212, 235
Dr No 148, 149
Dracula (1931) 35, 237
Dracula (1958) 107
Dracula (character)... 13, 62, 93, 208, 239, 240
dream palaces..........................6, 52, 252
Dromgoole, June...............................166
Duck Soup 57, 58, 60, 85
Dumont, Margaret............................141
Durbin, Deanna........................215, 216

E

Ealing Studios ...50, 77, 94, 112, 119, 238
Edge, Ron..............................35, 120, 164
Eisenstein, Sergei...38, 44, 58, 180, 235
Embassy Cinema, Bolton....................29
Enfants du Paradis, Les 126, 176
Extase 89

F

Fairbanks, Douglas 9, 138, 235
fat little guy in Milwaukee...148, 162, 165
Festival de Télévision de Monte-Carlo 156, 207, 242
Fields, Gracie 19, 109, 158, 165, 193
Film Industry Defence Organisation (FIDO) 112, 113, 142, 212
film noir.......................52, 100, 227, 237
Film Purchase Group...145, 146, 150, 152, 162, 167, 169, 172, 199, 200, 202, 205, 228, 246
 gentlemen's agreement...150, 163, 168, 173, 197, 199
 L. A. buying trips........152, 162, 165
Film Weekly 125, 226
Filmgoer's Book of Quotes, The...135, 136
Filmgoer's Companion, The...2, 7, 157, 173, 174, 176, 178, 181, 182, 189, 194, 195, 225, 231, 247
 1st edition 128
 2nd edition 131
 3rd edition 132
 4th edition 135
 5th edition 137

6th edition.............................136, 137
9th edition...................................142
interleaved author's copy 134
italics..135
Films and Filming...124, 129, 131, 225, 226, 239
Flynn, Errol......................141, 210, 235
Ford, John 10, 32, 202, 243
foreign language films...12, 45, 58, 86, 89, 126, 139, 155, 168, 175, 191, 193, 201, 214, 221, 222, 223, 225
Forman, Sir Denis....110, 111, 147, 189
Formby, George 20, 157
Forty-Second Street 12
four-by-three 3, 9, 99, 100, 153, 252
Fox, Sir Paul...146, 149, 162, 163, 170, 197, 198, 200, 247, 251
Frank, Alan 93, 166, 247
Frankenstein 35, 36, 93, 212
Frankenstein (character) ...13, 37, 62, 209, 239
Frankenstein Meets the Wolf Man 62
Freed, Arthur.....................63, 181, 235
Freer, Alan 55
French, Philip...137, 139, 140, 174, 177, 184, 190, 195, 238, 248, 249

G

Gable, Clark 8, 9, 95, 134, 141, 237
Garbo, Greta................................11, 141
Gascoigne, Bamber..........................114
Gatiss, Mark.....................................248
George, Gladys 181
Ghost of Sherlock Holmes, The........242
glances of expansive disdain....173, 199
Godfather, The 152, 181, 187, 191
Golden Age...3, 25, 27, 56, 60, 63, 102, 104, 107, 120, 122, 127, 160, 167, 168, 169, 186, 187, 188, 189, 191, 196, 202, 220, 246, 250, 251, 252
 beginning 9
 studios..13
 contract system...10, 52, 78, 95, 122, 214
 golden year (1939)........27, 168, 241
 zenith 32
 artistic nadir 52
 collapse 78
 end 95

289

golden oldies....156, 196, 217, 224, 251
Golden Square, London...110, 111, 120, 144, 171, 201, 233
Goldstein-Jackson, Kevin ...199, 200, 206
Goldwyn, Samuel...10, 100, 113, 202, 209
Gone with the Wind...21, 27, 41, 100, 154, 168, 169, 170, 172, 177, 181, 194
   auction 172
Goodman, Ezra 100
Grade, Lew.......................113, 117, 152
Granada Cinema, Kingston......104, 111
Granada Television...7, 110, 111, 113, 114, 115, 119, 124, 143, 146, 147, 157, 159, 166, 167, 189, 201, 208, 212, 213, 221, 225, 229, 232, 233, 244, 246, 247
Grand Theatre, Bolton 1, 17, 240
Grant, Cary.......9, 38, 56, 116, 191, 209
Grapes of Wrath, The... 32, 100, 127, 184, 243
Green, Benny 134, 136
Guardian, The ..120, 245, 246, 248, 249

H

Hall, Sir Peter...............................89, 103
Halliwell touch, the... 64, 71, 80, 127, 182
Halliwell, Clive 104, 251
Halliwell, Jim...7, 8, 13, 16, 17, 19, 34, 52
   death 226
Halliwell, Leslie
   birth...8
   first remembered cinema trip..........9
   cinemagoing on his own................25
   scholarship....................................27
   first day at school.........................30
   exercise books.....2, 34, 43, 49, 64, 125, 127
   first article published 45
   National Service 51
   meets George Webb 68
   Our Town......................................70
   Varsity editorship....................74, 76
   joins Rex Cinema 81
   wedding 103
   joins Granada..............................110
   publishes *The Filmgoer's Companion* 125
   appointed Granada film buyer 142
   first appearance on television 157
   joins Channel 4 201
   presents 'Home Front' and 'British at War, The' 213
   golden oldies on Channel 4 217
   NFT interview 225
   retirement....................................227
   London Film Critics' Circle award 244
   BAFTA award 248
Halliwell, Lily...2, 3, 6, 7, 8, 9, 13, 14, 16, 17, 18, 19, 20, 22, 23, 24, 25, 26, 27, 30, 33, 34, 38, 47, 52, 101, 103, 176, 238, 242
   death 102
Halliwell, Ruth ...103, 104, 111, 125, 132, 133, 135, 244, 247, 248, 251
Halliwell's Film Guide...2, 7, 126, 127, 136, 142, 173, 231, 236, 248, 249
   1970s..187
   1980s..193
   1st edition 178, 182
   5th edition 185, 194
   6th edition 194, 195, 247
   7th edition...........180, 193, 244, 247
   assessments.................................185
   italics...181
   star ratings 180
   Top Tens page 194
   Word on Shape, A 194
Halliwell's Handful (NFT film season) 220
Halliwell's Harvest 238
Halliwell's Hundred...... 80, 193, 236, 238
Halliwell's Movie Quiz 136, 138
Halliwell's Screen Choice (article)… 227, 228
Halliwell's Television Companion...142, 159, 177
Hamlet......................47, 48, 51, 55, 152
Hammer Films 107, 239, 240
Harlow, Jean 9, 141
Hassan 61
Hawks, Howard 32, 114
Hays, Will 10
Hayworth, Rita...........................84, 215

290

Heaven's Gate 192
Henry V 43, 44, 51
Hepburn, Katharine 56, 88
Hill Street Blues 206
Hilton, James 24, 242
Hippodrome, Bolton ... 6, 18, 20, 24, 34, 108
Hitchcock, Alfred ... 32, 111, 114, 117, 124, 125, 127, 202, 220
   British films 20
hokum 160, 182, 207, 212
Home Front 213
Hope, Bob ... 55, 68, 74, 85, 120, 121, 122, 215, 227, 230, 231
Horton, Edward Everett 12, 25, 214
House of Frankenstein 62, 80, 85
House of Wax 91, 92
Howden, Alan 172, 207, 217
Hutchinson, Tom 249

I

Incredible Hulk, The 159, 160, 172
Independent Broadcasting Authority (IBA) 109, 114, 148, 150, 152, 155, 169, 170, 173, 200, 201
International Film Encyclopaedia ... 139, 140
Internet Movie Database 130, 249
Isaacs, Sir Jeremy ... 149, 167, 201, 202, 203, 204, 205, 217, 247
Isle of Man 16, 21, 102
ITV
   big five 146, 199
   formation 110
   purchase group ... *See* Film Purchase Group

J

Jacobs, Prof. Lewis 138, 139
James Bond films 147, 148
James, M. R. 36, 105, 211, 242
Jaws 169, 170, 172, 184, 187, 192
Jaws 2 .... 169, 203, 207
Jennings, Humphrey ... 29, 39, 40, 157, 214
Jewel in the Crown, The 208
Jolson Story, The 215, 235, 237

K

Karloff, Boris 62, 125, 239
Katz, Ephraim 139, 140, 194
Kay, Peter 250
Kaye, Danny 68, 113, 114, 211, 240
Kelly, Chris 115, 158
Kelly, Gene .. 63, 68, 114, 118, 159, 181
Kine Weekly 83, 86
Kinema, Cambridge ... 66, 67, 68, 81, 84
King Kong 26, 50, 85, 86, 117, 119
King Kong (model) 120
Kings Row 32, 33
Kirkham 42, 242
Koh-i-noor restaurant 54, 97
Kojak 148, 164, 207, 226
Korda, Alexander 21, 40, 129
Kramer, Stanley 88, 97, 98

L

Lady Eve, The 56, 59, 60
Lady Vanishes, The 20, 184
Lake, Veronica 220, 231
Lanchester, Elsa 38, 129
Lane End, Buckinghamshire 202
Lang, Fritz 100
Laughton, Charles 11, 213
Laurel & Hardy ... 9, 15, 50, 105, 125, 144, 193, 211
Laurel, Stan 15, 50
Leatherbarrow, Stanley 36, 105, 242
Leigh, Vivien 46, 126
Let George Do It 19, 157
Lewis, Roger 239
Lewton, Val 36
Lido Cinema, Bolton 22, 30, 33, 34, 35, 44, 51, 190, 194, 250
lightness of touch ... 17, 60, 111, 193, 252
Listen to Britain 40, 214
Llandudno Resolution 112
London Can Take It 39, 213
London Film Critics' Circle 7, 244
Lorimar 197, 199
Los Angeles ... 118, 146, 156, 162, 164, 169, 172, 177, 205, 207, 218, 229
Los Angeles Times ... 131, 140, 180, 189, 246

Lost Horizon...4, 25, 52, 93, 108, 135, 184, 194, 212, 220, 242, 243, 247
Love Happy 57, 71
Lowe, Ronald..............................31, 42
Loy, Myrna 17, 153
Lubitsch, Ernst ...11, 59, 60, 64, 222, 230
Lucas, George 192, 203
Lugosi, Bela.............................235, 239

M

Madame Butterfly 9
Make Your Own Bed 108
Maltese Falcon, The 32, 136, 181
Maltin, Leonard 175, 178
Mamoulian, Rouben.......10, 22, 23, 100
Manvell, Dr. Roger 138, 139, 236
Marché Internationale des Programmes Télévision (MIP)... 154, 155, 156, 163, 168, 199
Marshall, Herbert.......................11, 59
Marx Brothers...11, 57, 58, 65, 68, 69, 71, 74, 85, 93, 94, 107, 135, 141, 193, 230
Marx, Groucho...............58, 69, 88, 116
Mass-Observation 29, 39, 40, 238
Matter of Life and Death, A... 45, 85, 220, 221
Maugham, W. Somerset...............46, 48
Mayer, Louis B. 11, 63, 236
MCA ..78, 142, 156, 162, 163, 169, 170
McDonald, Jeanette 215
McKemey, Denise ...103, 108, 133, 244
MGM...10, 58, 63, 78, 95, 120, 145, 150, 164, 168, 169, 170, 171, 175, 214
    characteristics 11
    Freed Unit.........................63, 77, 78
Miami Vice..207
Mills, John 107
Milne, Alasdair 149, 168, 170, 171
Ministry of Information .39, 40, 44, 214
Miracle of Morgan's Creek, The.....32, 60, 205
Monthly Film Bulletin...125, 175, 176, 194
Morecambe, Eric......149, 200, 231, 232
Morris, Desmond 111

Mountain of Dreams: The Golden Years of Paramount....................230
Mrs Miniver 38, 41
Mummy, The (character).....13, 209, 239, 240
Mummy's Hand, The..........................36

N

Nangle, John 185, 237, 238, 239
National Film Archive...110, 212, 231, 241, 249
National Film Theatre (NFT)......104, 125, 151, 160, 173, 205, 220, 221, 241, 246, 247, 251
National Service.............48, 51, 54, 242
Network............................150, 203, 204
New Statesman.................137, 180, 184
New York.................116, 118, 145, 211
New York Times 238
Next Week's Films...64, 65, 70, 71, 72, 75, 77, 96, 127
Night of the Demon 211, 242
Night on the Island, A 108
Night Train to Munich 212, 215
Norden, Denis 157

O

Observer, The............................102, 248
Odeon, Bolton...22, 23, 26, 29, 30, 43, 190, 194, 250
Odeon, Leicester Square 51, 94, 160
Odeon, Radcliffe 105
Old Boltonians' Dinner........61, 94, 104
Oliver!..149
Olivier, Laurence...43, 44, 51, 85, 92, 105, 209
On the Town...63, 68, 74, 85, 90, 117, 159, 235
optimism...13, 17, 18, 25, 52, 63, 132, 191, 215, 235
Our Town 69, 70
Oxford Companion to Film, The...139, 223

P

Paramount Pictures...10, 57, 58, 59, 81,

112, 119, 142, 143, 145, 189, 192, 207, 211, 230
characteristics 12
Parkinson, Sir Michael.............114, 120
Passing of the Third Floor Back, The
....212, 215
Peckinpah, Sam................151, 183, 188
Philadelphia Story, The...32, 56, 59, 60, 74, 85, 127, 155
Picturegoer...33, 41, 45, 63, 77, 79, 80, 98, 99, 138, 178, 225
Porter, Denise....................................103
Powell & Pressburger 44, 45, 85
Powell, William 17, 141
Prisoner of Zenda, The 112
Production Code...10, 12, 22, 60, 129, 151
Psycho...111
Public Film Buff Number One.....221, 245
Purser, Philip............................104, 234

Q

Queen Christina............................11, 19
Queen Elizabeth II 92, 109
Queen is Crowned, A 92, 93
Queen's Cinema, Bolton......6, 7, 8, 12, 13, 18, 19, 20, 22, 158, 242, 250
Quinlan, David.................130, 173, 191
Quinton, Anthony...131, 137, 178, 184, 195
quota quickies 18

R

Radio Times Film & Video Guide....248
Raging Bull 181, 205
Raiders of the Lost Ark 172, 217
Rank Organisation...43, 92, 101, 103, 105, 107, 109, 110, 212
Rebecca...............................32, 41, 108
Redgrave, Vanessa...................119, 121
Regal Cinema, Cambridge...........56, 63
Return to Shangri-La 242
Rex Cinema, Cambridge......66, 67, 68, 69, 70, 71, 72, 74, 77, 108, 110, 115, 166, 189, 196, 216, 225, 235, 238, 250, 251
3-D films...92

Blue Angel, The 76
Synchro-Screen..............................88
wide screens.................................101
Wild One, The 99
X-certificate films.................89, 102
Rialto Cinema, Bolton...6, 19, 37, 221, 222
Richards, Jeffrey 217, 238, 246
Richmond Film Society 241
RKO........10, 26, 36, 112, 119, 120, 214
characteristics 13
Robe, The 99
Rock Around the Clock 106
Rogers, Ginger 12, 80
Rotha, Paul...............................45, 129
Rugheimer, Gunnar ...144, 147, 148, 149, 150, 155, 161, 162, 165, 166, 167, 168, 169, 170, 171, 172, 198, 199
Running the Rex: Revelations of a Cinema Manager (article).............87
Russell, Ken 183, 189, 209

S

St. Catharine's College, Cambridge.....47, 53, 61, 94
St. Elsewhere....................................206
St. Mark's Church..............34, 36, 105
St. Simon's and St. Jude's elementary school......................................16, 31
San Francisco 180, 237
Santa Monica Civic Auditorium 121
Schickel, Richard.....................132, 137
Scorsese, Martin...45, 87, 186, 205, 251
Scott, George C................................138
Screen International 157, 218
Seats in all Parts 26, 86, 226, 238
Secret Life of Walter Mitty, The......68, 69, 113, 152
See 4 ....216, 227
Selznick, David O..............27, 112, 170
Semi-Tough 204
seven year contract................10, 52, 95
sex, violence and bad language......10, 185, 203, 218
Shangri-La...5, 23, 24, 25, 39, 81, 93, 135, 224, 241, 243, 252
Sheil, Peter.......................................241
Sherlock Holmes..............................126

293

Shipman, David 114
Sight & Sound 7, 90, 188, 225, 239
Sign of the Cross, The 11
Sing as we Go 18, 19, 126, 158
Singin' in the Rain 63, 78, 170, 235
Siskel, Gene 137
Six Million Dollar Man, The...148, 172, 226
sixteen millimetre film..........43, 57, 212
Slough 103
Sound of Music, The... 154, 167, 168, 199
Southern Television 109, 110
Spectator, The 7, 88, 134, 136, 225
Spielberg, Steven 153, 192, 237
Spraos, John 189
Star Wars .172, 187, 191, 192, 203, 206
Starsky and Hutch 148, 166
State Secret 68
Stewart, James 56, 62, 122
Story of Mankind, The 107, 184
Straw Dogs........................186, 188, 205
Strictly for Eggheads: Thoughts on Running a Specialised Hall (article) 90
studio system..33, 52, 78, 188, 189, 235
Sturges, Preston ...32, 60, 205, 230, 235
subtitles 214, 223
Sunday Telegraph, The 219, 231
Sunday Times, The...57, 139, 159, 170, 198, 238, 247
Supertrain 164, 165, 167
Synchro-Screen 91

T

Taylor, John Russell 177, 181
Technicolor 26, 44, 216
Teeside local radio 214
television
    effect on cinema attendance 78
    film packages...............143, 149, 151
    films on TV.........113, 115, 149, 190
    first broadcast 21
    five year ban 112, 142, 147, 152
    formation of ITV 110
    launch of Channel 4....................203
    mini-series...........161, 165, 207, 208, 218, 232
    panning and scanning 153

sex, violence and bad language ..151
    TV movies 152
Television Act...................................109
Thalberg, Irving 57, 187, 189
Thames Television….......146, 149, 159, 167, 199, 200, 206
Theatre Royal, Bolton..2, 6, 24, 34, 250
Thesiger, Ernest 37
Thin Man, The 17
Thing from another World, The 80
Things to Come 21, 71
Third Man, The 57, 180
thirty-five millimetre film...57, 64, 99, 210, 212
Thirty-Nine Steps, The 20, 220
Three-D 88, 91, 92, 189
Time Out Film Guide 248
Times Educational Supplement, The 177, 181
Times Literary Supplement, The......7, 128, 131, 137, 178, 184, 195, 227
Times, The..7, 30, 46, 82, 198, 217, 245
Took, Barry 233, 234
Top Hat 12, 52, 112
Tracy, Spencer 74, 120, 212
Trouble in Paradise 59, 60, 75, 88, 184, 194, 222
TV Times ..113, 115, 173, 204, 216, 227
Twentieth Century Fox...10, 99, 100, 120, 145, 167, 203

U

United Artists 112, 115, 147, 192
Universal Pictures...10, 35, 62, 106, 112, 119, 145, 153, 161, 162, 169, 208, 210, 212, 236, 240
    monster movies...13, 36, 38, 62, 208, 210, 239
University Challenge 113
Usher, Shaun 183, 191

V

V...208
Variety...160, 165, 176, 194, 195, 224, 232
Varsity...61, 62, 63, 64, 65, 66, 68, 70, 71, 72, 73, 76, 84, 85, 87, 88, 89,

90, 93, 94, 95, 96, 97, 98, 101, 102, 182, 225, 228, 242
Veidt, Conrad.....................23, 212, 215

W

Walker, John 247
Wardle, Irving...............46, 47
Warner Bros.....10, 49, 52, 112, 119, 134, 145, 251
   characteristics 12
Webb, George...66, 67, 68, 69, 71, 72, 75, 77, 81, 82, 83, 93, 94, 96, 98, 99, 101, 228, 250
Welles, Orson.....32, 33, 57, 86, 87, 139
West, Mae 118, 205
Whale, James 10, 36, 37, 209
What the Censor Saw (film season).205
Whicker, Alan..........................132, 232
Whitehouse, Mary............190, 204, 205
Who's Afraid of Virginia Woolf?...122, 123, 151, 152, 225
wide screens.....................100, 115, 194
Wilcox, Herbert 137
Wild One, The 97–99

Wilder, Billy 52, 60, 69, 70, 85
Winchester's...*See World Film Encyclopaedia, The*
Winds of War, The 207
Winner, Michael...96, 97, 147, 150, 203, 244
Winnert, Derek................................248
Woman of Substance, A 207
Wood, James......................................47
Woodstock...............................203, 204
World Film Encyclopaedia, The... 128–29
World War II ...29, 30, 33, 38, 39, 40, 41, 42, 44, 45, 49, 51, 62, 77, 80, 107, 158, 189, 203, 207, 212, 213, 214, 226
Worldvision Enterprises ..198, 199, 200
Worrall, Malcolm...............................35
Wright, Michael...55, 69, 92, 104, 107, 243, 247, 251

Z

Zanuck, Darryl F...............................11

Printed in Great Britain
by Amazon